Disaster Prepping

by David E. Stevens

for dummies®
A Wiley Brand

Disaster Prepping For Dummies®

Published by: **John Wiley & Sons, Inc.**, 111 River Street, Hoboken, NJ 07030-5774, www.wiley.com

For general information on our other products and services, please contact our Customer Care Department within the U.S. at 877-762-2974, outside the U.S. at 317-572-3993, or fax 317-572-4002. For technical support, please visit https://hub.wiley.com/community/support/dummies.

Wiley publishes in a variety of print and electronic formats and by print-on-demand. Some material included with standard print versions of this book may not be included in e-books or in print-on-demand. If this book refers to media that is not included in the version you purchased, you may download this material at http://booksupport.wiley.com. For more information about Wiley products, visit www.wiley.com.

Library of Congress Control Number: 2026935662

ISBN 978-1-394-38874-5 (pbk); ISBN 978-1-394-38876-9 (ebk); ISBN 978-1-394-38875-2 (ebk)

SKY10151892_040826

Table of Contents

Introduction

Most disaster preparation books assume the permanent collapse of civilization and promote a rural fortress retreat with a "Rambo" arsenal. If civilization ends, that may be the only path, but most people don't have the resources, time, or level of OCD required. Even if you *could* survive an apocalypse that results in a *Mad Max* world, would you want to? The good news is you . . . *probably won't*. A cataclysmic disaster bad enough to permanently wipe out civilization will likely take out you and me.

Instead, this book focuses on survivable disasters from minor blackouts to events that require some time for society to reboot. These disasters span everything from floods to asteroid impacts, earthquakes to artificial intelligence. In each case, you'll either stay and figure out how to get by for a while with little or no municipal infrastructure, or you'll evacuate. Both scenarios are covered with smart, simple, practical steps for those of us who aren't ready to remodel that abandoned missile silo.

With simple, inexpensive preparation, you can survive without power, water, and grocery stores for a week. With a little more effort and investment, you can get by more comfortably and extend your time to a month or more. Most of these preparations apply whether you live in rural Australia or a New York City apartment. They include leveraging technology, dual-use items that are useful with or without a disaster, and even things that are fun or might be good investments. This book also touches on more advanced strategies that move you toward permanent independence from municipal power and water. These include powering your home with solar panels or using an RV or vacation cabin as a survival destination and short-term rental.

The number of Americans who spend some of their household income on disaster preparation doubled to more than 20 million since 2017 and has expanded to include people from all walks of life. Categorizing yourself as a "prepper" isn't required, and since disaster preparation reduces dependence on municipal resources, it also tends to reduce environmental impact. This has brought together people with very different philosophical and political views but who share common goals.

About This Book

To effectively prepare, it's important to know what you're preparing for.

- Part 1 of this book identifies the different types of disasters you could face, their impacts, and developing a survival mindset. The rest of this book covers the resources needed to survive.
- Part 2 covers the basics: air, water, food, septic, and medical treatment.
- Part 3 covers shelter, power, communication, and defense.
- Part 4 covers evacuation, transportation, and money.
- Part 5 covers next-level preparation, such as achieving independence from municipal power and water, creating your own disaster retreat, and educating governments on how some of these disasters can be prevented.
- Part 6 covers fun things you can do while pretending to prep for an apocalypse.

Each chapter is broken down into two levels of preparation separated by cost. The third level is covered in Part 5:

- **Level 1:** Level 1 preparation is the least expensive and the fastest to implement. It'll get you through a week or two without power, water, or grocery stores. It covers simple hacks and dual-use items, some of which you already have or can buy inexpensively. For example, most water heaters contain enough water in their tank to provide a household with a week of drinking water. Or a small additional monthly fee on your phone plan allows you to use satellites to text when the cell phone network is down. Implementing Level 1 preparation should cost a few hundred dollars. This is budget preparation and is about getting by for a week or two . . . not comfort.
- **Level 2:** Level 2 preparation improves your survival conditions and increases independence from municipal infrastructure for about a month, but requires more investment and effort. This represents the most bang for the buck. It includes important things like keeping your refrigerator powered and dual-use items that are useful in or out of a disaster. For example, a $400 inflatable hot tub is fun and relaxing, but it can provide 250 gallons (1,000 liters) of water for flushing toilets, cleaning, and drinking (when treated). Implementing Level 2 preparation runs several hundred to several thousand dollars, depending on location and priorities.
- **Level 3:** Level 3 preparation strategies are covered separately in Part 5. These give more options and move toward permanent independence from the power grid and municipal water, but require a much greater level of investment and effort. However, some of these strategies may pay for themselves over time.

» **Level 4:** Level 4 preparation — remodeling that abandoned missile silo — isn't covered in this book, nor will this book prepare you for a Navy SEAL mission.

Foolish Assumptions

I've made a few possibly foolish assumptions about you:

- You're concerned about global or local disasters and their impact on infrastructure. Or . . . you really don't want to know any of that depressing stuff. You just want to be able to get through whatever might happen.
- You're new to disaster preparation but aren't ready for that abandoned missile silo or an appearance on *Naked and Afraid*. Or, you're a pro prepper looking for additional hacks, the latest tech, or a quick reference guide.
- You appreciate some level of self-reliance and not being completely dependent on municipal resources, or maybe you just want to reduce your environmental footprint.
- You're willing to look at everyday items from a different perspective and possibly "MacGyver" some things. Yes, "MacGyver" is now a verb in the *Merriam-Webster Dictionary*, defined as "to make, form, or repair with what is conveniently at hand."

Icons Used in This Book

Icons, the little pictures in the margins, are placed next to some of the paragraphs that may need extra emphasis.

TIP

This symbol indicates additional information that can make things easier to do, or shortcuts and hacks.

REMEMBER

This book is a reference, which means you don't have to commit it to memory, and there's no test at the end of class. However, sometimes there are important bits of information you may want to file away for future use.

WARNING

This symbol represents danger. It's used to emphasize any item or process that could get you or others into trouble.

TECHNICAL STUFF

Sometimes, we overshare. Technical or scientific information is used to explain the "why," illustrate a point, or give some background. While we find this stuff absolutely fascinating, you may not. Skipping these sections won't prevent you from applying the steps or strategies.

Beyond the Book

Additional resources and references will be covered, including several other exceptional books in the Dummies series. These books can provide more detailed information on related topics, such as "*Wilderness Survival For Dummies.*"

This book also comes with a free online Cheat Sheet, which highlights key skills, important items to have in your bug-out bag, and a list of vehicles that are effective during disasters and evacuations. Simply go to `www.dummies.com` and enter "Disaster Prepping For Dummies Cheat Sheet" in the Search box.

Where to Go from Here

You don't need to read this book from cover to cover, although that's not a bad idea. The chapters stand on their own; however, I do recommend starting with Chapter 1, which provides an overview of the entire book. Chapter 2 is all about understanding the potential global disasters you may face, ranked by their impact and likelihood. Chapter 3 zeros in on local disasters and specific impacts of both local and global disasters. Chapter 4 covers personal disasters that almost everyone could face sometime during their life.

Chapters 5 and on cover preparation strategy and resources by specific topic or area, such as drinking water, electricity, or evacuation. You can choose to read all the chapters or just choose the topics you're interested in and that apply to your situation. Inside each chapter, you can choose the level of preparation you wish to achieve.

I'm always looking for feedback, corrections, new ideas, and hacks for future editions. You can reach me at `disaster.prep.dummies@gmail.com` or `www.global-disasters.org`.

Finally, many of the top global disasters are actually preventable or can be mitigated. If you want to know more about how they might unfold and how we, as a society, can prevent some of them, read the last chapter or watch the TED talk, "How Do We Prevent Our Inevitable Extinction?" at `https://www.ted.com/talks/david_e_stevens_how_do_we_prevent_our_inevitable_extinction`.

1 Preparing for Prepping

IN THIS PART . . .

Understand your "why" for preparing, and evaluate and develop your survival mindset

Identify the potential global threats facing you based on their consequence and probability

Determine the most likely local disasters for your location and the immediate actions required

Consider the more common personal disasters, such as debt and job loss

IN THIS CHAPTER

» Summarizing the book

» Considering your "why"

» Developing a survival mindset

Chapter 1 Preparing for the Worst . . . or Something Less

The first and most important question is "why?" Why should you spend time, money, and effort preparing for a situation that might never happen? Believe it or not, I consider myself an optimist. I honestly believe people live longer if they have a positive attitude and outlook on life. With that said, I'm also an engineer, and you don't want your airliner or elevator designed by an optimist. Occasionally, considering potential negative outcomes can also help you live longer.

As a Navy F-18 pilot, I trained to drop nuclear weapons. Later in my career, I served as the Strike Operations Officer for the Persian Gulf during the Iraqi invasion of Kuwait. These occupations consist largely of planning and executing disasters. During Desert Storm, I saw the impact of destruction on a massive scale. I'm proud of my military service, but for my next career, I decided to focus on how we, as a society, might prevent or prepare for disasters. My TED Talk "How Do We Prevent Our Inevitable Extinction?" at `https://www.ted.com/talks/david_e_stevens_how_do_we_prevent_our_inevitable_extinction` provides an overview.

Prepping

The term "prepper" is sometimes perceived negatively. Some assume that preppers are all about themselves or that they are anarchists looking forward to the collapse of civilization. While there are always fringe people in every group, disaster preparation is actually positive for both local communities and society in general. During a disaster, those who have even a basic level of preparation will need little or no government resources, allowing those limited assets to go to those who are in dire need. Those who prepare are also in the best position to help others. Regardless of philanthropic motivation, a starving person can't help another starving person. Not to worry, just because you're making some disaster preparations doesn't mean you have to call yourself a "prepper." *Disaster Prepping For Dummies* is just a catchier title.

Understanding the threat

Before tackling disaster preparation, it's important to understand what disasters you might face. Conventional disasters like floods, tornadoes, earthquakes, and wildfires will be covered, but you may live in an area that's not prone to any of these. So, I'll start with global disasters. These include everything from pandemics to asteroid impacts, nuclear war to artificial intelligence. Even though most of these have a lower probability of occurring, they can affect anyone, no matter where they live. Because of this possibility, I believe everyone should work toward at least a basic level of preparation.

Much of the preparation covered in Chapters 2–4 is general to most situations, but some preparation is specific to the type, severity, or duration of a disaster.

- Chapter 2 begins by identifying and attempting to rank the top global disasters.
- Chapter 3 determines *your* most likely local disaster, such as a flood or fire, but also covers the specific impacts of both global and local disasters.
- Chapter 4 covers personal disasters such as a serious injury or illness, or the unexpected loss of a job.

Surviving with the basics: Air, water, food, septic, and medical

Part 2 has five chapters that cover the basics needed to survive: breathing, drinking, eating, eliminating waste, and maintaining your health. Chapters 5–13 are broken into levels of preparation based on cost and effort.

- Chapter 5 covers the air that you breathe. Air is something you don't think about until you don't have it. Most people can't hold their breath longer than 90 seconds, and consciousness is usually lost past 3 minutes. This chapter will cover ways to protect your ability to breathe when disasters create toxic or contaminated air.
- Chapter 6 covers water. After air, it is the most important resource. The average person can only survive about three days without water. This chapter covers places to source water, where to efficiently stockpile it, and how to treat it.
- Chapter 7 covers food. Most people can survive for up to three weeks without food, but dieting during a disaster is a bad idea. Your ability to remain alert and take action is affected, as well as your motivation and reasoning. This chapter focuses on which types of foods are optimal in a survival situation. It also covers how much food you need to stockpile based on your situation and disaster duration.
- Chapter 8 covers waste. What goes in must come out. It covers everything from getting rid of trash to what to do when your septic system no longer works.
- Chapter 9 covers how to maintain your health when emergency services are limited or non-existent. It focuses on basic first aid and supplies, as well as what medications or equipment you may want to have on hand.

Sheltering in place: Staying connected, powered, and protected

Part 3 covers the next set of priorities: shelter, staying connected, power, and defense. When possible, the best strategy is sheltering in place. You're familiar with the area, you have an existing shelter, and you can avoid the dangers of evacuation. The focus in this part is on how to stay in your home when power, water, and grocery stores aren't available.

- Chapter 10 covers your home and emergency shelter and is broken into two areas. The first area covers finding immediate temporary shelter during time-critical emergencies like tornadoes. It also covers basic items to have on hand to take care of immediate threats, such as fire. The second area focuses on ways to fortify your home to improve its ability to weather disasters, both natural and human-created.
- Chapter 11 covers how to stay connected if cell phone service and the Internet are lost. It's important to have access to emergency services, maintain your

connection with family and friends, and know what's happening to determine if you can stay or need to evacuate.

- Chapter 12 covers powering your important devices if municipal electricity is lost. This includes everything from phones and computers to refrigerators and heating or air conditioning. This could also include important medical equipment such as CPAP machines or oxygen concentrators.
- Chapter 13 covers protecting yourself, family, and friends when there's an interruption in first responder services. The emphasis is on situational awareness, training, and passive defensive measures such as security cameras. It also includes more active defensive strategies, such as pepper spray and stun guns.
- Chapter 14 briefly covers firearms.
- Chapter 15 highlights strategies for fixing and maintaining critical devices.

Evacuating: When, how, and with what

An emergency or disaster may require you to evacuate. Part 4 covers evacuation strategies, including what to take with you, how to travel, where to go, and funding.

- Chapter 16 focuses on deciding in advance under what circumstances you need to evacuate. It also covers what to take with you in the form of a "Bug Out Bag" and where to go.
- Chapter 17 covers different transportation options for evacuation, including your current vehicle, as well as emergency backups such as bikes and scooters.
- Chapter 18 covers ways to maintain the ability to purchase needed products or services when the power grid and Internet are down. Credit cards, debit cards, and even old-school checks won't be an option. This chapter looks at ways to stash paper currency and to protect and diversify financial assets and income.

Achieving independence from municipal infrastructure

Part 5 looks at more extensive strategies to move toward permanent independence from the power grid and municipal water. These Level 3 preparation options are considerably more expensive but, in some cases, may pay for themselves or even create income.

- Chapter 19 highlights ways to achieve permanent or long-term independence from municipal water. This includes standard approaches such as drilling water wells, but also introduces rain catchment systems, filtering surface water, and atmospheric water generators.
- Chapter 20 covers systems that can reduce or replace the need for municipal power, such as solar powering your entire home. While these strategies are expensive, they may be good investments.
- Chapter 21 covers how to identify the optimum evacuation location for a recreational vehicle (RV), or future cabin site, with emphasis on dual use as a survival retreat and a vacation destination. RVs can span anything from small camping trailers to luxury motorcoaches.
- Chapter 22 covers all the options for buying, modifying, or building a survival retreat/vacation cabin/short-term rental. It covers modifying or building it to operate efficiently off grid, but also to be attractive for vacations and short-term rentals.
- Chapter 23 covers vehicle categories, features, and technology that provide enhanced security and evacuation options but also make good daily drivers. Examples of vehicles — from motorcycles to trucks — that score well are highlighted. Internal combustion and electric vehicles are also evaluated for disasters and evacuation.
- Chapter 24 covers how many global disasters can actually be prevented or mitigated.

Having some fun while prepping

What if, after all this preparation, a disaster never happens? That would be terrible. It's important to play with dual-use items, learn how things work, and have some fun. Chapter 25 wraps up with a list of the top ten things to do while pretending to be disaster prepping.

TIP

I try to avoid identifying specific products unless they're truly unique or I've actually used them. I receive no compensation from any manufacturer or retailer for any product mentioned in this book, nor have I received any product for free. The products I *do* mention may not be right for your situation, and with new technologies introduced every day, you'll want to do your own research. I strongly recommend looking at reviews and using websites that don't accept advertising for any of the products they review. I often reference the nonprofit organization *Consumer*

Reports. They accept no advertising and have been around for more than 80 years. They do charge a small subscription for detailed reports, but that's how they can exist without advertising revenue.

Developing a Survival Mindset

The first resource you need to consider is yourself. You are the number one resource. It's important to evaluate your mental and physical state and what you may be able to do to improve it.

Surviving an apocalyptic disaster

The first question is, do you even want to survive a major disaster? That may sound like a dumb question since you're reading this book, but the answer may depend on the scale of the disaster, your motivation to protect family or friends, and your spiritual beliefs. This book isn't going to directly address your personal motivation or spiritual beliefs, but both can be important and directly impact your survival.

Disaster scale

The scale of the disaster is an important consideration. For example, let's say the Earth gets hit with a six-mile (10-kilometer) wide asteroid or comet (similar to the dinosaur killer). Statistically, getting hit by something that big is extremely unlikely, but it has happened before, and it will eventually happen again. The energy released would be the same as a global nuclear war — if it happened every day for 20 years. Most of the surface of the Earth would be incinerated, flooded by tsunamis, or destroyed by earthquakes. Anything that wasn't burned, crushed, drowned, or asphyxiated would freeze or starve as the Earth plunges into a decades-long ice age.

Short of living in an underground city or being a Mars colonist, it might be better not to survive the impact. As mentioned in the introduction, the "good news" is that you and I probably won't. If you do survive, you're looking at a post-apocalyptic world right out of a Hollywood movie, but worse.

Mad Max world

Many of the survival and prepper guides assume a permanent or decades-long collapse of civilization. Level 4 preparation isn't covered here because when you study disasters of this scale, they annihilate most of the Earth's population. Even if you survive the initial destruction, you're going to need a fortress home, room to grow crops, and an arsenal to protect it. This can be done, but requires extensive equipment, experience in multiple disciplines, and a group of people with expertise in farming, hunting, self-defense, machine repair, medicine, and at least one comedian.

This is an impressive aspiration, but it requires resources and a level of work that would prevent most people from having a job or business. There are professional preppers who are very successful at this, but it's usually their full-time occupation, and teaching how to do it may provide some or all of their income. There's nothing wrong with that. You and I can and should learn from them. However, the best laid plans of mice and men. . .

What if, after investing all that time, energy, and money, your survival compound becomes ground zero of the disaster? What if others take over your survival compound before you can reach it? Worse, what if an apocalyptic disaster never happens?

Preparing for the more likely disaster scenarios

This book assumes an extended but temporary suspension of utilities and food distribution rather than an apocalypse. Statistically, this type of disaster is much more likely, and it's a lot more likely that you and I will survive it. This means a period without infrastructure but not living forever in a post-apocalyptic movie. This also significantly simplifies your preparation. For example, instead of needing a non-GMO seed bank, room for crops, farming expertise, and agricultural supplies and equipment, you just need to stockpile some food. Depending on your resources and outlook, that stockpile could be for a week or a year. Even a year's worth of food is significantly cheaper than creating your own farm.

Additionally, many of these disasters, such as nuclear war, asteroid impacts, and volcanoes will create a climate scenario that may prevent anything from growing for a while. With that in mind, let's consider your survival mindset.

Mind: Learning to "MacGyver"

The human brain is phenomenally powerful. Here's a comparison of your brain to the state of the art in artificial intelligence (covered in Chapter 2). It's estimated that to match the reasoning power of a human brain would require hundreds of thousands of the most powerful processors pulling over a gigawatt of electricity.

That would require an automotive factory-sized building and consume the same power as a city of one million people. That's to replace one human brain that draws the equivalent of 35 watts. Your mind is your greatest asset . . . but it can also be your greatest enemy.

Attitude

This is a practical guide with specific action steps, not a psychological treatise. However, attitude is critical to your survival. Everyone's heard stories of people surviving under the most extreme conditions; conditions that any reasonable person would determine that there is no hope of survival or rescue. Yet they didn't give up and made it through alive. There are also plenty of stories about people in much less severe circumstances who simply gave up and died minutes or feet from rescue. I'm not going to tell you that with the right attitude you can survive anything, but believing survival is possible is essential. Without that belief, it doesn't matter how much technology or how many supplies you have.

MacGyvering

The other important mindset is thinking out of the box. Many of the ideas, steps, or survival items covered are things you already own, can be modified, or quickly purchased. It's often nothing more than looking at things from a different perspective. It helps to be able to MacGyver things. Your grandparents, great-grandparents, or great-great-grandparents survived things like the Great Depression because they didn't give up and knew how to do *stuff*. Plenty of tips and clever hacks will be covered in this book, but you'll certainly think of others, including dual-use items and new technology. I would love to hear your ideas, tips, and hacks at `disaster.prep.dummies@gmail.com`.

Humor

Large craniums and opposable thumbs are usually tagged as setting humans apart from animals and allowing the creation of civilization. I suspect our ability to laugh at ourselves should also make the short list of what made civilization possible. I've been told there is nothing funny about apocalyptic disasters. Actually, it's because of that statement that I think humor is required. For example, I heard a comedian say that for something to be *really* funny, someone has to get hurt. Well . . . *that* shouldn't be a problem during these disasters. See? That was a completely insensitive and inappropriate thing to say . . . but kinda funny. Humor can actually be a very powerful tool during terrifying situations.

POSITIVE IMPACTS OF HUMOR

As a military pilot, I went through several types of survival training, including the "helo dunker." This torture device simulates a helicopter crash in the ocean at night. You and six others strap into seats inside a giant metal cylinder suspended over a deep swimming pool. It drops into the water and sinks rapidly while rolling upside down (simulating a top-heavy helicopter crash in the ocean). By the way, to simulate night, you're blindfolded. The game plan is to wait until it stops upside down, calmly unstrap, find an exit door by feel, and swim "down" toward the surface. Keep in mind your fellow students are also blindfolded and attempting to do the same, which results in you getting kicked in the head. It's best to complete the exercise before you drown.

My flight school roommate was in the first group of victims. As the helo dunker hit the water and began to roll and submerge, he stuck his hand out a window and waved at us. Everyone busted up laughing. That small act of courage and humor broke the tension and eased the fear. The fact that I still remember this demonstrates its power. His name was Andy Logan. Years later, he was killed when his jet crashed on a low-altitude night mission. This drove me to create a new type of altitude warning system that ultimately resulted in my current career — trying to prevent the rest of the world from "hitting the ground."

Body: Evaluating Your Physical Condition

Your physical condition includes everything from your physical fitness to your medical health and diet.

Medication

Your medical health is very important in any survival situation. If you have a chronic condition, you'll want to stockpile some of your medications. Talk to your doctor and see if some of them can be consolidated. Even better, see if a combination of diet and exercise can reduce or eliminate some of them. Improving your health and fitness is a great survival strategy with or without a disaster.

Fitness

This isn't a diet or exercise book, but it might not be a bad idea to pick one up. My daughter is a certified fitness trainer . . . no pressure there. Let's be honest, most people don't have the discipline to work out regularly. Everyone knows that the best piece of fitness equipment to own is a treadmill, because you can drape lots of clothes over it as it sits idle. Joining a gym is better, but having someone kick your butt on a regular basis is probably the best solution for many. Not saying you need to do triathlons, but you don't want to be featured in a Life Alert "I've fallen, and I can't get up." commercial. Another way to improve your core strength and flexibility is doing things like yoga, yes, even if you're a gym rat. Guys, don't assume it's not a true workout. Talk to me after a sweat yoga session where a petite 100-pound woman asks you if you need help getting back up.

Spirit: Understanding the Impact of Spiritual Outlook

Here's a story I once heard. A major flood occurs. A man of great faith lives in a house right in the middle of a flood zone. As the water rises, neighbors come by in a truck and ask him if he wants a ride. He says, "No, God will save me." The water rises, and he has to move to the second floor. A boat comes by. He refuses and says, "God will save me." The water rises, forcing him to climb on the roof. A helicopter comes by and hovers overhead. He waves it away, yelling, "God will save me!" Finally, the flood washes his house away, and he drowns. When he gets to heaven, he asks God, "Why didn't you save me?" God says, "What are you talking about? I sent a car, a boat, and a helicopter."

Of course, everyone has an "expiration date," but if you're reading this book, I suspect you don't believe in giving up easily. You want to continue to make a difference and have a positive impact all the way to the end. Here are excerpts from two of my favorite poems:

"Do not go gentle into that good night . . . rage against the dying of the light." — Dylan Thompson

Or here's a little more dynamic version.

"Life should not be a journey to the grave with the intention of arriving safely in a pretty and well-preserved body, but rather to skid in broadside in a cloud of smoke, thoroughly used up, totally worn out, and loudly proclaiming, "Wow! What a Ride!" — Hunter S. Thompson

SURPRISING SPIRITUAL IMPACTS

A Navy fighter pilot and the Pope die on the same day. St. Peter meets them, gives them a tour of heaven, and finally brings them to one of their new homes. It's breathtaking with floor-to-ceiling windows, a giant swimming pool, and pickleball courts. The Navy pilot runs off to enjoy his new home. St. Peter goes a little further and points at another house for the Pope. It's very nice, but not as impressive as the Navy pilot's house. Very respectfully, the Pope mentions how amazing the last home was. St. Peter shrugs. "We've got a lot of Popes up here, but he's the first Navy fighter pilot we've ever seen."

All that to say, you probably don't want spiritual advice from a Navy fighter pilot. My educational background is in engineering and astrophysics. If you study quantum mechanics and cosmology, you quickly realize that these concepts are absolutely bizarre and non-intuitive. They make the precepts of most spiritual beliefs seem tame in comparison. Personally, I do believe in a supreme being and base a lot of that on quantum mechanics and cosmology, but this book applies regardless of your belief set.
I mention this because we can live weeks without food, days without water, minutes without air — but only seconds without hope.

IN THIS CHAPTER

» Understanding potential global disasters

» Ranking disasters by impact and likelihood

Chapter 2

Identifying the Top Potential Global Disasters

This chapter covers the top potential global disasters: asteroid/comet impacts, artificial intelligence, nuclear war, pandemics, solar superstorms, super volcanoes, and climate change. Most of these cataclysmic events are much less likely than local disasters such as floods, tornadoes, wildfires, and earthquakes that are covered in the next chapter. The reason global disasters are introduced first is that many people don't live in areas prone to local disasters like tornadoes, wildfires, or earthquakes, and may feel immune to these threats. Global catastrophes, however, can reach anyone anywhere. Additionally, most of these global events will result in the same impacts that the local disasters create, such as floods, fires, and earthquakes. This allows presenting the common impacts, the immediate actions, and the preparations in Chapter 3.

Ranking by Probability and Consequence

To make this list, a disaster must have the potential to create a worldwide impact and be possible during your lifetime. The first step is to attempt to rank these potentially cataclysmic events based on their probability and consequence. This is the same science your insurance company uses to calculate your premiums. What is the probability or likelihood that something bad will happen, and if it does happen, how bad will it be? For example, the consequence of being attacked by a great white shark is extremely bad. The likelihood for most people, however, is ridiculously tiny. You're more likely to die from being hit on the head by a falling coconut.

Likewise, it doesn't matter if it's extremely likely if it's not that dangerous. This ranking is an estimate, and new discoveries and technology can change the probability and ranking overnight. The good news is that, unlike the local disasters, six of the seven global catastrophes are preventable or can be mitigated. Chapter 24 covers real-world solutions that governments can apply to prevent many of these from happening. Sorry, the zombie apocalypse didn't make the cut.

TECHNICAL STUFF

Most people would rather have a root canal than take a statistics and probability course. They weren't my favorite either. Statistics can illuminate but also mislead. For example, you may have heard that most car accidents happen within a few miles of your home. This is often used to suggest that you get complacent when you're close to home and need to be more vigilant. That may be true, but the reason most accidents happen within a few miles of your home is that's where you are most of the time. It would be odd if accidents didn't happen more frequently near home. So, although this statistic is true, it's not useful information. I mention this because the probability of some of these potential disasters may be surprising. Don't hesitate to challenge the numbers, but before you do, please review how probability works. Yes, there is a *Probability For Dummies*.

1: Asteroids/comets: Increasing odds of a catastrophic impact

The probability of a major asteroid or comet impact is extremely low, so how did it make the top of the list? There are three reasons.

- It's one of the only threats that has the unquestioned ability to cause the greatest global destruction, up to the extinction of most life on Earth. The dinosaur-killing impact didn't just take out the dinosaurs; it wiped out about 70 percent of all species on the planet. The energy released was the same as that of a global nuclear war . . . if it happened every day for 40 years!

- Despite the low probability, it could happen with only a year or two of warning. Astrophysicists have done a remarkable job of finding and tracking the largest asteroids that could threaten the Earth, but they haven't found them all. Even when they do, comets are wildcards. Due to their distance from Earth, new comets are impossible to detect until they're inbound, at which point they may be less than two years from impact. On average, a new comet is discovered every week.
- The impact rate was recently and terrifyingly updated.

Determining the impact rate

Historically, the impact rate was estimated by counting craters or tracking known asteroids and comets. Since impacts land on top of each other, and craters on Earth are eroded, they're very hard to count accurately. Additionally, most comets come from outside the solar system, so unless it has visited us in modern times, we won't see it until it's inbound.

TECHNICAL STUFF

The ability to estimate the impact rate improved dramatically by a fortunate accident. The Nuclear Test Ban Treaty banned atmospheric testing of nuclear weapons in the 1960s and set up a monitoring system that uses a global system of special microphones to "listen" for atmospheric explosions. This classified data was finally released to the public. The good news — there haven't been any atmospheric nuclear tests. The bad news — they recorded dozens of huge atmospheric explosions caused by small asteroids or comets blowing up in the upper atmosphere. Fortunately, most of them exploded over the oceans. However, several of these were 10 times more powerful than the Hiroshima bomb. For the first time in history, astrophysicists had actual impact data they could plot on a graph (see Figure 2-1).

The difference between the slope of the older estimated impact rate and the new one based on the International Monitoring System data is only a few degrees. However, this is a logarithmic graph, meaning each graph block is 10 times higher than the previous one. For example, a 10-megaton blast big enough to destroy a city was estimated to occur every 1000 years or so. The new data suggests it occurs roughly every 100 years. This means that asteroid or comet impacts may be 10 times more frequent than we thought. The reason we haven't lost a city every 100 years may simply be because cities only cover 1 percent of the Earth's surface. Most of these blasts happened over the ocean or unoccupied land. The B612 Foundation, founded by former astronaut and Stanford physicist Dr. Ed Lu, created a video that highlights these impacts (see `https://www.youtube.com/watch?v=Z36qXGzJWII`).

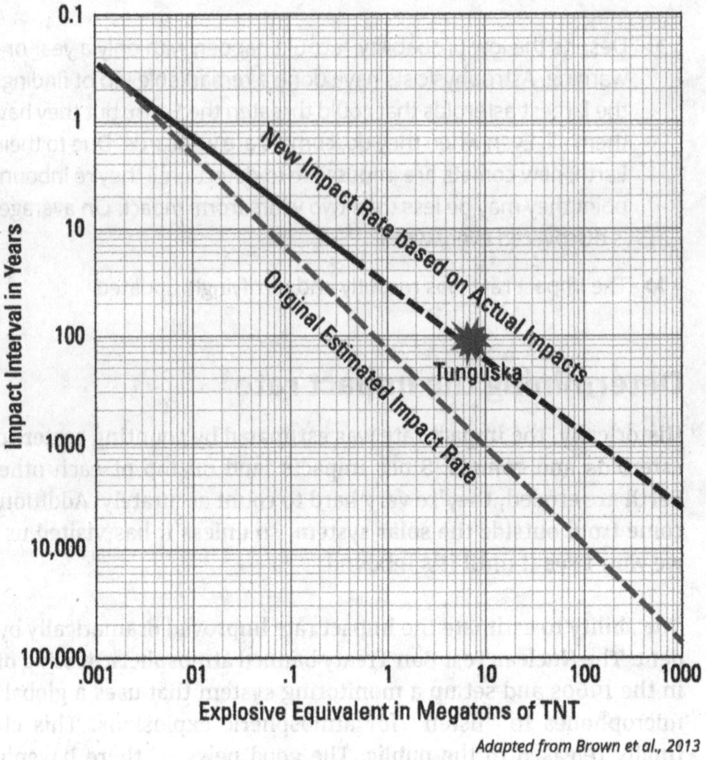

FIGURE 2-1: The impact rate based on Nuclear Test Ban Treaty International Monitoring System data.

HISTORY OF IMPACTS

The dinosaur-killing asteroid was about 6 miles (10 km) wide, or about the size of Mount Everest. I visited the area near the impact point at Chicxulub, Mexico, and then drove for more than an hour to get to the rim of the impact crater near the Mayan ruins at Uxmal. After 66 million years of erosion, the 110-mile-wide (177 km) crater wall is still visible.

The newly discovered Eltanin impact hit one of the deepest parts of the ocean 2.5 million years ago near South America. It released more energy than all the nuclear weapons in the world combined. The impact pumped so much water, sulfur, and dust into the atmosphere that it may have started a cycle of extreme winters that covered much of the northern hemisphere under a mile of ice. To put this in perspective, it's taken two centuries for humanity to put enough greenhouse gases into the atmosphere to raise the global temperature 1.8°F (1°C). That's bad, but a one-kilometer-wide asteroid could cause a 14°F (8°C) drop in a few days.

Almost every ancient civilization has a "myth" about a great flood. Because 71 percent of the Earth is covered in oceans, it's a likely impact point. A one-kilometer-wide asteroid would vaporize more than one million cubic kilometers of ocean, as shown in Figure 2-2.

The water would have to come back out of the atmosphere in the form of rain, which could take . . . oh, I don't know . . . maybe 40 days and 40 nights. This is purely speculative, but new research does suggest an impact or shotgun blast of multiple small impacts may have occurred 12,400 years ago. This coincides with a mini-ice age called the Younger Dryas, when the woolly mammoth, saber-tooth cats, and possibly the Clovis Indian Culture became extinct. This connection is still hotly debated, and I defer to the archeologists and anthropologists. However, we know impacts have occurred throughout Earth's history and statistically, would have happened during the thousands of years of humanity's rise.

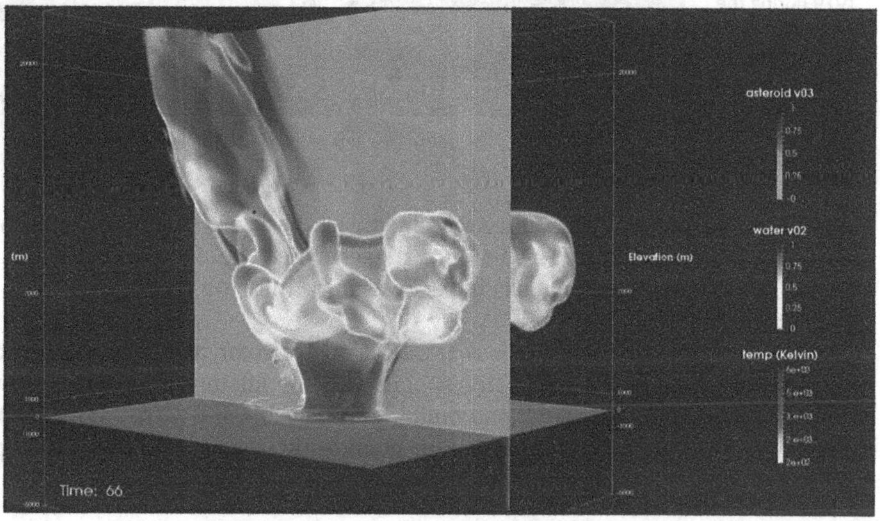

FIGURE 2-2: Los Alamos Laboratory simulation of a one-kilometer-wide asteroid ocean impact.

US Government - Los Alamos National Laboratory/`https://www.space.com/36451-asteroids-bad-at-making-waves.html`/last accessed on Feb 13, 2026

Examining the Tunguska event

Figure 2-3 is a photograph of the Tunguska event in 1908. The photograph was taken more than 20 years after the impact. An estimated 160-foot (50-meter) wide asteroid or comet blew up several miles above the ground, releasing hundreds of times the energy of the Hiroshima bomb. It flattened 830 square miles (2,150 square kilometers) of forest. If it had come in over a city, it would have obliterated it. On the other hand, if it *had* taken out a city, we might have an asteroid deflection system in place today.

FIGURE 2-3: Photo taken in 1929 during the Leonid Kulik expedition of the 1908 Tunguska event.

Leonid Kulik/https://en.wikipedia.org/wiki/Tunguska_event#/media/File:Tunguska_Ereignis-1.jpg/ Public domain / last accessed on Feb 14, 2026

Scientists assumed that an impact the size of Tunguska happened every thousand years or so. The new data suggests this type of impact could happen every century, and the Tunguska impact was more than 100 years ago.

More recently, the 2013 Chelyabinsk meteor, about half the size of Tunguska, blew up in the upper atmosphere with 500 kilotons of energy. It injured 1,600 people and damaged 7,000 buildings. Chelyabinsk fits the higher impact rate from the Nuclear Test Ban Treaty monitoring system data. Equally important, it caught scientists completely unaware.

More recently, in February of 2025, asteroid 2024YR4 was estimated to have a 1 in 43 chance of hitting Earth in 2032. Twice the size of the Tunguska impactor, the blast would carry four times the energy, surpassing the largest nuclear weapon. Closer tracking shows it will miss Earth, but this type of near miss also supports the higher impact rate. More concerning is an extrapolation of the higher impact rate to asteroids big enough to set a continent on fire and plunge the Earth into a nuclear winter.

Assessing risk

Asteroid and comet impacts aren't just possible, they're inevitable. If you doubt that, look at the moon. Not only is it covered in impact craters, but it was actually created by a massive impact. On top of that, almost every shooting star (meteor) you've ever seen comes from the Earth traveling through the debris cloud of a comet — a comet that has crossed Earth's orbit in the past. In other words, these are comets that just missed us.

There are more than 100 named meteor showers. Figure 2-4 shows a close-up picture of a real, 2.5-mile-wide (4 km) comet taken from the Rosetta spacecraft in 2014. It won't hit Earth, but if one of this size did, it would take out almost all of us.

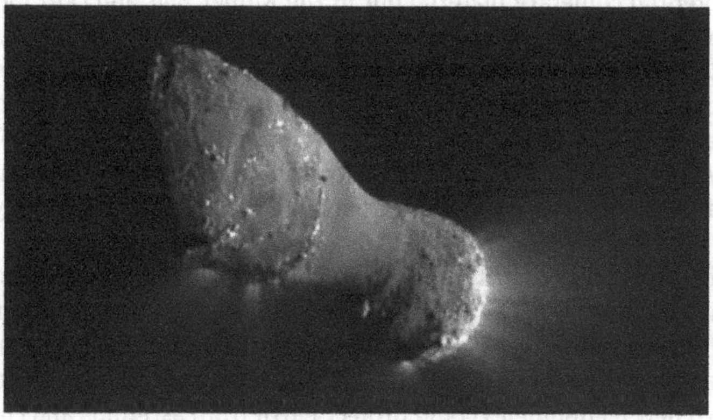

FIGURE 2-4: A close-up picture of a comet taken from the European Space Agency (ESA) spacecraft Rosetta in 2014.

NASA/https://science.nasa.gov/solar-system/comets/103p-hartley-hartley-2/Public domain/last accessed on Feb 14, 2026

Predicting probability

This may be surprising, but you are statistically more likely to die in an asteroid or comet impact than in an airplane crash. Although there are dozens of fatal airplane crashes every year, the odds that you will be on *that* particular airplane are extremely low. The problem with a large asteroid or comet impact is that *we're all on the same airplane*. Even a small probability of a major impact is amplified because it applies to everyone. It's not just the risk of an asteroid or comet landing on your head; if that were the case, you wouldn't need this book. The problem is that for every person killed, there will be thousands who are injured or displaced.

Although the odds of a dinosaur-killer-sized asteroid or comet hitting the Earth during your lifetime are extremely low, the probability of one big enough to set a continent on fire, while still low, is quite a bit higher. These asteroids or comets may be ten times smaller, but they're also roughly ten times more likely. Then there are even smaller impacts that could take out a city like the Tunguska impact. The odds that you will be in that city are much lower, but the likelihood of one of these impacts is roughly 100 times higher.

The good news is that NASA and other agencies are successfully identifying most of the large asteroids that could be a threat to Earth. The bad news is that they can't do this with comets. Unless a comet has visited the inner solar system and made a loop around the sun since we've had telescopes, we won't know of its existence. Unlike asteroids, new comets from outside the solar system are impossible to detect . . . until they're inbound.

TECHNICAL STUFF

Comets appear to be rare, but just the opposite is true. If all the dangerous asteroids were marbles, they'd fill a dump truck. That's a lot of marbles, but if all the potential cometary material out in the Kuiper Belt and Oort Cloud were marbles, they'd fill a line of dump trucks parked nose-to-tail and extending for over 60 miles (100 km). On average, one new comet is discovered every week. Scientists have recently discovered that comets can even come from other stars. In November 2025, comet 3i/Atlas was the third interstellar comet to slice through our solar system from another star. To quote one of the world's leading impact experts, Dr. William Napier, the Earth exists in a cosmic shooting gallery.

The problem is that finding a new comet with Earth in its crosshairs might only give us a year or two before impact. That isn't enough time to launch a Bruce Willis on an *Armageddon* deflection mission. Current strategies require at least seven years to rendezvous with and deflect a large asteroid or comet. Fortunately, two new technologies could protect Earth from asteroids and comets that are discovered very late. One uses a directed energy beam. The concept is called DE-STAR (Directed Energy System for Targeting of Asteroids and exploRation) and is highlighted in the "How Do We Prevent Our Inevitable Extinction?" TED talk. The other technology uses kinetic energy with penetrating impactors as a last line of defense. Details of this technology are covered in Chapter 24. Unfortunately, the development of these technologies currently receives very little funding.

The specific impacts of an "impact" result in many of the effects created by local disasters such as fires, earthquakes, and flooding. These effects are covered in Chapter 3.

2: Artificial general intelligence: Arriving sooner than you think

The term *artificial intelligence (AI)* is overused, describing everything from motion detector flood lights to ChatGPT. The term *artificial general intelligence (AGI)* is more specific and refers to a machine with the ability to understand and learn any intellectual task that a human being can. AGI is tougher to rank as a threat — not because no one knows the probability of it happening, but because no one can be sure of the consequences.

On our current path, AGI will achieve the same computational capability as a human brain within a few years. That's not easy to achieve because the human brain is surprisingly powerful and compact. With current technology, it would take ten million cutting-edge processors in huge factory-sized buildings, pulling more than a gigawatt of power, to match your three-pound brain. That would cost well over $1 trillion. However, two years later, that might be $500 billion, then a year later, $50 billion. Moore's Law has been correctly predicting the doubling of computing power every two years. That means the arrival of human-level AGI is now simply a question of money rather than time. When the believed payoff is greater than the price, AGI becomes inevitable. More importantly, very shortly after that, superintelligent AGI will follow. With the huge drive to be first and the current investments, we are only a few years away.

Matching our IQ

An AGI with *my* intelligence isn't much of a threat, but these systems have something you and I don't. They can access and process thousands of times more information and do it in a fraction of a second. Because of this, even though they don't yet have our IQ, they can already do things that humans can't. AGI is proving to be better at discovering new materials, genetic combinations, encryption, etc. However, it goes both ways. A rogue nation or a malevolent human with access to these systems can use them to accelerate the development of more powerful cyberattacks, deadly viruses, or lethal weapons.

TECHNICAL STUFF

Nobel Prize–winning physicist Sir Roger Penrose and Dr. Federico Faggin, the father of the microprocessor, believe that consciousness isn't simply the result of total processing power. They believe that an AGI with human-level intelligence doesn't necessarily mean it will be sentient or conscious. In other words, it won't automatically have free will and be able to initiate action rather than just respond to instructions. They believe consciousness is tied to quantum processes that operate in the human brain. New research recently demonstrated that these quantum processes can occur in the microtubules that form the skeleton of your cells. Since operational computer chips don't use quantum processes, they believe they cannot be conscious. If Penrose and Faggin's hypothesis turns out to be correct, consciousness and the ability to initiate action may require more than just brute-force processing power. However, even if this idea is correct, the hottest area of computer chip development today is . . . quantum chips.

Assessing risk

The next step is when AGI exceeds our intelligence. At that point, it should be able to design more capable AGI systems, which could then develop even smarter ones that could then do the same. You get the idea. Humans have had about the same IQ for thousands of years. An AGI might be able to design its successor and double its IQ every year. That exponential increase could give it a thousand times the computational ability of a human brain within a few years. This is referred to as the Singularity, which is the point at which AGI becomes so much more intelligent than humans that it becomes impossible to predict the outcome or humanity's future. A superintelligent AGI might be able to cure cancer, reverse aging, and make fusion power a reality . . . but it could also decide to keep us as pets. That may sound absurd, but the IQ difference between a human and a chimpanzee is only about 60 points. Yet that relatively small difference was enough to create more than eight billion of us and a permanent place on the endangered species list for the chimpanzee. Even if a superintelligent AGI isn't conscious and able to initiate action like taking over the world, a malevolent organization or country could still employ it.

A WORLD OF ABUNDANCE

Another potential outcome in the next ten years will be a world where all products and services are universally available and ridiculously cheap. AGI and humanoid robots would work faster and more efficiently than humans at a fraction of the cost. The potential disaster may not be a *Terminator* future, but a much more personal disaster with the loss of most jobs. This is covered in Chapter 4, and how this could unfold is covered in Chapter 24. Yeah . . . I don't get invited to many parties anymore.

PULLING THE PLUG ON AGI

Pulling the plug on AGI in the future may not be as easy as it sounds. Simple AI algorithms already influence what people think and believe. Most of the population now gets their view of the world from social media platforms like Google, YouTube, Instagram, and the like. These platforms generate profit through advertising, so they need to maximize exposure to their ads. That means keeping you on their platform as long as possible by making sure you're happy with what you're viewing.

The AI algorithms track what you're accessing and feed you more of the same and feed you nothing that doesn't support your interest or social/political view. Additionally, they know people are more likely to click things that make them indignant, so the algorithms prioritize videos, podcasts, and posts with inflammatory subjects. This isn't a malevolent AGI with an agenda; it's just a collection of simple AI algorithms that work behind the scenes to increase advertising exposure and profit.

Of course, the net result is that it often appears to you that a whole swath of the population must be completely insane or clueless . . . and *that* swath is thinking the same about you. The point is that simple algorithms already influence beliefs. A superintelligent AGI might easily be able to influence everyone into not "pulling the plug." Add the rapid development of humanoid robots, as shown in Figure 2-5, that can run and have enough dexterity to catch a baseball, and an AGI may be able to physically prevent us from "pulling the plug."

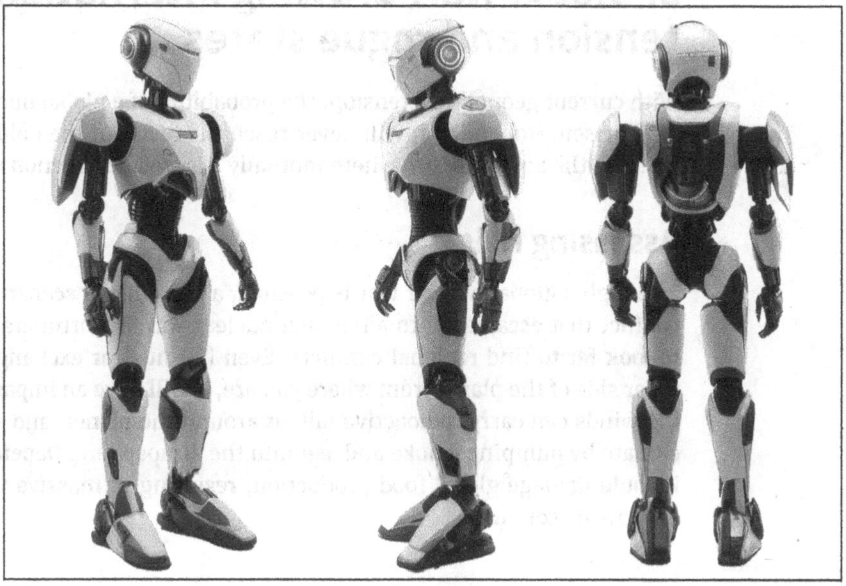

FIGURE 2-5: Humanoid robot.

ramses/Adobe Stock Photos

Predicting probability

A 2024 study of biorisk (potential for harm from viruses, bacteria, or toxins) conducted by the Forecasting Research Institute surveyed the top experts in the field. They predicted AI might match the best virologists in one out of six areas of research by 2034. By the first half of 2025, AI matched the best experts in half the research areas. This should cause concern, particularly in this field of research. Most economic forums also suggest that by the end of 2027, AI will begin having a profound positive effect on U.S. and global gross domestic product (GDP), but with a proportionally negative effect on employment due to the replacement of workers.

Unless there's a global movement to regulate how AGI evolves, it will surpass human intelligence in less than ten years from when this book was published. Continued massive investment could push it to within five years. Currently, AGI is ranked as the number two potential global threat. Only uncertainty about the consequences prevents it from moving to the number one position. Chapter 24 highlights how this might unfold and what steps governments and individuals can take to prevent us from becoming pets.

3: Global war: Growing international tension and rogue states

With current geopolitical tension, the probability of a global nuclear war has definitely risen. Hopefully, it will never reach the levels of the Cold War between the U.S. and the Soviet Union, where mutually assured destruction was a given.

Assessing risk

Although a global nuclear war is possible, a more likely scenario would be a local conflict that escalates into a regional nuclear war. Unfortunately, you don't have to look far to find regional conflicts. Even if a nuclear exchange happens on the other side of the planet from where you are, it will have an impact on you. Prevailing winds can carry radioactive fallout around the planet, and it would affect the climate by pumping smoke and ash into the atmosphere. Depending on the scale, it could damage global food production, resulting in massive waves of refugees, and crash economies.

MUTUALLY ASSURED DESTRUCTION (MAD)

I remember as a young Navy fighter pilot seeing a nuclear attack profile for the first time. Using a fighter instead of bombers in a nuclear war would be a last resort. Unlike high altitude bombers, the attack profile I was training for had me coming in extremely low, pulling straight up at the target, and lobbing the warhead. Then, I was supposed to try to fly away before the bomb fell back toward the ground and detonated. Imagine taking a grenade in your hand, running right up to the enemy, stopping, pulling the pin, and throwing it straight up in the air. Now, imagine turning around and running away as it falls. Yeah . . . that's exactly what *I* was thinking. The joke among pilots was that they should just make the bomb release button detonate the nuke while it's still attached to the jet. It would save time and eliminate the stress of trying to escape the blast. Bottom line, the actual use of any nuclear weapon anytime is a terrible idea for everyone.

Another scenario is the use of an electromagnetic pulse (EMP) weapon. These are nuclear warheads that are detonated over 20 miles above the ground. At that altitude, they produce no blast effect and limited heat and radiation damage. The energy is in the form of a huge gamma ray burst. When it collides with air molecules in the atmosphere, it produces a massive EMP strong enough to overload and destroy unprotected power grids hundreds of miles from the blast. The effect is similar to a massive solar superstorm except that an EMP warhead also destroys unshielded electronics and electronically controlled devices such as cell towers, cars, computers, and cell phones. While a nuclear war with EMP warheads is possible, a solar superstorm, covered in the next section, is inevitable.

Predicting probability

There are currently at least nine nations that have nuclear weapons and several working to develop them. Currently, the countries with nuclear weapons are Russia, the United States, China, France, the United Kingdom, India, Pakistan, Israel, and North Korea. The stated purpose of nuclear weapons is deterrence. Ironically, all the countries with nuclear arsenals also happen to be on one of the other nuclear nations' target lists. So, if you live in or near one of these countries, you may want to have a friend or a vacation cabin in a rural area or look for property in nearby countries that don't have nuclear arsenals.

4: Biological threat: Expanding biotechnology and pandemics

Rising in danger in comparison to nuclear war are pandemics and biological threats.

Assessing risk

These threats include natural pandemics, genetically modified organisms, and new biotechnology such as a gene drive and mirror-image life.

PANDEMICS

COVID was a wakeup call — one that was responsible for an estimated seven million deaths globally with a mortality rate of roughly one percent. COVID was transmitted via air and had a fairly long incubation period. These two factors allowed it to spread rapidly. However, there are strains of Ebola that have mortality rates of 90 percent. Ebola is spread via bodily fluids instead of respiratory transmission, so it's less contagious. However, a worst-case scenario would be a respiratory or airborne virus with a long incubation period and a high fatality rate. This could mutate naturally or be engineered. Chapter 5 covers ways to protect the air that you breathe.

BIOTECHNOLOGY

Other threats are the potential malevolent use of biotech, including new technologies such as gene editing with the application of gene drive or biological life synthesis, such as mirror-image life.

Gene drive is a very powerful and useful tool. It's been used to try to prevent mosquitoes from spreading disease. For example, a mosquito's DNA was edited such that it cannot carry the malaria parasite. Then, a gene drive was inserted into the gene sequence, which makes that trait permanently dominant. No matter what mosquito this modified mosquito breeds with, its offspring and their offspring will carry that trait forever. Over time, this should change the entire mosquito population such that they cannot carry malaria. The potential benefits are very high, but this technology can be applied to any organism, including humans. This means that any genetic trait could be introduced into a population. Over time, that trait would become permanently engineered into that population.

Mirror-image life is an even more concerning biological technology. All of the biomolecules that make up life on Earth, like DNA and proteins, have a "handedness" to them, just like your right hand is a mirror image of your left hand. Proteins can either be left-handed or right-handed. No one knows why, but all life on Earth has left-handed proteins and DNA. Laboratories have recently been able to create right-handed proteins. It is possible, although it hasn't been achieved yet, to synthetically create an entire organism composed of right-handed instead of left-handed proteins. This is called mirror-image life. They would be identical in their function but would be unrecognizable by any Earth organisms.

This has potentially positive applications, such as getting certain proteins that fight cancer into the body without them being attacked by the body's immune system. Of course, you can see the other side. If you create right-handed bacteria, no organism on Earth would recognize them. Even the most treatable bacterial infection, if redesigned as a right-handed organism, would be completely invisible to all antibodies or antibiotics. In the extreme case, a right-handed organism could multiply unchecked throughout all ecosystems, crowding out all the other life on the planet. That's unlikely, but it highlights the dangers of biological synthesis.

Predicting probability

Applying what the world learned from the COVID pandemic, the probability of a catastrophic pandemic has been slightly reduced. However, there is a wildcard.

Trying to build a nuclear weapon requires very sophisticated resources and technology that are out of the reach of most terrorist organizations. Biotechnology, however, has advanced to the point that any well-equipped lab can conduct basic gene editing. With that capability, rogue nations or terrorist organizations have the potential to create biological weapons.

5: Solar superstorm: Taking out the global power grid

Solar flares and coronal mass ejection (CME) events carry a huge amount of electromagnetic energy. Earth's magnetic field and atmosphere protect life on the planet from these storms, but not our infrastructure or technology, as shown in Figure 2-6. A solar flare is an intense, localized burst of electromagnetic radiation from the sun. CMEs are massive eruptions of magnetized plasma and radiation from the sun's surface. The sun produces these frequently, but they're only dangerous when these narrow bursts happen to be pointed at us. Solar flares travel at the speed of light and can disrupt communication, navigation and impact power grids. CMEs are slower but can carry much more energy. If a massive CME's plasma strikes the Earth, it could take down the world's power grids.

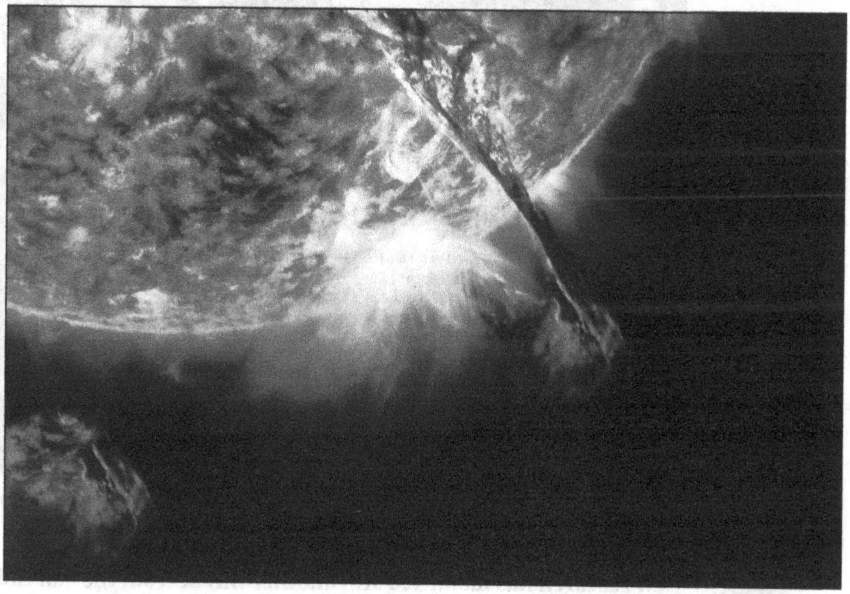

Artsiom P/Adobe Stock Photos

FIGURE 2-6: Coronal mass ejection event.

Assessing risk

If a large CME struck the Earth, the electromagnetic pulse (EMP) created could take out the world's entire power grid by overloading and burning out the electricity generation and distribution equipment. This would shut down power, water, communication, and transportation, requiring months or years to repair or replace the equipment. Unlike the EMP from a nuclear weapon, it wouldn't damage most electronic devices, such as phones or computers, unless they're plugged into the power grid without any surge protection. However, without power, communication, and transportation, food production and distribution would stop, causing starvation and massive civil unrest.

Unlike asteroids, nuclear war, and AGI, nothing can prevent a solar superstorm, but the effects can be mitigated by fortifying power generation and distribution infrastructure. Chapter 12 covers the Geomagnetic Storm Impact Scale, along with preparations you can make to protect your home and electronic equipment. On the positive side, constant surveillance of the sun provides up to 12 hours of warning of a coronal mass ejection headed toward Earth. Solar flares tend to be less damaging but have only minutes of warning. Figure 2-7 shows the Geomagnetic Storm Impact Scale from `spaceweather.gov`.

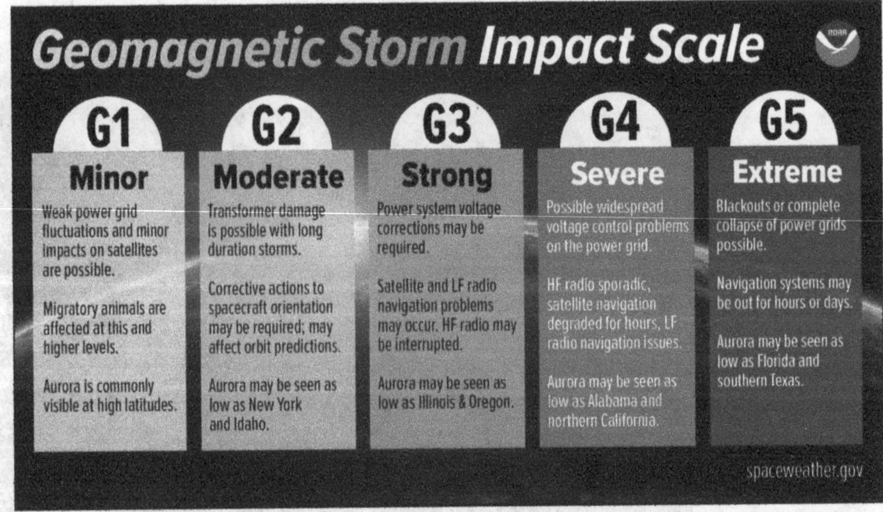

FIGURE 2-7: Geomagnetic Storm Impact Scale.

NOAA/`https://www.weather.gov/wrn/winter-space-sm`/Public domain/last accessed on Feb 14, 2026

TECHNICAL STUFF

New research has identified still another threat from the sun called a solar particle storm. These events appear to be very rare, with the last major one occurring about 14,500 years ago, but they bring a blast of radiation that not only causes the problems mentioned above but can also penetrate the atmosphere and bring dangerous levels of radiation. However, getting indoors, preferably under a concrete or metal roof, should provide protection.

EMP AND AGI

Here's a final ironic thought. If a superintelligent AGI decides to take over the world, the one thing that would probably take it out would be a solar superstorm. Even if it survived, the loss of the global power grid should put it to sleep. However, I wouldn't depend on that as a backup plan.

Predicting probability

Solar superstorms are inevitable and not preventable. They've hit Earth many times in the past and will again. The last large one wasn't that long ago. Known as the Carrington Event of 1859, it created such a strong EMP that it affected the limited technology of the time. Telegraph operators received electric shocks, and it set fire to their equipment. It also produced an aurora borealis that could be seen as far south as Cuba. The Carrington Event wasn't one of the few or even the strongest solar superstorms that Earth has experienced. New research suggests that there have been many storms, and some were at least ten times more powerful.

6: Super volcano: Exploding cubic miles of ash

Super volcanoes are geographic areas that have huge magma chambers lying under an inactive or semi-active volcanic region. They're the most violent volcanic eruptions on the planet, blowing out over a thousand cubic kilometers of magma and ash. If you take the destruction shown in Figure 2-8 and multiply it by 1,000, you'd have a super volcano eruption.

A super volcano eruption would be catastrophic for anyone nearby, but also for the Earth's climate. Each of these sites has erupted in the past (tens to hundreds of thousands of years ago), and volcanologists believe that for all of these, it isn't a question of if they will erupt again but simply when. Super volcano sites include Yellowstone in the U.S., Taupo in New Zealand, and Toba in Indonesia.

TECHNICAL STUFF

Most of Earth's mass extinctions are attributed to climate change caused by massive volcanic eruptions or extraterrestrial impacts. The majority of volcanic activity occurs at the junction of tectonic plates as they collide or move away from each other. Recent research on the oldest impact crater in Australia suggests that the tectonic plates may have been created billions of years ago by massive impacts. Some volcanoes and super volcanoes are not on the edges of the tectonic plates but actually in the middle. For example, Yellowstone is far from the edge of the North

American Plate. A recent hypothesis suggests that these hot spots might also have been caused by a weakness or flaw in the crust or underlying mantle caused by a past extraterrestrial impact. If this turns out to be true, most mass extinctions might actually be caused directly or indirectly by impacts.

FIGURE 2-8: Volcanic eruptions.

visoot/Adobe Stock Photos

Assessing risk

I'll use Yellowstone as an example since it's the closest to where I live. If Yellowstone were to erupt with the same energy it did 631,000 years ago, it would be truly catastrophic for the Western United States, as shown in Figure 2-9.

THE POWER OF VOLCANOES

I had the opportunity to observe a volcanic eruption in Hawaii. It was fascinating watching the lava roll across the ground. It slowly crept over the top of a highway and set a palm tree on fire. It then poured into the ocean with explosive steam fountains, creating new land. Even from a safe observing distance, I could feel the intense heat on my face. As it devoured everything in its path, I realized this uncontrollable force of nature completely ignores human engineering.

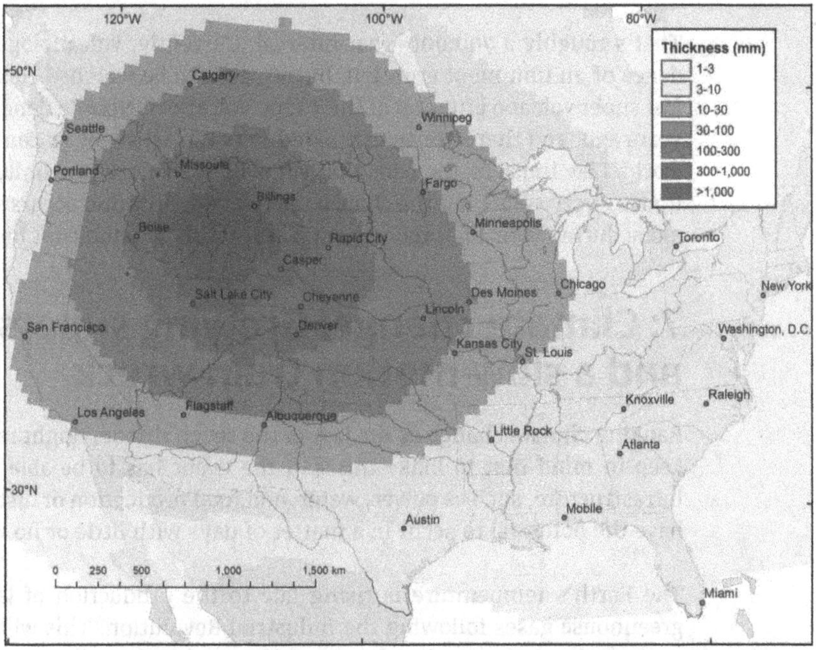

FIGURE 2-9: USGS estimation of the Yellowstone super volcano eruption ash distribution.

USGS/https://www.usgs.gov/volcanoes/yellowstone/modeling-ash-distribution-yellowstone-supereruption-2014/Public domain/last accessed on Feb 14, 2026

The eruption would either be one gigantic explosion or a cascade of explosions within a short period. If you were within 60 miles (100 km) of the eruption, the pyroclastic flows, ejected molten rock, or the ash and gas would probably kill you. Despite the low population density in this region, estimates put immediate deaths at 90,000. If you survived the initial blast, you would have to run from the toxic gas and burning ash that would blanket 400 miles (650 km) from the eruption with 1 foot (0.3 m) or more of ash.

Unless you were able to outrun it, you would likely succumb to asphyxiation. Even airplanes and automobiles with internal combustion engines would be shut down by ash ingestion (an electric vehicle wouldn't be affected, covered in Chapter 17). Eventually, the ash would cover the entire United States and much of Canada. As much as six inches would fall as far east as Chicago and as far west as Los Angeles. The cloud would then be carried around the planet, shutting out the sun and creating a nuclear winter that could drop global temperatures dramatically and destroy crop production.

Predicting probability

Yellowstone's last major eruption was more than 631,000 years ago. Before that, two previous eruptions occurred 1.3 million and 2.1 million years ago, respectively.

That's roughly a 700,000-year interval. Currently, volcanologists don't see evidence of an imminent eruption, but it needs to be watched closely. However, the last super volcano eruption of the Taupo volcano in New Zealand was about 25,000 years ago, and there are an estimated 12 potential super volcano sites around the world. Like impacts, the odds that you will be in close proximity to a major eruption are very small, but the chance that a major eruption occurs somewhere on the globe during your lifetime, although still small, is quite a bit higher.

7: Climate change: Growing superstorms and a slow-motion train wreck

Ranking climate change as the last of the seven threats might raise eyebrows, but keep in mind that to make this list, the event has to be able to damage global infrastructure, such as power, water, and food production or distribution, and also have the potential to occur in a matter of days with little or no warning.

The Earth's temperature is rising due to the production of large quantities of greenhouse gases following the Industrial Revolution. This will result in significant sea level rise, major climate shifts, and potentially more violent weather. Large swaths of coastline will be inundated, areas that were once farmland will become deserts, and deserts may become tropical forests. The Earth has actually operated for over 90 percent of its existence without icecaps, snowcapped mountains, or glaciers. In other words, the current global climate is the exception, not the rule. However, that does nothing to lessen the impact that a major climate shift will have on our current civilization.

Assessing risk

The key difference between this threat and the others is that most of the impacts of climate change will happen over decades. The most aggressive prediction for sea level rise still requires several decades to inundate coastal cities. In other words, this is a slow-motion train wreck. Even if there isn't enough time to slow the progression, there is enough time to prepare for the impact. All the other potential cataclysms can happen in a matter of days or hours. To put this in perspective, an asteroid or comet a kilometer across or a super volcano eruption would completely reverse global warming in a few days . . . but not in a good way. It would create a nuclear winter or small ice age that could last years or decades, making the worst future effects of climate change look like a walk in the park. That's why asteroid and comet impacts and super volcanoes are ranked above climate change.

Predicting probability

Climate change made the list because it can generate superstorms, such as unusually massive hurricanes. Climate change is also likely to increase the number of hurricanes, tornadoes, floods, and wildfires. According to the Weather Channel, the number one weather-related death in the U.S. isn't from storms or floods. Instead, it's actually caused by excessive heat. As storm and flood warnings have improved, the average deaths from these have decreased, but heat-related deaths have remained steady or increased over the past three decades. Another reason climate change made the list is that, along with AI, it is one of the two global threats that are actually in progress. The odds are 100 percent that you and I will feel the impacts of climate change. All the other threats, except nuclear and biological war, are guaranteed to occur but haven't yet. Finally, climate change will be the net result of three of the other cataclysmic disasters.

Estimating the Odds of Global Disasters

When these potential global disasters are combined, the probability of at least one of them occurring during your lifetime is no longer insignificant. An adage says, "Those who fail to learn from history are doomed to repeat it." Most of these global disasters are preventable or can be mitigated. Unfortunately, governments are currently doing little in any of these areas. Chapter 24 covers how these cataclysmic disasters might unfold and what governments can do to prevent most of them.

It's hard to wrap your mind around the possibility of these disasters actually happening. They're often the subject of science fiction stories, including mine, but all that's required is to look back in time. Anthropology makes it clear that humanity's rise hasn't always been smooth. Sudden changes such as droughts and floods, some of which may have been initiated by one of these disasters, have been a factor in the demise of many civilizations. The odds that any one of these will directly impact you are extremely low. Unfortunately, there are seven of them, as shown in Figure 2-10.

THE *FUZED* SERIES

The *Fuzed* series is a set of reality-based thrillers, highlighting four of these global disasters in action-adventure stories that avoid putting people to sleep with statistics. Although fiction, they utilize a technical advisory board of the world's leading experts to accurately depict the top preventable threats along with real-world solutions that governments can develop.

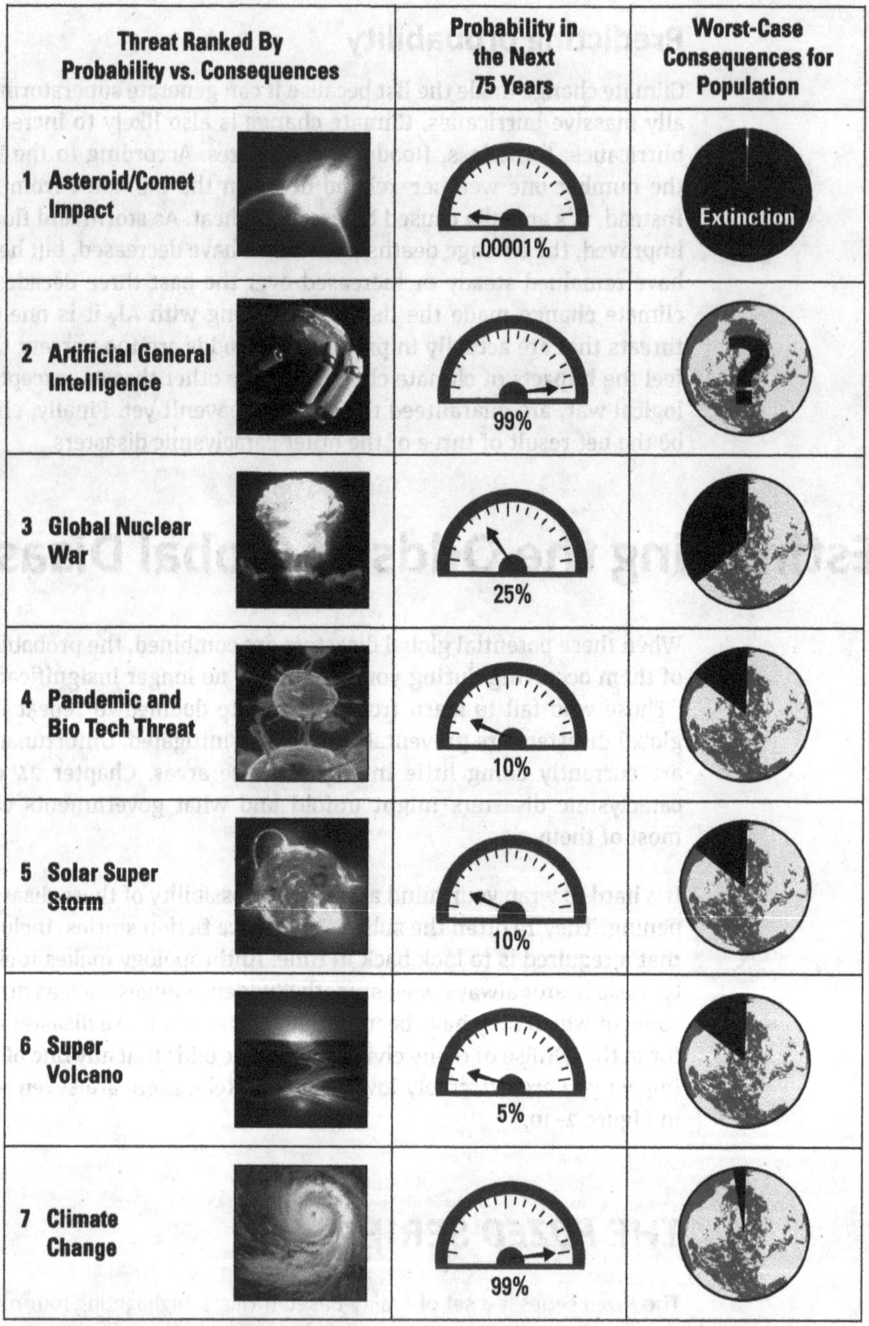

Threat Ranked By Probability vs. Consequences
Probability in the Next 75 Years
Worst-Case Consequences for Population
1 Asteroid/Comet Impact
00001%
Extinction
2 Artificial General Intelligence
99%
?
3 Global Nuclear War
25%
4 Pandemic and Bio Tech Threat
10%
5 Solar Super Storm
10%
6 Super Volcano
5%
7 Climate Change
99%

FIGURE 2-10: Top seven global disasters ranked by probability and consequence.

IN THIS CHAPTER

» Determining which local disasters apply

» Estimating your vulnerability

» Understanding the risk

» Determining immediate action and preparation

Chapter 3 Identifying Local Disasters and Their Impacts

You survived Chapter 2 and all the potential global disasters. This chapter highlights more common local disasters such as floods, hurricanes, tornadoes, wildfires, nuclear/industrial accidents and earthquakes. Most of the effects of the global catastrophes from Chapter 2 are the same as what you would experience during these local disasters. The biggest difference is that global disasters make evacuation more challenging. Even if you're certain that none of the local disasters in this chapter apply to where you live, a global disaster can create similar risks and dangers and require similar action and preparation.

In the previous chapter, global disasters were ranked based on two factors: probability versus consequence. These two factors will eliminate the need to consider many local disasters based on your location. For example, in Calgary, Canada, hurricanes won't make your threat list, but ice storms might. However, in addition to probability and consequence, a third variable, specific to your situation, is added.

Evaluating Vulnerability

In addition to probability and consequence, a "vulnerability" factor is added. This vulnerability factor was created by former Army Ranger Brian Duff, author of the book *Mind 4 Survival*, and who served as this book's technical editor. The new equation is

$$\text{probability} \times \text{consequence} \times \text{vulnerability} = \text{threat score}$$

This threat score considers your situation and preparation.

Here's an example: Let's say you live in central Oklahoma, also known as being part of "Tornado Alley." The probability of a tornado is higher than anywhere in the U.S. Based on this, you might assess the probability of a tornado as a 4 out of 5 (with 5 being the highest probability and 0 being the lowest).

Knowing that the consequence of a direct hit by a major tornado can be catastrophic, you might also give the consequence a 4 out of 5. The probability times the consequence would be $4 \times 4 = 16$. Now add the "vulnerability" factor. If you live in a house built out of insulated concrete forms, highlighted in Chapter 22, or you have a basement or tornado shelter in your home, your vulnerability might only be 1 out of 5. That would create a total threat score of $4 \times 4 \times 1 = 16$.

However, if you live in a mobile home, the vulnerability score would probably be 4 out of 5 since mobile homes have little chance of surviving tornadoes. This creates a total threat score of $4 \times 4 \times 4 = 64$. You can see that vulnerability makes a big difference in the score and your risk.

Based on your location, you can skip many of the threats listed in this chapter and then rank any local disaster that applies using this scoring system, as shown in Table 3-1. This will help you determine how much time and energy you want to put into preparation based on your risk.

TABLE 3-1 **Threat evaluation formulae: probability × consequence × vulnerability = threat score**

Threat	Probability 0 to 5	×	Consequence 0 to 5	×	Vulnerability 0 to 5	=	Threat Score
		×		×		=	
		×		×		=	
		×		×		=	
		×		×		=	

Hurricanes/Typhoons: Surging Water Carries Away Houses, Cars, and People

I live on the Texas coast, which is an area that's been hammered by hurricanes in the past. I designed our beachfront house to survive a Category 5 hurricane, but it doesn't matter how well it's built if it gets knocked over by a house that wasn't as well built. I recently rode out a Category 1 hurricane to test several ideas and technologies. There wasn't a mandatory evacuation, but I did have an evacuation plan and carefully monitored the hurricane's progress, wind speed, and storm surge. The peak winds stayed under 80 mph. I learned a lot, but I strongly recommend against riding out any hurricane. In other words, do as I say, not as I did.

WARNING

In 2023, off the western coast of Mexico, Hurricane Otis went from a Category 1 to a Category 5 in less than 24 hours, surprising forecasters. Those in Otis's path had less than a day to evacuate from the catastrophic impact. With rapidly rising tides, evacuation routes are often submerged long before the hurricane makes landfall.

Classifying hurricanes

When you go from a Category 1 to a Category 5 hurricane, the wind speed doubles from 75 mph (120 kph) to over 156 mph (240 kph), as shown in Figure 3-1. However, the force that the wind exerts is the square of the wind's speed. What that means is that although the wind speed doubles, the force hitting you or your house is FOUR TIMES higher. To put that in perspective, an F-18 jet takes off at the same speed as a Category 5 hurricane's wind. In other words, those winds can lift a 30-ton fighter into the air.

FIGURE 3-1: Hurricane category wind speed and storm surge height.

Olga Izvekova/Adobe Stock Photos

Considering storm surge

As dangerous as those winds are, they're not the deadliest threat. A friend of mine who had a beachfront house north of Galveston was watching Hurricane Ike in the Gulf of Mexico in 2008, which was predicted to come ashore as a Category 1 or Category 2. His brand-new house was built to code on 10-foot-tall pilings, so he planned to ride it out.

The morning before the hurricane made landfall was quiet with almost no wind or waves. Despite the calm conditions and predictions, he had an uneasy feeling and decided to leave with his wife that morning. A few hours after he left, the wind remained low, but the water slowly rose until it covered the only highway off the peninsula. As predicted, Hurricane Ike made landfall as a Category 2 storm, but it had a Category 5 storm surge, responsible for $38 billion in damages. The bottom of his house was 16 feet above sea level, but the 20-foot storm surge didn't read the building codes. When he came back a few days later, his house was completely gone. Even the pilings and concrete slab they were embedded in were missing.

Assessing risk

With hurricanes and typhoons, the primary risk is storm surge, which is responsible for 90 percent of hurricane fatalities. The large battering waves sweep houses and people away. After storm surge, the wind is the next biggest danger, primarily from flying debris. A piece of lumber can become a deadly projectile able to penetrate the wall of a home.

Post hurricane or typhoon, the biggest risk is no emergency services and the inability to travel or evacuate on damaged or submerged roads. If you stay, you may face long-term loss of the power grid, municipal water, and access to stores for food and bottled water. This can result in the risk of heat stroke, dehydration, or illness.

WHY PEOPLE IN THE SOUTHEASTERN U.S. DIE EARLIER

There may be an even higher long-term risk of hurricanes and tropical cyclones. Recent research is summarized in a 2025 PBS *Terra* program titled "Did Scientists Just Figure Out Why People Die a Decade Earlier in the Southeastern US?" The study suggests that the long-term impacts of hurricanes and tropical storms can last for years after the event. While direct deaths from storm surge and winds have been significantly reduced by more accurate forecasting, long-term indirect deaths may contribute to the lower life expectancy in the Southeastern U.S. The factors that contribute to reduced lifespan include:

- Contaminants created by the release of chemicals into the ground and water from flooding of industrial areas and spikes in pathogens such as bacteria, viruses, and mold.
- Reduction in local government function during the recovery years, such as suspension or reduction in health care service, sanitation, and law enforcement.
- Long-term economic impacts, including the loss of local businesses and industry, with the resulting loss of jobs, reductions in household income, and the need to relocate.
- Finally, stress reduces lifespan. The initial trauma, combined with loss of a business, job, housing, or forced relocation away from family or social support, can be extremely stressful.

Taking immediate action

If you're in the direct path of any hurricane or typhoon, the strategy is simple — evacuate. Don't wait until the last minute. Evacuating early avoids having your exit route blocked by rising water or massive traffic jams. Assume the hurricane can make landfall at least one category higher than predicted. Even if it's only predicted to be a tropical storm, assume it could develop into a hurricane. If, due to your location and the predicted path or strength of the storm, you believe you can ride it out, monitor the storm closely. Sudden changes in its path, strength, or time over your location can have a dramatic impact. Have an evacuation plan and be ready to execute it at a moment's notice. Remember my friend and his former beach home.

Preparing

Check your insurance before the storm season begins. Understandably, flood and windstorm insurance require 30 days from purchase or change to become active and cannot be bought or changed if a named storm is predicted to impact your area. Hurricanes and typhoons are now tracked extensively and accurately.

If you live in an area at risk, stay informed and have an exit plan. Decide in advance under what conditions you will evacuate and where you'll go. Part 4 covers evacuation transportation, destinations, and what to take with you. If you're not in the direct path of a hurricane or typhoon or you are far enough inland that evacuation isn't necessary, Part 2 will cover strategies to get through the extended interruption of municipal infrastructure.

Chapter 10 covers strategies to help fortify your doors and windows against extreme wind and flying debris.

Heat Waves: Overheating Is the #1 Cause of Weather-Related Fatalities

If you ignore the potential long-term impacts of hurricanes and typhoons on life expectancy, heat-related deaths actually surpass other weather-related fatalities. While major catastrophic weather events can eclipse heat deaths in any given year, heat-related deaths have remained a constant, silent killer over the past three decades. These deaths particularly affect the most vulnerable of the population — children, the elderly, and those with chronic medical conditions.

According to the National Oceanic and Atmospheric Administration (NOAA), heat-related deaths are likely to increase. The Earth's average surface temperature has increased by about 1.8°F (1°C) since the 1970s. That doesn't sound like much, but it's an average across the globe. Many locations are much higher or lower. It's now common to have record-setting temperatures in many areas each summer.

Assessing risk

Not surprisingly, most heat-related injuries and deaths are due to heat stroke and dehydration. When core body temperature exceeds 104 degrees, or you become substantially dehydrated, you're facing a potentially lethal situation. These effects are particularly acute in children, the elderly, or those with preexisting conditions, including diabetes and cardiovascular issues. A good way to evaluate the risk is by using the Heat Index, which operates with a "feels like temperature" paradigm. In addition to the air temperature, it includes the effects of the air's relative humidity since the body's ability to cool by perspiring is massively impacted by high humidity.

Taking immediate action

Be aware of the Heat Index. If it's predicted to be extreme, drink plenty of water even when you're not thirsty, and drink liquids with electrolytes, such as sports drinks. Wear light colored, loose-fitting, breathable clothing that allows air to circulate. Avoid exertion, stay out of the sun, and seek air-conditioned spaces. Taking frequent baths or showers in cool water can also help.

Preparing

This is all good advice, but many of these actions aren't possible during a disaster when electricity or water pressure is lost. Parts 2 and 3 of this book cover strategies and preparations to protect you and your family from the heat when municipal water and power go down.

PREVENTING HEAT STROKE/DEHYDRATION DURING HEAT WAVES

In addition to the previous immediate action steps, you can do the following to protect yourself from heat stroke:

- Your body can dissipate more than 1,000 watts of heat by sweating. This means it's critical to stay hydrated.

(continued)

(continued)

- You can also cover sun-facing windows and move to the lower level of your home.
- If any strenuous work is required, do it at night if possible.
- Make sure you have several battery-powered fans, and if the humidity isn't high, you can use evaporative cooling by spraying yourself with a water mist. See Exploring Power Options (Level 2) in Chapter 12 to learn how to provide power for cooling.

Floods: Drowning Is the #1 Cause of Storm-Related Fatalities

Although hurricanes and tornadoes get the greatest media coverage, flash floods can be equally catastrophic and more deadly with less advanced warning. Floods can be the result of hurricanes or other storms, but are usually created by extreme or prolonged rain. When you consider all weather events globally, after excess heat, floods are the #1 cause of death, killing more than 6,000 people a year.

In 2025, a massive rain event in central Texas caused parts of the Guadalupe River to rise 35 feet in less than 40 minutes. Unfortunately, much of this occurred at night. Even if you're an Olympic runner, outrunning a river at night that expands from 100 feet wide (30 meters) to over a mile (1.6 km) in a matter of minutes is next to impossible. The speed and force of the water can sweep away not just people but entire houses. Flood currents move faster than most people can run. No matter how good a swimmer you are, you're going to be carried rapidly downriver with tons of dangerous debris.

WARNING

You don't have to face a catastrophic flooding event to be at risk. A large percentage of drowning deaths occur when people attempt to drive their car across a flooded road. Moving water is surprisingly powerful. As little as six inches can knock you off your feet. Twelve inches can sweep away a car.

REMEMBER

When facing flooded roads or paths, remember and share the cheesy but accurate phrase, "Turn around; don't drown."

Assessing risk

For floods, the primary danger is clearly being swept away and drowning. The secondary threat is being trapped in your home or other location and unable to evacuate. Isolated without electricity, drinkable water, or food, you are at risk primarily from heat stroke and dehydration. Additionally, flood waters often contain toxins, bacteria, and viruses.

Taking immediate action

If you encounter a flash flood while traveling, don't try to cross that water — turn around, don't drown. Delay is better than death. If the flood is coming to you and you're on foot, the only strategy is to get to higher ground. If the flood source is a river or drainage canal, move perpendicular to it. Climbing a tree or other structure should only be used as a last resort since floods can sweep away trees and almost any other structure.

If you're trapped or isolated by the flood, use your phone to let first responders know your location and situation. If you can't get through to them, call or text several people who can relay that information in case your phone dies. Be sure to include your location. If your location isn't tied to a specific address or landmark, use a GPS marker. Chapter 11 covers a way to use your phone to communicate even when the cell phone network is down or unavailable.

Preparing

Determine in advance if your home or even your vacation spot is located in a flood plain. Create a specific escape or evacuation plan. If there's any question about the weather, make sure you have a way to be notified via a weather app or weather radio, even when you're sleeping. Specific evacuation strategies are covered in Part Four. If you aren't directly in the path of a major storm or flood and evacuation isn't necessary, Part 2 covers strategies to get you through an extended interruption of municipal infrastructure, while waiting for the flood waters to subside.

Tornadoes: Blowing Away Structures and Creating Deadly Projectiles

Tornadoes give you very little time to prepare or evacuate. Here, the goal is simple: survive the storm. It's straightforward if you have a basement or a tornado shelter. If you don't, it requires immediate action, which means prior planning.

Early on, I learned that 60 percent of all military tactical jet fatalities occur from pilots flying into the ground, despite the fact that fighters have ejection seats. The problem is that pilots spend too much time trying to save the aircraft and wait too long to eject. I taught my flight students to make the decision when to eject *before* they strap into the jet. There's not enough time when the situation is at hand. They must determine, in advance, when to pull that ejection handle. The same applies to immediate emergencies like tornadoes. You need to figure out exactly what you're going to do now, when you have time to think without adrenaline.

Tornadoes are classified by their top wind speed using the Enhanced Fujita Scale (EF) shown in Figure 3-2. Chapter 10 covers options if you don't have access to a tornado shelter.

Enhanced Fujita scale

Scale	Wind speed mph	Wind speed km/h	Frequency	Information
EFU	N/A	N/A	3.11%	**No observable** damage
EF0	65-85	105-137	52.82%	**Minor** damage: Small trees are blown down and bushes are uprooted. Shingles are ripped off roofs.
EF1	86-110	138-177	32.98%	**Moderate** damage: Small trees are uprooted. Roofs stripped from shingles.
EF2	111-135	178-217	8.41%	**Significant** damage: Medium trees are uprooted. Whole roofs ripped off frame houses.
EF3	136-165	218-266	2.18%	**Severe** damage: All trees are uprooted. Roofs and outside walls are blown away from frame homes.
EF4	166-200	267-322	0.46%	**Devastating** damage: Trees partially debarked. Frame homes are completely destroyed.
EF5	>200	>322	0.05%	**Incredible** damage: Trees are debarked. Frame or brick homes are swept away.

Dimitrios/Adobe Stock Photos

FIGURE 3-2: Enhanced Fujita Scale (EF Scale) tornado categories by wind speed.

Assessing risk

Movies suggest that the biggest danger is being sucked off the ground and into the tornado. Large tornadoes can indeed tear the roof off a house and demolish it. However, the primary cause of death in a tornado is actually flying debris. With wind speeds over 200 miles per hour, a 2 × 4 (39mm × 89mm) piece of lumber can penetrate a cinderblock wall, and EF5 tornadoes have thrown automobiles more than 300 feet (100 meters).

Taking immediate action

If you're outside or in your car and can find a sturdy building, abandon your car and get inside the building. Go to the lowest level and stay away from windows. If you can't find a safe structure, look for a ditch or low spot on the ground that can provide some protection from flying debris. Lie flat with your face down and cover your head. A bridge with a highway underpass may look like it provides protection, but it can funnel the wind, creating even higher wind speeds. If there is no ditch or low spot and you're stuck in your car, fasten your seatbelt, duck down below the windows, and protect your head.

If you're inside, get yourself and your family to your basement, a tornado shelter, the lowest level of a nearby sturdy building, or someone else's basement. If none of this is available, go to an inside room with no windows, like a closet or a room with small windows, like a bathroom. If a bathtub is available, get in it and stay low. Regardless of where you end up, protect your head with a mattress or cushions if possible.

Preparing

Chapter 10 covers simple strategies to fortify your doors and windows against extreme wind and flying debris, ways to create a more survival room inside your home, and basic tornado shelters. Part 2 covers strategies to get through the extended interruption of municipal infrastructure after the storm passes.

Wildfires: Driving Winds Push Fires and Kill by Smoke Inhalation

Fires can be caused by an impact, war, or a volcano, but it's more likely to occur from a wildfire. Wildfires have recently swept across the Western and Central U.S. as well as parts of Canada, Europe, and Australia.

Assessing risk

The average speed of a wildfire driven by wind is about 14 mph (23 kph), but with extreme winds, wildfires can expand at more than 25 mph (40 kph). That's a problem since the average person can only run about 12 mph (19 kph). The heavy smoke can obscure escape routes and be disorienting. Most people who die from wildfires succumb to smoke inhalation.

Taking immediate action

If you live in the Western U.S., download the Watch Duty app. Watch Duty is a nonprofit organization of active and retired wildland firefighters, first responders, dispatchers, and reporters. The app creates extremely accurate and up-to-date maps of the status of all major fires from the Pacific to the Mississippi River. There may be similar apps in your area or local emergency service notifications.

If you're notified of an approaching fire or identify one that could be a threat, evacuate as soon as possible. Don't wait. Wildfires driven by wind can rapidly cut off escape routes.

Preparing

If you live in an area prone to wildfires, you want to clear areas around your home of any flammable material. You can also set up a sprinkler system around your home. Sprinklers are not going to put out a wildfire, but they may provide some protection if engaged early by saturating the ground around your home. It's worth a try, but don't stick around to see if it works. Chapter 5 covers critical items such as masks and supplemental oxygen that can protect you during an evacuation. Part 5 covers more advanced fire-suppression systems and vehicles that are particularly effective in these situations.

Earthquakes: Collapsing Roofs and Walls Cause Most Fatalities

You should already know if you live in an earthquake zone. If you're not sure, do the research. Everyone in California and Alaska recognizes the risk . . . or should. However, you might be surprised if you live elsewhere. For example, Memphis, Tennessee, is in an active earthquake zone.

You can access a global seismic risk map at `www.globalquakemodel.org/product/global-seismic-risk-map`. You can also find risk maps specific to your region or country. Additionally, areas that have a high earthquake risk may also have a higher risk of volcanic activity.

Assessing risk

The largest cause of injury and death in an earthquake, not surprisingly, is the collapse of walls and ceilings, followed by falling objects and glass.

Taking immediate action

Unless you're near the exterior door of your home and the area in front of your home isn't surrounded by structures that could collapse or fall on you, it's best not to try to get outside during the earthquake. The actions you should take immediately are as follows:

- **Drop:** Get down to the floor on your hands and knees.
- **Cover:** Seek cover under a sturdy desk or table. If there is no sturdy furniture, get next to an interior wall away from windows, mirrors, and tall furniture.
- **Hold On:** Hold on to the legs of a table or desk, or protect your head and neck with your arms if you're next to a wall. Stay in this position until the shaking stops.

Preparing

Chapter 10 covers furniture that can provide more protection and home modifications that can increase survivability during an earthquake.

Industrial/Nuclear Accidents: Poisoning the Air You Breathe

If you live near or downwind of a chemical or nuclear power plant, there is a risk of exposure to toxic or radioactive material. The worst industrial accident in history occurred in 1984 in Bhopal, India. A chemical plant that produced pesticides had a catastrophic failure that released tons of deadly gas. It immediately killed over 2,250 people and injured another half a million in the surrounding area.

Chernobyl was the worst nuclear power plant disaster. Although not on the same scale as Bhopal, 134 plant workers were hospitalized with acute radiation poisoning, and 28 died within 3 months. Downwind of the plant, thousands were exposed to radioactive material in the air before they could be evacuated. Over the following 20 years, about 6,000 cases of childhood thyroid cancer occurred in the affected population, a large fraction of which were attributed to the disaster.

Assessing risk

Unless you're close enough to be injured in the blast, the risk is entirely respiratory. Breathing in toxic gases can kill immediately by lung damage or suffocation, and also cause long-term lung and organ damage. Breathing in radioactive particles can cause acute radiation poisoning; at lower doses, inhaling radioactive particles can increase your probability of cancer, particularly thyroid cancer.

Taking immediate action

If you live in the vicinity of a chemical or nuclear plant, be aware of warnings such as plant sirens. Make sure your phone's Wireless Emergency Alert, covered in Chapter 11, is active and ensure that your phone settings don't prevent it from alerting you at night. If you know where the plant is located and the prevailing winds, get upwind from the plant as soon as possible. The key is to avoid breathing in any of the gases or particles during your evacuation.

Preparing

Chapter 5 covers preparation, such as using gas masks and supplemental oxygen, which can protect your lungs while evacuating. Chapter 9 also covers potassium iodine pills that can be taken during a nuclear accident to protect your thyroid by blocking the absorption of a common radioactive element.

Blizzards/Ice Storms: Freezing without the Power Grid

Hurricanes and tornadoes tend to take the headlines, and it's often assumed that climate change will make extreme winter weather, such as blizzards and ice storms, a thing of the past. Although the Earth's average temperature is increasing, one of the biggest effects is the shifting of weather patterns. The term "climate change" is accurate. It impacts things like ocean currents, which can warm or cool nearby land masses. Some areas will become hotter and drier, but other areas will see more precipitation and cold periods. With or without climate change, extreme winter weather can always be a threat.

Assessing risk

A major blizzard or ice storm can make roads inaccessible and take down power lines. This can quickly become a disaster if it shuts down emergency services, the power grid, and the ability to heat your home when the temperature is below freezing. The disaster can be amplified during extended periods below freezing without heat due to frozen or ruptured water pipes. A worst-case scenario is being isolated with no power, heat, water, or the ability to evacuate.

Taking immediate action

Keep a close eye on developing weather and ensure you have enough basic food and water. Also, make sure your vehicle is ready for evacuation and filled with gas or charged.

Preparing

Chapters 6 through 9 cover ways to prepare for an extended loss of power — water, food, and emergency services. Chapters 16 and 17 cover evacuation and transportation options.

Active Shooter: Running, Hiding, Attacking

The FBI defines an active shooter as an individual or individuals engaged in killing or attempting to kill people in a confined and populated area. In most cases, active shooters use firearms, and there is no pattern or method to their selection of victims.

Assessing risk

Due to the lack of a pattern, this threat is impossible to predict. The only common factor is that they usually occur in a "confined or populated area." This unfortunately includes schools but can be any location where people gather from nightclubs to concerts. The only preventative measure is to try and be more aware of your surroundings when in any confined or populated area.

Taking immediate action

Below are the actions recommended by law enforcement. These actions may seem obvious, but it's important to review them because when adrenaline is flowing, it's critical to already have a plan in mind. It's also easy to skip simple steps like silencing your phone when hiding.

1. **Running: Evacuate if possible.**
   - If you're far enough away from the gunfire or attacker, get away. Try to plan your escape route to avoid being seen by the attacker. If you're inside a building, run outside and move far away until you're in a secure place.
   - Leave your belongings behind and take others with you, but don't stay if they won't go with you.

- If law enforcement is present, keep your hands up and open as you exit so that they can see that you have no weapons.
- If law enforcement isn't present, when it's safe to do so, call 911. Don't assume someone else did. Information such as the number of shooters, their description, location, and type of weapons may be critical.

2. **Hiding: If you can't evacuate, hide.**
   - If the shooter is too close and you can't evacuate, hide, find a place that:
     - Puts a wall and door between you and the shooter.
     - Allows you to take an alternate escape path.
     - If outside, somewhere that blocks gunfire, like a brick wall or a large tree.
   - If in a room, lock doors, turn off lights, and barricade with furniture.
   - Silence phones and any electronic devices and remain quiet.
   - Remain in place until you receive an "all clear" signal.
3. **Attacking: If you can't evacuate or hide — attack.**
   - If you can't evacuate or hide and your life is in danger, take action.
   - Act aggressively and try to incapacitate the shooter.
   - Use anything around you as an improvised weapon or something to throw, such as a fire extinguisher or chair.
   - If there's more than one of you, a group attack is much more effective.

TIP

Understand that gunfire may sound artificial. Assume that any popping sound is gunfire. If two or more of you are hiding in the same place, spread out to avoid offering easy targets.

REMEMBER

When you're in places where you regularly spend time, such as work or large venues (concerts and sporting events), take a minute to visualize possible escape routes.

Preparing

Due to the random nature of most active shooter situations, it is hard to prepare in advance. Clearly, if your country or state laws allow you to carry defensive devices from pepper spray and stun guns to firearms, and you have the training to handle them, this is a good option. Chapter 13 covers defensive strategies and devices.

WARNING

If you are carrying a firearm in one of these situations, it's very important to make sure that when law enforcement arrives, you aren't confused with the attacker.

Cyberattack: Shutting Down the Digital Economy and Your Bank

Cyberattacks are usually associated with attempts to steal money or data, or damage a company's operations, finances, or reputation. While all that is true, cyberattacks can actually damage or shut down infrastructure. Almost all modern infrastructure is controlled by software, including everything from the power grid and water treatment plants to cell phone networks and airports. There have been several successful attacks that caused shutdowns of power, water, airports, and the like. There have also been attacks that cause permanent damage, such as the 2010 Stuxnet virus, which destroyed more than 800 uranium enrichment centrifuges in Iran by causing them to overspeed.

Assessing risk

The primary risk of a cyberattack is the temporary loss of municipal infrastructure, such as the power grid or water distribution systems, but it could also directly impact transportation, complicating evacuation. Another and more personal impact could be the theft of your assets or identity (see Chapter 4).

Taking immediate action

If you're notified of a cyberattack or data breach, change your passwords immediately. If you suspect your computer has been infected, disconnect it from the Internet to prevent additional damage or theft of personal information. Using another device, change your passwords.

Preparing

The primary personal threat is the theft of your assets or identity. Hackers frequently target bank, credit, stock brokerage, and cryptocurrency accounts. For every improvement in digital security, hackers find another avenue or approach. Chapter 4 covers many protective measures you can take.

TIP

Don't keep all your financial assets in one account. Financial experts recommend spreading your assets across at least three financial institutions. In the event of a cyberattack, it's unlikely all three financial institutions will be successfully attacked at the same time.

IN THIS CHAPTER

- Identifying potential personal disasters
- Evaluating your vulnerability
- Avoiding personal disasters when possible
- Mitigating the impact

Chapter 4
Avoiding Personal Disasters

Personal disasters can be anything from a major vehicle accident to the loss of a job. These disasters don't carry the same shock and awe as global or local disasters, but can be every bit as devastating and are more likely to occur sometime during your lifetime. This chapter looks at strategies that can be taken that might help reduce their impact.

Evaluating Your Vulnerability

It's impossible to list every situation, and in-depth coverage is outside the scope of this book. However, because of their likelihood, this chapter highlights practical considerations and preparations to prevent or mitigate these disasters.

- Loss of assets through fraud, cyberattack, or identity theft
- Loss of your job
- Spiraling debt
- Serious illness or injury
- Loss of your significant other

Almost any of these can happen to anyone, but some of these personal disasters may be more likely or have a larger impact depending on your life stage. You can use the same formulae from Chapter 3 (see Table 3-1) to determine your susceptibility to these.

Avoiding Fraud, Identity Theft, and Cyberattacks

Last year, more than $12 billion was stolen by digital fraud. Almost two-thirds of all credit and debit card holders have been victims of fraud at least once, and one-third have experienced identity theft. I've found false charges on my credit card, and the odds are good you have, too. Although not usually catastrophic, some people have lost their life savings. Digital fraud is one of the most likely personal disasters. Below are steps to reduce your risk.

Creating strong passwords

Using "I don't remember" as your password might not be the best idea. Likewise, don't use words or phrases that someone visiting your social media sites could figure out . . . like your pet octopus's name. You want at least 15 characters with upper and lowercase letters, numbers, and symbols. Try not to reuse passwords across accounts.

Password managers create unique, complex passwords for every account and auto-fill your passwords. However, they are subscription services and are only as good as your master password, which, if compromised, puts all of your accounts at risk.

TIP

For critical financial accounts or master passwords, enable multi-*factor authentication*. This slows down the login process by requiring additional verification steps (like a code sent to your phone or an authentication app), but it provides an important extra layer of security.

Protecting personal information and documents

Think carefully before posting sensitive information such as your address, phone number, or birthdate on social media. Also, avoid sharing personal information over the phone unless you initiated the contact and are certain you can trust the recipient. Store financial and personal documents in a safe place. Evacuation considerations for storing and transporting these documents are covered in Chapter 16. If you still get paper bills and receipts, shred them and any other important documents before discarding them.

Shopping online safely and avoiding phishing scams

Here are some basic steps to improve online safety:

» Only shop on secure websites with "https" in the address bar and a padlock symbol. Sites with URLs starting with "http" are not secure.

» Don't click links in unsolicited emails, pop-up windows, or from social media sites. Visit the company site by typing its URL directly into your secure browser.

» Use a credit card instead of a debit card because credit cards offer better protection against fraudulent charges.

» Legitimate companies don't send emails or texts, and they don't call to ask you to verify purchases, account numbers, or passwords. If you receive one of these emails, texts, or calls, don't click anything or give out your information via email, text, or phone. Instead, contact the company using a phone number or website you know is real. A classic example is an email or text "confirming" an expensive purchase you never made with a link or telephone number. It's a scam often referred to as "phishing."

» A newer type of fraud is referred to as *spear phishing*. Much more insidious, the attack is tailored to you. By first researching your social media and that of your friend group, scammers can collect enough information to impersonate family and friends. Here's an example: You know your child or grandchild is vacationing in another country. You receive a message that claims to be from them. They say they drank too much, got arrested, and unless they can get $1,000 immediately, they're going to spend a month in jail. The message includes plenty of personal information that appears authentic. Be careful what you post on social media, and make sure you confirm identity before sending money.

Securing your Wi-Fi and installing antivirus software

Protect your home Wi-Fi network by enabling encryption and using a strong password. If you use public Wi-Fi, understand that it isn't secure and use a VPN (Virtual Private Network) for sensitive activities like bank and credit card transactions. Use reputable antivirus software and keep all your computer's operating system and browser software updated to protect against security vulnerabilities and malware.

Checking bank statements and credit reports

Check regularly for unauthorized charges or withdrawals from bank and credit card statements. Report any suspicious activity immediately. Monitor your credit report. You can get a free copy from each of the major credit bureaus (Equifax, Experian, and TransUnion) once a year by going to `annualcreditreport.com` or calling 1-877-322-8228.

You can also place a free, one-year fraud alert on your credit reports by contacting the credit bureaus. It then requires businesses to verify your identity before granting new credit. You can even freeze your credit reports, which prevents new accounts from being opened. Of course, you'll have to unfreeze your credit reports if you want to open a new account yourself.

Third-party companies such as Credit Karma can help with real-time monitoring of your credit and accounts. Some of these companies don't charge but come with financial advertising, while others don't advertise but charge a small monthly fee.

Losing Your Job

Here's a terrifying statistic: Fifty-four percent of Americans don't have enough emergency savings to cover even three months of expenses. About a quarter of Americans can't go one month without income. These numbers are almost identical in Canada and European Union nations. Only about a quarter of all households have enough emergency savings to cover six months with no income.

Preparing for AI

In my younger years, I didn't have six months or even three months of emergency income, so I'm not throwing stones. However, the world is changing rapidly. The Industrial Revolution eliminated most jobs that required unskilled labor, but artificial intelligence is poised to eliminate many of the remaining jobs over the next decade. Chapter 24 illustrates how AGI is likely to unfold and its direct impact on jobs, from radiologist to stockbroker.

Building emergency savings

Of course, the standard answer is to save three months, or preferably six months, of income for emergencies. As a teenager, I was also told that if I saved a few hundred dollars every month, I'd be a millionaire before I was old. Yeah, I didn't do that either. The real question is, how did the individuals who have six months of emergency savings achieve it? Many years later, my very successful business mentor taught me that those who've become financially independent have two major things in common:

- They have more than one source of income.
- Some or all of their income is passive. In other words, they can make money while they're sleeping.

DEVELOPING MORE THAN ONE SOURCE OF INCOME

To prepare for the potential of a sudden job loss, it's hard to argue with having another source of income. It's estimated that about one-third of all American adults have a "side hustle." This is usually a small business that provides a product or service. There are literally thousands of books on how to choose and start a small business. One factor to consider when choosing a business or asset is whether it can create passive income.

CREATING PASSIVE INCOME

The simplest form of passive income is dividends and interest from investments. If you have enough financial assets to achieve a significant income from this, you probably also have six months of emergency funds. If not, a good goal is to build a business or asset that will eventually generate income that continues without you having to work at it every day. Oddly enough, the first one that comes to my mind is book royalties; however, this also includes ongoing income from any original content, such as music, video, podcasts, and patented inventions.

If you have capital, other sources of passive income include income-producing real estate, such as an Airbnb. With little or no capital, a successful, global network marketing business with a multi-decade track record can provide ongoing income and business education. A great resource for exploring how to build a passive income business is the #1 selling personal finance book in history, *Rich Dad, Poor Dad*, by Robert Kiyosaki. It's been translated into 51 languages. See Chapter 18.

Spiraling Debt

There are many reasons debt can get out of control. Everything from massive student loans to increasing housing costs. The tipping point is often a personal disaster, such as a job loss, illness, or major repair. With high interest rates compounding, debt can quickly spiral out of control. The ultimate disaster you're trying to avoid is complete financial collapse or bankruptcy. Here are some preemptive steps you can take to prevent debt from becoming a personal disaster.

Budgeting

Not surprisingly, the first and most important step is to create a budget. The problem with that advice is that creating a budget is impossible if you don't know where the money is really going right now. A great way to determine this is to first document every single penny you spend on anything for 30 days. That includes a Starbucks coffee or a Netflix movie. Use your phone to make notes or carry a little notebook with you. You may be very surprised at the result and find it much easier to reduce or eliminate small expenses that add up fast. Also, check your credit card and bank statements and eliminate any services that you don't use. These are often subscriptions you've completely forgotten that you signed up for . . . but the service provider hasn't forgotten your credit card. Asking for a new credit card with a new number can also help identify and eliminate parasitic subscriptions.

Using the "snowball" method to reduce debt

When it comes to paying down your debt, a commonly recommended approach is the "snowball" method. You pay off the smallest debt first and make minimum payments on the other debts, so you can put extra money toward the small one. When you pay it off, you apply all of that former payment to the next smallest, accelerating the debt reduction. The reason you start with the debt that has the smallest balance instead of the highest interest rate is that it gives you faster victories. These little victories help keep you motivated and on track on your way to eliminating debt.

If the debt remains so high that you can only make minimum payments on any debt, even the smallest event can tip you into financial disaster. Here are several options to avoid bankruptcy. They're listed in order of severity.

» **Consolidating debt:** If you have good credit, you may be able to get a debt consolidation loan with a lower interest rate and lower monthly payments. This simplifies the repayment process and saves money with reduced interest and may spread payments over a longer period, making them more manageable.

WARNING

If the behavior that created the debt in the first place isn't changed, this will just make room for more debt, creating a bigger train wreck in the future. Cut up the credit cards. You may not want to close the credit card accounts because that may affect your credit score. However, if it takes closing them to stop using them, do it.

» **Restructuring debt:** If you have a lot of high-interest loans like credit cards, and a debt consolidation loan isn't an option, you can work with a nonprofit credit counseling agency. They'll help you create a budget and repayment plan and negotiate with your creditors to try to get lower interest rates and/or monthly payments. You pay the credit agency, and they pay your creditors. This simplifies the repayment process and usually gets you out of debt faster. However, credit counseling agencies do charge a monthly fee, and they'll probably require you to close your credit card accounts. This process may also drop your credit score, unless your score is already very low, in which case, it may raise it. The key is to find a reputable credit counseling agency. Just because they're a nonprofit doesn't necessarily mean they know what they're doing. Check them out with the Better Business Bureau and read all the reviews.

- **Settling debt:** If you have a level of debt that you believe will be impossible to ever repay, you can try debt settlement. Debt settlement companies negotiate with your creditors to lower the amount you owe. They make it clear to the creditors that if they fail to accept a lower payoff, you may have to declare bankruptcy, preventing them from receiving any repayment. The upside is that you avoid bankruptcy. The downside is that creditors don't have to negotiate and may still pursue collection efforts or wage garnishment. Using a debt settlement company will also trash your credit score, but you can rebuild it much sooner than if you end up with a bankruptcy. The debt settlement company also charges you a fee (usually a percentage of the total debt).

  It's critical to get a reputable company with good references and reviews. Avoid companies that promise quick fixes or pressure you into signing up for their service. You don't have to use a credit counseling agency or debt settlement company. You can negotiate directly with creditors. Before you attempt this, it's critical to educate yourself. There are many excellent books, podcasts, and classes that you can take.

- **Declaring bankruptcy:** Bankruptcy is usually the last resort. It's a several-month-long legal process that can eliminate some or all of your debt and give you a fresh start. However, you will have to prove your inability to pay, may need legal representation, and bankruptcies usually require you to sell many of your assets. A bankruptcy will also stay on your record for seven to ten years, which could affect everything from your insurance rates to the ability to buy a home.

Suffering a serious injury or illness

This disaster is self-explanatory. Whether a serious illness or injury, it can directly affect you or a member of your family. If it's you, it may restrict or eliminate your ability to earn income. If it's a family member, it will impact your time and finances. The short answer is to make sure you have sufficient insurance, particularly medical and life insurance. The longer answer may be achieving another stream of income, as mentioned in the "Losing Your Job" section and covered in more detail in Chapter 18.

Losing your significant other

Unfortunately, if we live long enough, losing someone close is inevitable. The impact can be emotionally devastating, but it can also affect you financially, particularly if the individual was your significant other. This book won't attempt to address the loss, but the short answer for preparing for the financial impact is life insurance. Long-term disability can also be added to these policies. When you're young, term life insurance is relatively inexpensive. Get advice from a trusted financial advisor and shop around. Regardless, if there are children involved, it's critical to have this type of insurance.

Loss can also include the severing of a significant other relationship, such as divorce. Life insurance doesn't apply. In the case of either death or divorce, the financial disaster can be similar to the unexpected loss of a job. The long-term strategy is to develop another source of income, preferably a business or asset that can evolve into passive income, covered in Chapter 18.

2 Surviving — Basic Life Support

IN THIS PART . . .

Protect your lungs from toxic air

Determine how much water to stockpile based on the number of people in your household

Learn how to filter and treat water

Identify the best diet, foods, and storage for longer-term disasters

Create a backup plan when the sewers back up

Treat injuries and illnesses when emergency medical services aren't available

IN THIS CHAPTER

» Using N95 masks

» Upgrading personal air filtration

» Supplementing with pure oxygen

» Sealing your home from contamination

» Using ultraviolet (UVC) to sterilize air

Chapter 5

Breathing When the Air Is Toxic

Sounds silly to list air as a resource, but it's the most important one. You can live about three weeks without food, three days without water, but you can only maintain consciousness for about three minutes without air. What could threaten your ability to breathe, poison you, or contaminate the air? A major volcanic eruption can put millions of tons of ash in the atmosphere in a matter of hours. A more likely scenario would be a wildfire or an industrial or nuclear plant disaster. A respiratory virus from an epidemic or pandemic could also be a threat.

For wildfires, volcanic eruptions, or chemical/nuclear plant disasters, the solution is to evacuate, but that may take time. During an epidemic, pandemic, or other biological threat, you may need to stay home. This chapter will cover ways to protect your lungs, whether you have to evacuate or shelter in place.

The chapter is broken into two levels of preparation. The first section of this chapter is Level 1 preparation. It covers ideas and products that cost less than $100 to buy and implement, and some strategies have no cost. The total cost for this level of preparation should be several hundred dollars, depending on your situation.

The Level 2 section expands on this with additional ideas and products that will cost several hundred to a couple of thousand dollars, depending on your situation, location, and priorities. Level 3 preparation is covered separately in Part 5 and moves toward permanent independence from municipal infrastructure.

Level 1: Protecting Yourself from Toxic Gases, Bacteria, and Viruses

This section focuses on basic, inexpensive items to protect yourself from airborne contaminants, toxins, and pathogens.

Stocking N95 masks and knowing their limitations

Everyone who lived through the COVID pandemic is familiar with wearing a medical mask (see Figure 5-1). They provide some very limited protection from bacteria and viruses. It's difficult for any mask to directly filter out viruses because viruses are incredibly tiny. A material with small enough holes to catch viruses would be too dense to breathe through. What masks *can* do is filter out particles that bacteria or viruses "ride on," such as tiny liquid droplets from coughing, sneezing, or breathing. Since most respiratory illnesses are transmitted this way, masks can help.

The biggest limitation is that these masks make a poor seal around your nose and mouth. Some of the air you breathe comes from around the outside edges of the mask. From an infection standpoint, their best use is to prevent the *wearer* of the mask from transmitting an infection to others, rather than protecting the wearer *from* others.

For house fires, wildfires, volcanoes, or industrial/nuclear accidents, N95 masks provide almost no protection. All they can do is help keep some ash and fire combustion particles, including those that might contain radioactive material, out of your lungs. However, with a large amount of ash or smoke particles, the mask will quickly become saturated, preventing you from getting sufficient air.

WARNING

Most fire-related deaths occur from smoke inhalation. Smoke inhalation usually causes death by breathing toxic gases like carbon monoxide or cyanide compounds from combustion. These gases prevent the absorption of oxygen, causing suffocation. Medical masks have zero ability to filter out any of these toxic gases.

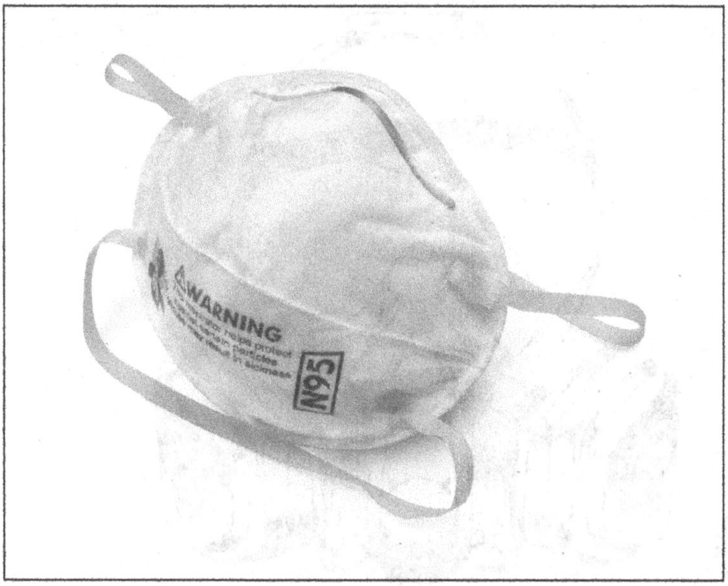

FIGURE 5-1: N95 mask.

lunx/Adobe Stock Photos

N95 masks should only be used to reduce biological exposure or filter out large combustion particles or ash. They can also be used when you're doing work around the home, like sanding furniture, but there are better choices. Since N95 masks are very inexpensive and easy to store, it's good to have a supply of them on hand. Better options are covered next.

Upgrading to a paint respirator for better filtering and dual use

True gas masks are covered in Level 2 preparation, but a budget alternative is a good-quality paint respirator mask, as shown in Figure 5-2. The large filter cartridges provide better filtration and airflow, and the adjustable straps create a much better seal around the nose and mouth. Paint respirators are designed to protect you from fine dust or paint fumes. Like medical masks, paint respirators have no ability to filter out toxic gases or help if there's insufficient oxygen, but they are more effective than medical masks at filtering out ash, chemical fumes, or particles carrying biological or radioactive agents.

Paint respirator masks usually cost around $40, but they're reusable with replaceable filter cartridges. They can be found at hardware stores or online and are dual-use. Using these masks for their intended purpose of painting or sanding gives you some practice and will probably make your lungs last longer.

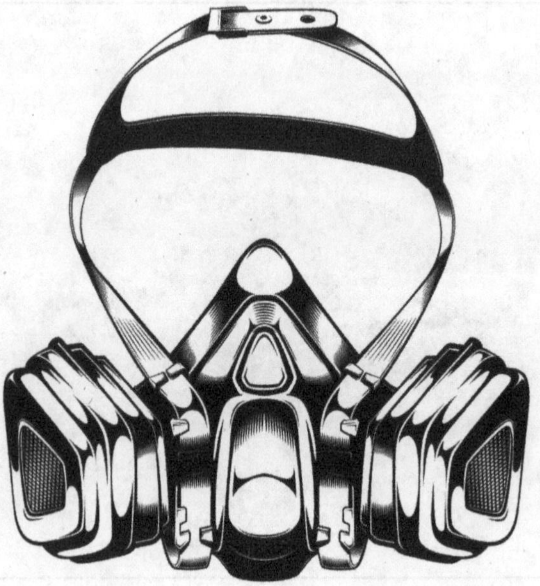

FIGURE 5-2: Paint respirator mask.

Yevhen/Adobe Stock Photos

Escaping with small cans of pressurized oxygen

If you are in an environment with toxic gases such as carbon monoxide or combustion products such as cyanide gas, or there's a lack of oxygen, medical masks or paint respirators are useless. The only solution is to have your own air. Fortunately, you don't need to keep a scuba tank in your closet. You can buy small disposable cans of oxygen (see Figure 5-3). They're usually used to enhance workouts, during hiking at higher altitudes, or to get a competitive advantage in synchronized swimming. A good example is Boost Oxygen, which comes in a variety of sizes and is available at many sporting and general retail stores. Ten-liter cans are about the size of a large can of spray paint and cost around $15. They also come in smaller five- and three-liter cans. These small cans can be lifesavers in some disaster situations.

Humans consume about 250mL of oxygen per minute at rest and about ten times that during heavy activity. It's safe to assume that if you're using one of these in an emergency, you'll be sucking air at a high rate. A ten-liter can should still give you about four or five minutes at max consumption. That's not a lot of time, but it might get you out of a smoke-filled or toxic gas area. They also come in smaller five- and three-liter bottles that can be stashed in a bedroom nightstand or a car glove compartment. Here are examples of situations where these small cans of oxygen could be important.

FIGURE 5-3: Small, disposable can of oxygen.

Have a nice day/Adobe Stock Photos

- If you wake up to find your house on fire and your bedroom completely filled with smoke, a few minutes of air should be enough to get yourself and your family out of the house. Fire escape strategies are covered in Chapter 10.
- If you're caught in a wildfire and your only escape route is on foot or in your car through a dense smoke-filled area. You should turn your car's ventilation to recirculation or off . . . unless you have a Tesla with Bioweapon Defense Mode. Yes, believe it or not, that actually exists and will be covered in Chapter 23.
- If there's an industrial or nuclear power plant accident nearby, these may provide enough air to get upwind of the chemical or radioactive release. If you're in your car, your oxygen consumption should be lower, allowing you to extend the time.
- If you live in the shadow of a volcano or within 100 miles of a potential super volcano, you might want to stockpile a batch of these.
- If your significant other loves bean burritos.

A common question is whether these little cans of oxygen can be used if you drive your car off a bridge and into deep water. I'm a scuba diver, and since these cans don't have a pressure regulator or mouthpiece, they won't work underwater. Therefore, I recommend only driving your car into the shallow end of a swimming pool.

Seriously, if your car is in the water and sinking rapidly, you won't be able to open the doors against the outside water pressure until the interior fills. That may be a good time to get one of these cans out and take several deep breaths before exiting to extend the time you can hold your breath.

Improving air filtration with central air HVAC systems

More advanced home air filtration will be covered in the next section, but for Level 1 preparation, if you have a central air heating and cooling system, you can upgrade your furnace/air conditioner filter. With central air HVAC (heating, ventilation, and air conditioning), all the air is pulled through one or more intakes where the filter or filters are located. Basic HVAC filters trap lint and dust but aren't effective at filtering out smoke particles, bacteria, or viruses. However, you can replace them with better filters. They're a little more expensive, and the additional filtering capability can reduce airflow, making your HVAC work a little harder to move the air.

REMEMBER

Keep in mind that air filtration helps, but it can't filter every cubic inch of air in your home. Even in the best insulated homes, outside air seeps in all the time, and the act of breathing constantly introduces potential pathogens. However, constant filtration through high-quality filters will reduce smoke and any airborne biological material.

Most home air filters use the industry standard MERV (minimum efficiency reporting value) rating system to identify how effective they are at removing air contaminants. Home Depot and 3M have their own proprietary rating systems of Filter Performance Rating (FPR) and Microparticle Performance Rating (MPR). Their equivalent is shown in parentheses below.

Your current filter is probably either a MERV 8 or MERV 11. Moving to a MERV 12 or 13 will work to eliminate smoke, bacteria, and viruses from the circulating home air. However, in addition to the higher cost, it can slightly reduce air flow. A possible compromise is to have a MERV 13 filter standing by while using a MERV 11 most of the time. If there's smoke or a biological threat, just switch out the MERV 11 with the MERV 13 and set the HVAC fan to run continuously. You can also switch to the MERV 13 when you have someone in your home who has any type of respiratory illness, such as a cold or flu. Below are the HVAC filter MERV ratings with the proprietary MPR and FPR ratings in parentheses:

- **MERV 8 (MPR 600, FPR 5):** Captures particles from 3 to 10 microns like lint, dust, and mold spores.
- **MERV 11 (MPR 1000-1200, FPR 7):** In addition to the MERV 8 capabilities, it filters out pollen and pet dander, which helps for allergy sufferers. Most HVAC systems can use these filters without any loss of airflow.
- **MERV 12 and 13 (1500-1900, FPR 10):** In addition to MERV 8 and 11 capabilities, it filters smoke particles, airborne bacteria, viruses, and smog (not carbon monoxide or toxic gases). However, MERV 13 does reduce airflow, potentially increasing heating and air conditioning costs slightly.
- **Higher than MERV 13 (MPR 2000+, FPR 11+):** Most house HVAC systems don't have enough suction power to use these filters. However, HVAC systems can be designed for these or designed to use thicker filters that provide more filtering area and improve airflow.

Improving air filtration if you don't have central air

Many homes use mini-split HVAC systems to heat and cool the air in individual rooms. These systems are common outside the U.S. and are becoming more popular in the U.S. because of their higher efficiency and ability to control individual room temperatures. The drawback is that they don't recycle all of the house's air through a central filter. Each unit uses a small washable filter that isn't designed to trap smoke particles, bacteria, or viruses. Achieving the higher filtration levels for viruses requires more expensive standalone air purifiers that are covered in the following Level 2 preparation section.

Level 2: Securing the Air in Your Home for Longer-Term Disasters

Level 2 preparation requires a bit more investment and sometimes a little more effort, but it is the most bang for the buck.

Upgrading to a gas mask

Although a bit of a fashion risk, a genuine gas mask is unquestionably the best way to protect yourself from contaminated air. Most of these use replaceable NATO (North Atlantic Treaty Organization) standard filters with much better sealing and full-face coverage to protect your eyes from irritant chemicals and toxic gases. Masks, as shown in Figure 5-4, are very effective against airborne bacteria, viruses, toxic fumes, and some toxic gases. However, they still can't protect you from carbon monoxide or a lack of oxygen. These masks start around $250 and go up from there.

FIGURE 5-4: Gas mask.

Tohamina/Adobe Stock Photos

Sealing doors and windows to reduce air infiltration

You can't keep all outside air from entering your house. Houses are actually designed to allow some airflow in and out. If they didn't, there would be an excessive build-up of carbon dioxide from your breathing. With that said, most houses allow too much air to pass through, which can allow smoke, toxic gases, or biologically contaminated air into your home, while increasing your heating and cooling bill. The most common entry point for outside air is around your doors and windows.

Using technology to locate air leaks

Fortunately, this can be fairly easy to identify and address. There are a couple of ways to find major air leaks in your home, but with current technology, the fastest and easiest way is simply to buy an infrared (IR) digital thermometer. You point the plastic gun-shaped thermometer at the area in question and pull the trigger; the surface temperature at that spot appears on the thermometer's screen.

It sounds expensive, and at one time it was, but today you can buy a basic one from a hardware store or online for less than $40. This is an optional tool, but if you suspect you have a leaky home, this could pay for itself with reduced heating and cooling costs.

Finding air leaks thermally

To use a digital thermometer to find air infiltration points, you'll need to wait for a hot summer day when the outside air is much hotter than the inside air. You can also do this in the winter when the outside air is much colder than the inside air. Start by pointing the gun at the interior walls separating interior rooms. This will give you a good estimate of your home's inside temperature. Then, while still inside, point the IR gun at an exterior wall that has windows or exterior doors. Depending on how good your wall insulation is, there may or may not be much of a temperature difference. Keep checking temperatures as you move along the wall toward exterior doors and windows, particularly right around the door and window frames. If there's hot air coming in, you should see a spike in the temperature.

Fixing air leaks

The next step is to seal as many of these entry points as possible. For example, if you find hot or cold spots right where the door meets the door frame, an easy fix is to replace the door gaskets with new ones. Door gaskets are the flexible material inside the door frame that the door rests against when it's closed.

Exterior caulking around doors and windows can often stop or reduce air infiltration. If you still have hot or cold spots after caulking, you might need to temporarily remove the interior trim around the doors and windows and fill the gaps with expanding foam. However, every house is different and requires varying techniques and materials. You can have the leaks fixed professionally, or if you're handy, you can watch DIY YouTube videos that cover techniques and materials for your particular type of house construction.

Installing an ultraviolet air purifier

In addition to using higher MERV filters, if you own your home and have central air, you can install an ultraviolet air purifier (see Figure 5-5). These use the ultraviolet C band (UV-C). UV-C isn't your dance club's black light; instead, it's a high-energy form of ultraviolet that is extremely effective at killing pathogens like bacteria and viruses.

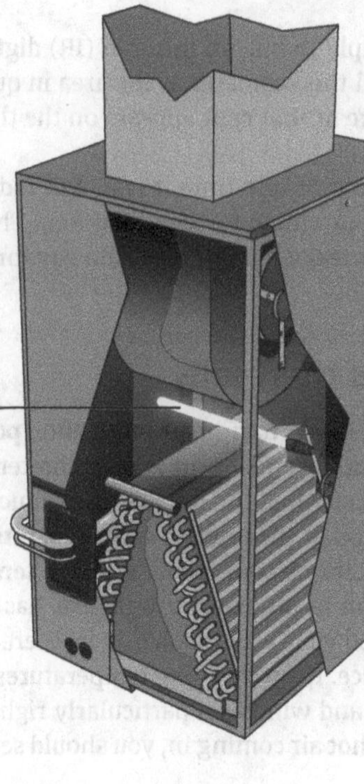

FIGURE 5-5: UVC air sterilizer installed inside an HVAC air handler.

Earth's ozone layer filters it out and prevents it from reaching the Earth's surface. Having your house's air travel through a UV-C sterilizer is not only good during a pandemic, but it also reduces the chance of spreading a regular cold or flu to other members of your household. You can get one of these to add to your existing HVAC's air handler for about $100, with another roughly $100 to install it.

WARNING

If you're handy, you can install it yourself, but make sure the bulb is never powered on during installation. UVC can cause blindness and burn skin in a matter of minutes. To prevent looking like Deadpool, avoid any direct exposure to UV-C.

Buying a standalone air purifier

If you don't have central air, there's a large variety of standalone air purifiers. Having one of these units, even if you do have central air, is also a good idea. They can be used in areas that might be higher risk, such as a bedroom with a sick individual or a family room where people congregate. Many of these units do a good job of removing dust, some smoke, and basic odors, but to reduce biological threats narrows the options to higher-end models.

Their price is determined by the amount of area they can clean and their ability to effectively remove the smallest particles. Keep in mind that neither central air filters nor these standalone air purifiers can filter every cubic inch of air in your home. However, using these standalone air purifiers in common areas or in bedrooms can significantly reduce airborne pathogens and smoke particles.

TIP

As with many products covered in this book, there are a bewildering number of air purifiers on the market. If your primary concern is smoke, look for a unit that is certified to remove particles down to about 0.01 microns. If you're considering an air purifier that can reduce pathogens, viruses can be as small as 0.004 microns. Look for a unit that not only removes 99.99 percent of airborne contaminants but is also certified to remove particles as small as .003 microns. These units often cost over $1,000 but may be worth the price if you're concerned about biological threats. For both smoke and airborne pathogens, I use an Atmosphere Sky, but do your own research.

Expanding your portable oxygen supply

If you live in an area that's more susceptible to air contamination, such as near a chemical or nuclear plant or near an active volcano, having additional portable oxygen could be important. This also applies if you or one of your party has a chronic lung condition such as asthma or COPD (chronic obstructive pulmonary disease). Other medical equipment will be covered in Chapter 9.

Small high-pressure tanks can hold a lot more air than the small portable cans covered in the Level 1 section. For example, a 20 × 5-inch diameter (51cm × 13cm) tank, as shown in Figure 5-6, weighs about 6 pounds (3 kg) but can hold more than 400 liters of compressed air.

That's 40 times what the small cans from the Level 1 section hold. Instead of four to five minutes at max consumption, these bottles should last up to three hours. If you're sharing it with another, it would last half that time. If you're driving or riding in a car, and you're not at max consumption but using it as supplemental oxygen, it could last much longer.

The tank shown in Figure 5-6, along with a regulator and filling it, will cost around $200. In the U.S., buying pure oxygen to fill the tank requires a prescription, which you should be able to get from your physician. Aviation oxygen, used as supplemental air in aircraft, can be purchased without a prescription. For large quantities of oxygen, this is more cost-effective than the small cans. However, if you don't live next to a volcano, nuclear or industrial site, or have someone with a chronic lung issue, it's more convenient and less expensive to purchase a batch of the little portable cans of oxygen.

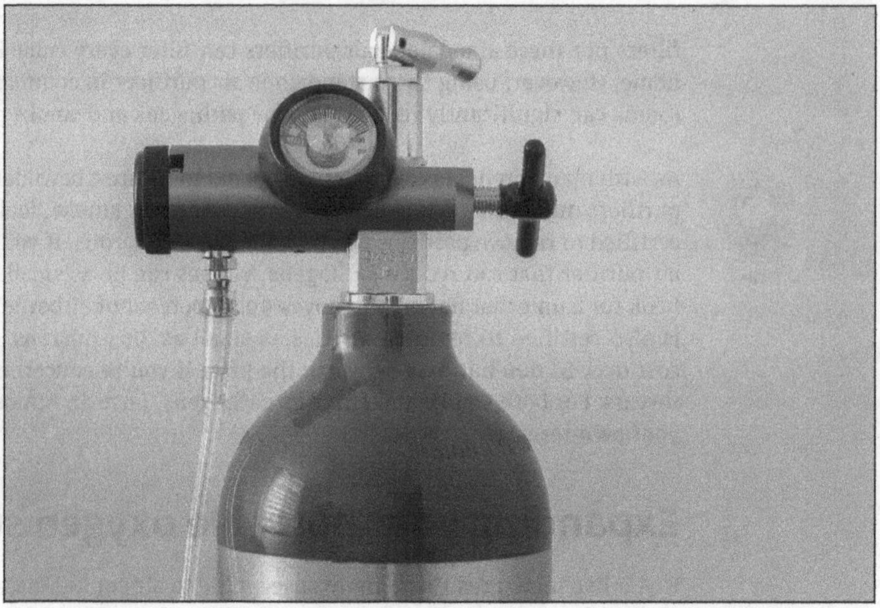

FIGURE 5-6: Six-pound pressurized oxygen tank.

christian vinces/Adobe Stock Photos

Considering your vehicle's need for air

If you happen to live in the shadow of a volcano or within 100 miles (160 km) of a potential super volcano, you might want to consider an electric vehicle. Internal combustion engines, by definition, need air for combustion. When the atmosphere is filled with ash, the vehicle's air filter will quickly become clogged, starving the engine of air. Even airliners can lose engines when flying through heavy ash clouds. An electric vehicle needs no combustion air and isn't vulnerable to ash ingestion. See Chapter 23.

IN THIS CHAPTER

» Determining how much water you need

» Getting immediate access to water

» Filtering and sterilizing

» Extending the supply beyond a week

» Making water out of thin air

Chapter 6
Drinking When the Faucets Run Dry

Your body is about 60 percent water. After air, water is the most important resource you need to survive. You can go at least three weeks without food, some of us . . . a bit longer, but only about three days without water. This chapter will cover finding, storing, treating, and even making water out of air. It will also cover a surprising source of water that you may already have, along with strategies to stockpile water with minimal expense.

One of the first things lost during any disaster is electrical power. Municipal or city water requires electricity to pump and maintain pressure. Those giant water tower tanks you see in most towns provide pressure from gravity, but with no new water pumped in, they empty quickly, and water pressure is lost. However, water pressure can also be lost due to issues with the water treatment plant, damaged pumping equipment, or broken pipes. Even if you have a well, you're still dependent on electricity to power the pump. Power options are covered in Chapter 12.

The first section of this chapter covers how much water you need. The second section covers immediate sources that will get you through a week or two with no municipal water. The third section covers longer-term Level 2 sources that require a little more investment and time. However, these preparations should allow you to get by with no municipal water for a month or more. Moving toward permanent independence from municipal water is covered under Level 3 preparation in Part 5.

Determining How Much Water You Need

For Level 1 preparation, the first step is to figure out how much water you'll need for drinking, flushing toilets, and basic hygiene. To illustrate this, we'll start by calculating water needs for two people for two weeks. At the end of this section, however, a formula will allow you to tailor this example to the number of people in your party and how many days you want to cover.

Calculating water for drinking

REMEMBER

Here's a good rule of thumb: You need a minimum of one gallon (4 liters) of drinking water per person per day. You may be thinking that you don't drink that much water, but your total daily intake includes all the liquids you consume, such as coffee, tea, soda, fruit juice, and milk.

When you apply the rule of thumb for two weeks, you end up with 14 gallons (53 liters) per person. For two people, that's 28 gallons (106 liters). Keep in mind, this is a minimum. In situations with extreme exertion or heat, your body can sweat two gallons a day.

Also, this doesn't include water for flushing toilets or cleaning.

Calculating water for flushing

After water pressure is lost, the toilet tank that supplies the water for flushing won't be refilled, and water must be manually poured into it. Most toilets require about 1.6 gallons (6 liters) to flush, but some require more. You may want to experiment by turning off the water to your toilet and flushing it. Then, see how much water you need to refill the tank. When you have to add water to the tank for each flush, you will only flush when absolutely necessary — meaning when there is solid waste.

REDUCING FLUSHING WITH DIET

Continuing the gross theme, diet can affect your body's "output." Consuming fiber is generally considered a good thing for a healthy diet . . . unless you have limited water to flush toilets. Carbohydrates often contain fiber, which increases the frequency and amount of solid waste your body produces. This isn't the best situation when trying to conserve water for flushing. Protein and fats do not contain fiber. The best survival diets usually involve a significant reduction in carbohydrates in favor of protein and fat. This type of diet is often referred to as a low-carb or Keto diet. I won't get into the health aspects or pros and cons here, but reduced-carbohydrate diets have additional advantages when food and water are in short supply. This will be covered in detail in Chapter 7.

TIP

Here's a gross but simple rhyme to help family and friends remember to minimize flushing: "If it's yellow, let it mellow. If it's brown, flush it down."

For two people, you need at least two flushes per day. For example, I'll assume the standard 1.6 gallons per flush. For two flushes a day for two weeks, that's 45 gallons (170 liters). If you have a pressurized tank or the tank is inside the wall, you may have to flush by pouring water directly into the bowl. It's best to practice this with a *clean and empty* toilet bowl. You can see that the largest requirement for water is flushing toilets. Chapter 8 covers alternatives where there is insufficient water or the septic or sewage system fails, and you can't flush the toilet.

Calculating water for cleaning

You also need a little water for basic hygiene. You should have about one quart (1 liter) per person per day. This water is used for brushing your teeth and a sponge bath, not a shower. Putting hand sanitizer in the bathrooms will also reduce the water needed for washing hands. For two people and two weeks, this adds another seven gallons (27 liters) to the water required.

WATER FOR COOKING

What about water for cooking? If the loss of water pressure is accompanied by loss of electrical power, your primary plan will be to eat foods that don't require much, if any, preparation. Cooking requires electricity, gas, or other fuels, which you may not have or may want to conserve.

Calculating water example and worksheet

The total in this two-person, two-week example is 28 + 45 + 7 = 80 gallons. Below is a formula you can use to calculate the water required for your situation by entering the number of days and the number of people in your residence.

Minimum Water Required Example

Days		People				
				Drinking		
			x	1 gallon	=	28
				Flushing		+
14	x	2	x	1.6 gallons	=	45
				Washing		+
			x	0.25 gallons	=	7
				Subtotal		80
				Minus Hot Water Heater	–	30
				Total Gallons Required	=	50

Minimum Water Required Calculation Worksheet

Days		People				
				Drinking		
			x	1 gallon	=	
				Flushing		+
	x		x	1.6 gallons	=	
				Washing		+
			x	0.25 gallons	=	
				Subtotal		
				Minus Hot Water Heater	–	

Acquiring Immediate Water When Water Pressure Is Lost (Level 1)

This section covers Level 1 preparation to get you through a week or two without municipal water. Although loss of water pressure can be from natural disasters like earthquakes or long-term loss of electrical power, short-term loss is often a simple break in a water line. These are usually fixed within a few days, but during a natural disaster that can extend to a week or more. Even without water pressure loss, water can become contaminated from natural disasters like flooding or pipe damage that allows organic material to enter the water supply.

With a little out-of-the-box thinking, you can ensure enough water for drinking, cleaning, and flushing for one week with minimal expenditure and time. How you obtain this water depends on whether you can stay in your home or have to evacuate. Evacuation strategies are covered in Part 4. For this section, I'll assume you can stay in your current residence and start with the water sources you may already have at hand. Then, ways to efficiently stockpile water will be covered, wrapping up with inexpensive items that will allow you to drink water from almost any source.

Accessing water that you may already have

Most homes have water resources that you don't normally consider.

Drinking your water heater

Unless you have a tankless water heater, most water heater tanks hold 30–75 gallons (100–300 liters). You can usually access that water by a faucet at the bottom of the tank, as shown in Figure 6-1. If you can drink water out of your faucet, the water in your water heater is also safe to drink. Most water heaters come with a normal faucet and handle, but others come without the handle that goes on the valve stem. If that's the case, you'll need to buy a faucet handle that fits the valve stem or use a tool such as a vice grip to open the valve.

WARNING

Do not open the valve at the top of the tank. That's a pressure relief valve and may spray hot water under pressure. Additionally, if you're on city water, during a pressure loss, there can be a brief period of negative pressure that could suck water out of your tank. To be on the safe side, shut off the water heater's inlet valve. When water pressure comes back, don't forget to turn it back on.

TIP

Vice grips are a very versatile tool and highly recommended to have on hand or in your bug-out bag.

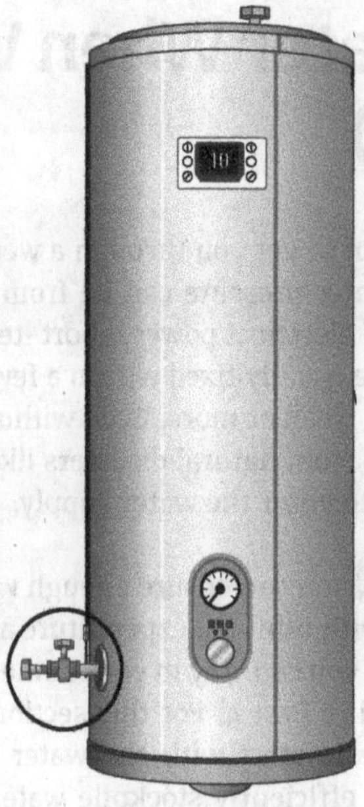

FIGURE 6-1: A standard water heater showing the access faucet (circled) at the bottom of the tank.

Ariestia/Adobe Stock Photos

There may be some sediment in the initial flow because the faucet is designed to drain the water heater tank from the bottom, but the sediment is sterile and will settle out in the container you drain it into. In some cases, the valve is so close to the floor that a small hose must be attached to the valve to get the water into a container. A small RV hose designed for potable water should be used.

Water heaters are sized for the number of expected occupants in a home, usually 15 gallons per person. If it's sized correctly, a full water heater should provide about two weeks of drinking water per person, but that doesn't include flushing toilets or washing.

WARNING

Your water heater could be tankless, meaning it heats the water as needed and doesn't store any water in a tank. Or, in some countries, the hot water is also used for heating and comes from a centralized facility for apartments and condominiums. In these cases, it's critical to stock additional water.

Your toilet tank

A final and admittedly last-ditch source of immediate water is the toilet tank. The tank is the reservoir of water your toilet holds for flushing and sits above the bowl where waste goes. It usually holds less than two gallons and shouldn't be used for drinking unless absolutely necessary — and then only after it's sterilized.

Stockpiling water

Water is cheap but can become extremely precious during a disaster. While existing sources, like your water heater, can help provide drinking water, more water is needed for flushing toilets, cleaning, or longer periods without water pressure.

2.5-gallon (10-liter) containers

The simplest option is to stockpile water by buying prefilled 2.5-gallon (10-liter) containers. Many of these containers have their own handle and dispenser, and they're rectangular, making them easier to stack. The 2.5-gallon containers weigh about 21 pounds (10 kg).

TIP

If you have any mobility issues, one-gallon (4-liter) jugs of water also work.

Our two-people/two-week example requires a total of 80 gallons. If the water heater was sized correctly for two occupants, it should contain 30 gallons, meaning you still need 50 gallons of water. If you use 2.5-gallon containers, you'll need 20 of them. If you don't have access to your water heater or have a tankless model, you'll need 32.

Dealing with the weight

In the example, 20 of the 2.5-gallon containers are required. When you stack three of them on top of each other, they're about six feet (1 m) high and take up about 14 square feet (1.3 square meters) of floor space. Water weighs 8.34 pounds (3.75 kg) per gallon. Twenty 2.5-gallon containers weigh 417 pounds (190 kg). You may be wondering if that's too much weight for your floor to support. If the containers are stacked three high, it works out to about 32 pounds per square foot, which most floors can easily handle. If they couldn't, your 250-pound friend would have already fallen through your floor.

WARNING

Don't stack these containers more than three high. Although the floor may be able to handle the weight, the pressure on the bottom container is high and might cause it to deform or leak. Also, being able to move the containers when they're stacked that high becomes more challenging. If there are other heavy items on the floor where you plan to store these containers, it's best not to put all of the water containers in the same location. If you have a very old home or any questions about the structural integrity of your floor, have it checked before stacking water. One last word of warning: Water leaks aren't good for floors. Keep sharp objects — or children with sharp objects — away from these containers.

Fill your own containers

Another option is to fill your own containers. There's a large collection of containers that can be purchased at home improvement stores or online. Make sure they're designed to hold potable water and don't have any oils or other contaminants inside them. You also want containers that are stackable, easy to pour into and out of, and not too heavy to lift. Picture yourself carrying these or holding and pouring the contents into a sink or toilet tank. Keep in mind that strong, stackable plastic containers are considerably more expensive than purchasing the 2.5-gallon prefilled containers. They should be checked every six months, and if not chemically treated (covered later), the water should be replaced every year.

Finding a good storage location

Figuring out where to store all this water is very dependent on your residence. If possible, it's best to keep the water containers away from hot areas due to the potential for plastic leaching into the water (see the sidebar below).

If you have a basement, it's a perfect place to store water . . . aside from having to carry the containers up and down the stairs. Attics are usually a bad location because of poor access and temperature extremes. They could either freeze and burst the containers in the winter, or the summer heat can cause plastic chemical leaching. Also, the attic floors may not be rated for the weight.

Good storage areas include pantries, utility rooms, and closets. Storage in bedrooms under the bed may be possible, depending on the bed height. A garage can be used if the temperature doesn't go below freezing in the winter and if the primary use of the water will be flushing and cleaning, not drinking. This eliminates any concern about possible heat-induced plastic leaching.

You also want to stash some small water bottles of one liter or less. Packs of six to twelve are portable enough to carry or throw in your car, and you can put several in each bug-out bag. Bug-out bags are covered in Chapter 10.

Bathtub water bladder

If you have a bathtub, it's often suggested that you fill it with water. This is a great idea if you have time to do this before losing water pressure. However, bathtubs aren't sterile and could contaminate the water for drinking. Even if the tub is cleaned prior to filling, the water in the tub will be exposed to the air with everything from sneezes to tiny droplets from the flushing of a nearby toilet.

A very clever and inexpensive solution to this is a water bladder that fits inside a bathtub called WaterBOB, shown in Figure 6-2. It's important to fill it right away with a power grid-down situation since water pressure may be lost quickly.

FIGURE 6-2: WaterBOB bathtub bladder holds 100 gallons (378 liters) of water.

Image courtesy of WaterBOB.

This product allows the water to be kept clean by keeping it out of contact with the tub's surface or the air. The water can be easily pumped out of the bag as needed. Since bathrooms are designed to hold the weight of a full bathtub with a person in it, the weight on the bathroom floor shouldn't be an issue. The downside is the loss of the bathtub for cleaning, but during a water emergency, showers and baths should be paused anyway. The other consideration is that this bladder can only be filled while there's water pressure, so you should still stockpile water in case pressure is lost immediately.

ASSESSING THE SAFETY OF BOTTLED WATER

There is growing concern with the quality of bottled water and the bottles themselves. The source or filtering method of some brands may not be the best. Additionally, some plastics can leach compounds into the water that may include heavy metals, BPA, phthalates, and microplastics. This process is accelerated when exposed to higher temperatures, which might be the case if the water can't be stored in an air-conditioned space. Non-profit organizations like Consumer Reports test bottled water for these types of contaminants. Water bottlers change manufacturing processes and sources, so before you purchase large quantities of water, it would be a good idea to check out the latest ratings with independent organizations like Consumer Reports, NSF International, and the Environmental Working Group.

(continued)

(continued)

Fortunately, a good percentage of your water reserve will only be used for flushing toilets or cleaning. Long-term health impacts don't apply if you're not consuming lower-quality water. If you have limited space, some of your water reserve can be stored in unconditioned areas that get hot, such as garages. For the drinkable portion, spend a little extra to get higher-quality water in non-PET (polyethylene terephthalate), hard plastic bottles and store them inside. Keep in mind that even the drinkable water will only be used in an emergency when long-term health impacts are secondary to access and quantity. If you have to consume the "flushing/cleaning" water, you can always run it through a filter, which is covered in the next section.

Treating contaminated water

During a disaster, you may lose water pressure and, depending on the duration of the disaster, eventually run out of stored water. This requires finding other sources of unknown quality. Or you may still have municipal water pressure, but due to power loss, it may not be properly treated. You may also find yourself in a situation on the go where your only water source is questionable or clearly contaminated.

Water contaminants fall into two broad categories.

- Biological organisms like bacteria, viruses, and parasites can cause severe illnesses such as dysentery.
- Toxins like lead, pesticides, and microplastics can be toxic or have long-term health risks.

The best water treatment usually involves filtering the water through membranes with tiny holes and through compounds such as carbon-block filters. This filtering can also be combined with either ultraviolet or chemical treatment. The membrane and carbon take out most of the toxins and biological organisms, and the ultraviolet or chemical treatment kills what might have escaped the filter.

Although you want to eliminate contaminants that cause long-term health issues, for disasters, the biggest threat is usually bacterial or viral infections. You can't afford to be incapacitated by illnesses that cause severe diarrhea and vomiting. These treatable diseases can also be life-threatening if medical services aren't available. I'll cover some of the medications you want to have on hand in the next chapter.

The following sections discuss common techniques for purifying water for consumption.

Filtering on the go

A fast and inexpensive option for purifying water for consumption while you're on the go is a water filter straw. A good example is the LifeStraw shown in Figure 6-3. It's for individual use and uses membranes that have extremely small passages to capture contaminants like bacteria and parasites. You put the bottom of the straw into the suspect water and literally suck the water through the membrane. The membrane also removes many common toxins such as heavy metals, microplastics, and pesticides. A filter straw is a must-have for your Bug-out-bag. The LifeStraw can filter up to 1,000 gallons and only costs about $20.

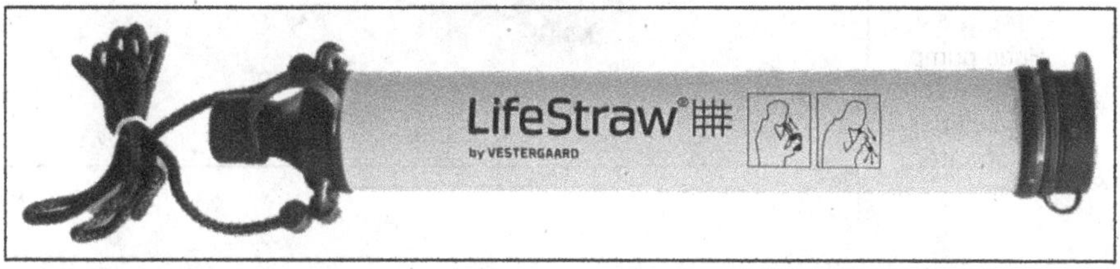

FIGURE 6-3: The LifeStraw is an example of a portable water purification device.

WARNING

Due to the extremely small size of viruses, this type of filter isn't as effective at removing them. For viruses, chemical treatment, UV, or boiling is more effective.

Filtering at home

You may be thinking that you already have a good residential water purification system, either a whole-house filter, an under-the-counter, or faucet-mounted system. That's a good thing, unfortunately, they require water pressure, and many of them also require electricity, the two things that you may not have. Additionally, if you read their manual carefully, you will find that none of them are designed to handle anything but municipal water. In other words, even if they could filter water from your roof or a pond, they aren't certified to filter water with potentially high levels of contaminants.

The solution is a hand pump or gravity filter, not to be confused with the inexpensive pitcher filters you put in your refrigerator. Although they work on the same principle, the pitcher filters are designed primarily to reduce chlorine and lead and improve the taste. They're definitely not certified to protect you from significant toxins, bacteria, or viruses. Gravity filter systems designed to handle a wider range of water are covered in the next section.

For Level 1 preparation, a simple hand-pumped camping filter is effective and relatively inexpensive. The best versions of these will be more effective at eliminating contaminants, such as viruses, than the filter straw and can produce larger quantities in a shorter period (see Figure 6-4).

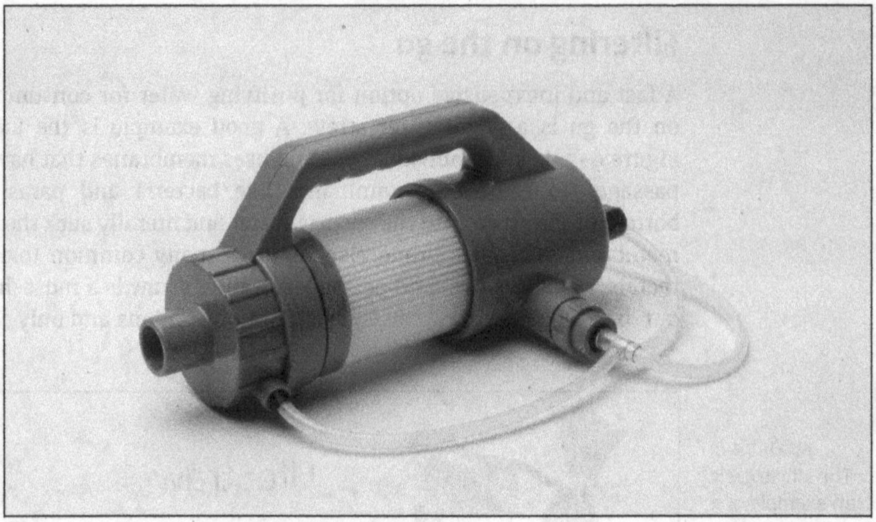

FIGURE 6-4: Hand-pump water filter for larger quantities of water.

salahudin/Adobe Stock Photos

Treating chemically

For Level 1 preparation, sterilizing additives are a simple and inexpensive way to disinfect larger amounts of potentially contaminated water. Sterilizing additives are chemicals in tablet or liquid form, usually based on chlorine or iodine. You drop a tablet or a few drops into a bottle and allow 30 to 60 minutes for it to disinfect the water. These chemicals effectively kill biological organisms like bacteria, parasites, and viruses.

However, you should keep in mind that you are also a "biological organism," so it's best not to drink water treated this way on a regular basis. The same chemicals that kill bad bacteria in your water can also kill the good bacteria in your gut. However, any potential digestive issues or potential long-term health risks are minor compared to the effects of dehydration or dysentery.

Potable Aqua is a good example of this type of disinfectant and has an added advantage. It uses a two-part process with the first tablet using an iodine-based disinfectant to kill biological contaminants. After 30 minutes, the second tablet is added to neutralize the iodine. This reduces the negative impacts on your digestive system and eliminates the delicious iodine flavor. It costs about $9 USD and treats 6 gallons (25 liters). Keep in mind that chemical disinfectants cannot remove contaminants like heavy metals, pesticides, or microplastics.

TIP

For larger amounts of water, the easiest and least expensive chemical treatment is chlorine bleach. It only requires a 1/8 teaspoon (8 drops) per gallon (4 liters) for clear water and 1/4 teaspoon (16 drops) per gallon for cloudy water. Let it stand for at least 30 minutes before using. Bleach also has many other uses, such as disinfecting surfaces and medical implements.

WARNING

Never use bleach that's "scented," "colorfast," has added cleaners, or is "non-splash." All of these versions have additional chemicals that you don't want to ingest. An unopened bottle of bleach loses effectiveness after a year and should be replaced no later than every 18 months. If the container is open, it's only good for 6 months.

Boiling water

Boiling water is also an effective way to sterilize water for consumption if you have access to a pot and a heat source. Bringing water to a rolling boil for at least one minute (three minutes if you are at a higher altitude) will kill almost all bacteria, viruses, and parasites. Although effective, boiling water requires a lot of energy (electricity or gas), which may not be available or may be better used for other purposes. In the next section, I'll cover more elaborate systems that treat larger amounts of water using both chemical treatment and filters without electricity.

WARNING

Chemical treatments, UV, or boiling water will not remove contaminants like heavy metals, microplastics, pesticides, or other toxins. Water that may contain these contaminants should also be filtered.

For an overview of water quality issues, health risks, and types of treatment, see *Water Treatment For Dummies*.

TIP

WASHING CLOTHES WITH NO WATER PRESSURE OR ELECTRICITY

With limited water reserves, washing clothes is a low priority and may require a mindset adjustment. You can get by for a while without washing clothes, even longer if you're a teenager. However, if you do have access to sufficient water but no electricity to run your washer and dryer, there is a simple, inexpensive option. You need a large five-gallon (20-liter) bucket and can buy a manual clothes washing plunger online. It looks like a big toilet plunger, or you can make one out of a regular toilet plunger by cutting some holes in it. When you combine a bucket of water, detergent, and a bit of exercise, it gets high marks for cleaning clothes. Of course, the clothes then need to be rinsed, squeezed of excess water, and hung up to dry. A mop bucket with a ringer also works for this purpose. Welcome to your ancestors' world.

Having a few five-gallon plastic buckets is important, regardless of whether you use them for washing clothes. They can be stacked and have many uses, including collecting water from other sources.

Securing Water for Longer Duration Disasters (Level 2)

If you have a water well, you can skip this section and go right to Chapter 12 on how to provide power to keep that pump running. However, groundwater can also become contaminated by natural or human-caused disasters, so you may want to read "Creating a larger water reserve" in the next section.

Long-term loss of municipal water can be caused by damage to water treatment facilities or pipelines due to natural disasters such as floods, earthquakes, and wildfires, or human-made disasters from war to terrorist attacks. There have also been municipal water systems that have been found to contain dangerous levels of toxic compounds such as lead. All of these can eliminate municipal water for weeks or longer. It's difficult to stockpile enough water for more than a week or two, particularly if you have more than two people in your home. The ideas that follow are Level 2 preparation and require a bit more time and investment than the previous section.

Creating a larger water reserve

If you have a hot tub or a pool, you're all set. If not . . . get one. No, you don't have to install a pool or buy a $7,000 hot tub. You can buy an inflatable hot tub from a big box store or online for $500 or less. Hot tubs are a great dual-use item. They're awesome for relaxation as well as creating an emergency backup water supply of about 250 gallons for flushing toilets and cleaning. When treated, the water can even be used for drinking.

WARNING

These small hot tubs weigh over 2,000 pounds (900 kg) when filled. If installed on a deck or floor, make sure the deck or floor can support the weight.

Collecting and treating water

Other sources of water could come from rain off a roof, rivers, lakes, or ponds. It's critical to have an effective filtering system that can take out biological and toxic contaminants.

A good option for filtering larger quantities of water is a large gravity filter that requires no electricity. You pour the untreated water into the top, and it slowly drips through a multi-element filter to a container at the bottom, as shown in

Figure 6-5. They're similar to the pitcher filters sold in stores but are much bigger, use more extensive filtering, and produce up to 20 gallons a day. They cost about $200 or more. If the water source is visibly dirty, prefiltering it through cloth can help prevent the water filter from clogging early. The filtered water should also be treated with one of the chemical disinfectants.

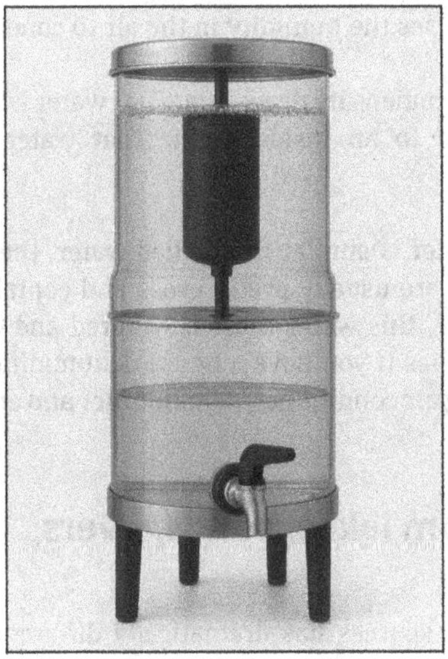

FIGURE 6-5: A gravity filter can produce 20 gallons per day without electricity.

Generated with AI using ChatGPT-OpenAI

Another option is to choose a higher-end gravity filter that includes an ultraviolet treatment in the tank or spigot to do the final sterilization. This eliminates the need for chemical treatment but does require a small amount of electricity.

Finding new sources of water

Even if you have an inflatable hot tub for long-duration disasters, additional water may be needed. The next step is to locate other potential water sources.

Collecting water from your roof

Although there are rain catchment systems, which I will briefly cover in Part 5, this can be as simple as putting a large bucket under a gutter downspout. During a rain, it's important not to collect the initial water, particularly if it hasn't rained in a day or two. Let it run for a while to flush the roof of biological debris such as bird droppings. Once the water is collected, pour it through a screen or fabric to filter the larger particles and then pump it through a filter. It must still be chemically disinfected before consumption.

Collecting water from your air conditioner

If you've lost municipal water but have electrical power and air conditioning, one potential water source in the summer is your air conditioner. The process of cooling the air in your house causes the humidity in the air to condense.

Every air conditioner has a condensate drain line. That water is usually allowed to drain outside or channeled to an inside drain. That water can be captured in a bucket.

Although the condensed water is similar to distilled water, the cooling coils and lines that it drains through are usually pretty gross and contain lots of dirt and biological growth. Therefore, this water must be filtered and disinfected before consumption. This also applies if you have a house dehumidifier. Of course, this assumes you have a working air conditioner/dehumidifier and enough humidity to produce the condensate.

Collecting water from lakes, ponds, rivers, or streams

Clearly, water from natural sources has dramatically different levels of purity, from mountain streams to swamps. If the water is visibly dirty or cloudy, it should be screened through a cloth before pouring into any filtration system. This prevents the filter from becoming clogged early. Regardless of the source, the water must be disinfected.

Using an atmospheric water generator

Having an inflatable hot tub may not be an option if you live in a condominium or apartment, and you may not have access to water off the roof or any other outside body of water. An atmospheric water generator, shown in Figure 6-6, literally creates water out of thin air.

Atmospheric water generators are basically dehumidifiers that condense water out of the air using cooling coils and then filter it for consumption. They produce very pure water similar to distilled water. The only requirement beyond electrical power is that the relative humidity should be about 40 percent or higher. As the humidity drops, so does their output, meaning that these systems aren't effective if you live in a desert climate.

FIGURE 6-6: Atmospheric water generator.

Generated with AI using ChatGPT-OpenAI

The smaller units can sit on a countertop and produce a couple of gallons of water a day under optimal conditions. They're portable enough to be carried in a car or RV. The least expensive units are a little more than $1,000 and require about as much power as a small window air conditioner. Larger units use outside air and can produce more than 100 gallons a day with a proportional increase in price. This is an expensive way to produce a small amount of water. However, if you compare it to the cost of drilling a well or installing and maintaining a rain catchment system (Part 5), this is cost-effective for a permanent source of drinking water.

These aren't the best options for making enough water to wash or flush toilets. However, flushing doesn't require drinkable water, so water from your roof or other non-potable sources can be a good complement to an atmospheric water generator. In Part 5, Level 3 strategies will be covered to include wells, rain catchment, and larger atmospheric water generators.

TECHNICAL STUFF

Hydrogels are a developing technology that has great potential. They absorb water directly from the air at night when it's cool. In the day, when the sun heats up the gel, it releases all the stored water. This technology can be used even when the humidity is under 30 percent. Unlike atmospheric water generators or desalination, hydrogel technology uses very little energy and can be easily powered by an integrated solar panel. Several companies with prototypes should be commercially available soon. This is definitely something to keep an eye on for the future.

Chapter 7

Eating When the Grocery Stores Shut Down

This may surprise you, but grocery stores only stock about three days of food. "Just in time" inventory allows them to carry a wide variety of foods that customers demand with the store's limited shelf space. This means that if the supply chain stops and there are no more delivery trucks, the shelves will be bare in a few days. Popular items like bottled water and toilet paper may be gone within the first 24 hours.

The topic of food for disaster or survival situations can be an entire book in itself and often is. This chapter covers the basics, including the amount of food needed as well as the best types of food for storage and diet. You can inexpensively stockpile your own pantry to get you through a week for Level 1 preparation. There are also prepackaged survival foods that can be bought in bulk, providing easier storage for longer-duration disasters, which are covered in the Level 2 section. It's always easier, faster, and more cost-effective to stockpile food rather than attempting to grow it. It takes about 4,000 square feet (370 square meters) of garden under perfect conditions to feed one person for one year. However, if farming is of interest, *Backyard Homesteading For Dummies* is an excellent reference.

WARNING

I need to provide a disclaimer here: Although I married a medical professional, I am not one, nor have I played one on TV. Therefore, you should carefully research any suggestions I make that involve your diet or health. If you have a medical condition or any health questions, consult your physician first . . . and never run with scissors.

Determining How Much and What Kind of Food You Need

The average number of calories needed per day is about 2,500 for men and 2,000 for women, but it depends on many factors such as size, activity, and age. What's equally important is the type of calories. I can happily get all my 2,500 calories from 16 Reese's Peanut Butter Cups, though that's a really bad idea. It's important to carefully consider the nutritional value and protein/fat/carbohydrate breakdown of foods for sustainable nutrition and storage in disaster situations.

Forget the old food pyramid; for survival, fat is your friend

The old food pyramid was recently turned upside down, placing protein, healthy fats, and vegetables at the top and carbohydrates at the bottom. During a disaster, there are significant benefits to reducing the intake of simple carbohydrates and replacing them with protein and fat. Understandably, you may question the wisdom of a diet high in fat, but this book focuses on situations where grocery stores may not be available for a week or more. You're trying to prevent starvation and malnutrition rather than improving your cholesterol level. With that said, the new food pyramid suggests that reducing carbs has health benefits as well. I'll stay away from any debate about the health benefits of these types of diets and refer you to authoritative books on the subject, like *Keto Diet For Dummies*.

Finally, although having extremely low body fat can highlight those six-pack abs, a normal level of body fat is generally considered healthier and provides your body with important reserve fuel.

Carb reduction

For disaster preparation, replacing carbohydrates with protein and fats is based on practical considerations.

- **Fat is fat on energy:** Fat carries more than twice as many calories (nine per gram) as carbohydrates (four per gram). That's important when your pantry becomes your only grocery store. You can store more calories per cubic foot.
- **Fiber:** Carbohydrates often contain fiber, which is normally a good thing. However, fiber, by definition, produces more solid waste. This means you have to go to the bathroom more often, which is bad if you have limited water to flush toilets, not to mention toilet paper. Remember what disappeared first from store shelves during the COVID pandemic.
- **Blood sugar:** Simple carbohydrates are burned quickly and tend to spike blood sugar. Blood sugar levels often overcorrect downward, making you feel hungry sooner; think donuts. Fats and proteins don't spike blood sugar and, therefore, extend the period of time before you feel hungry.
- **Reduced consumption:** The combination of a higher caloric value per gram of food, combined with extending the time between hunger pangs, increases the time you can survive without access to grocery stores.

Vegetarian and vegan diets

Vegetarian and vegan diets present additional challenges to stockpiling food for disaster preparation. That's not to say you can't maintain a vegetarian or vegan diet in a survival situation, but fresh vegetables aren't an option for long-term storage, and long-shelf life food possibilities are more limited, even if you aren't trying to reduce carbohydrates. Remember that your food stockpile is intended to be used only in an emergency situation. Unless the vegetarian or vegan diet is required for significant health reasons, it might be worth considering pausing it during a disaster. However, I will cover non-meat foods and plant-based protein powders that have reduced carbohydrates and can be easily stored.

CARNIVORES VERSUS OMNIVORES

My father was a veterinarian and scientist. He wrote the authoritative textbook on *Comparative Physiology of the Vertebrate Digestive Systems* . . . a real cliffhanger in the comparative physiology world. He once told me that the size of the digestive system of a carnivore, like a tiger, is much smaller than that of a herbivore, like a cow. A cow is a true vegan and has a four-chambered stomach that takes up a large percentage of its body. Cows must feed almost continuously to get sufficient calories, even with relatively sedentary behavior.

Carnivores, on the other hand, have high caloric needs for hunting and powering larger brains, and they do this with smaller stomachs and intestines. This is accomplished by

(continued)

(continued)

having a more streamlined and specialized digestive system designed to process only fats and proteins. Higher caloric content also allows longer periods between feedings. Humans are omnivores. Omnivores can consume both meat and plants, which is great. However, my father pointed out that the human digestive system is much closer in size to a tiger's than a cow's.

Testing the best types of survival foods

Here's a test you can run for yourself. Pick a few days and make sure all your meals consist of only fat and protein; for example, a breakfast might consist of eggs and bacon or sausage. It would exclude biscuits, bread, orange juice, or anything else that contains carbohydrates, even including the sugar in your coffee.

Now, base your other meals on only fat and protein. If you're unsure about what falls into this category, you can look online to find out which foods are low-carb or keto. For this experiment, you're trying to get as close to no carbs as possible. Yes, it is actually possible to live without bread, pasta, or sugar for a day or two.

WARNING

Once again, if you have any medical conditions or medications that require specific diets, you shouldn't try this without checking with your physician.

You then want to note how long after each meal that you begin to feel hungry. Also, note when and how often you need to use the bathroom. To get a real feel for this, you should try this over a few days. After that test, if you wish, pick a few days with a diet high in carbohydrates, such as a breakfast with pancakes, waffles, or cereal. See how long it takes before you feel hungry again and how often you need to use the bathroom.

With fat's high caloric content and its ability to satiate appetite, not only is food storage improved, but the amount of food you consume without being hungry usually decreases, extending your food supply even further.

Acquiring Basic Survival Foods for a Week or Two (Level 1)

The most cost-effective strategy is to create your own survival pantry from the grocery store by using foods that you already eat but stockpiling an extra week or two. You're really just buying a week or two of groceries in advance, and you can slowly build this stockpile up over time to spread out the cost.

Identifying the right types of food

For disaster preparation, you are looking for several things in food:

- No refrigeration needed
- Long shelf life
- Minimum preparation required
- High calorie content per weight and volume
- Minimum carbohydrates and fiber

Long storage life

Most foods that don't require refrigeration will last at least a year. If you stick to stockpiling foods that you actually like to eat and eat the oldest first, you'll be replacing them often enough that you will always have foods that are about a year from their expiration date. Keep in mind that the "best by" dates are tied to the taste, not whether the food is safe to eat. With that said, eating a can of chili someone bought in preparation for Y2K is a bad idea. (If you don't know what Y2K is, ask your parents.)

However, if you primarily eat fresh foods, foods that require refrigeration, or foods that require a lot of preparation, like pasta, you'll need to stockpile foods that you don't normally eat. Since you don't eat them as often — out of site out of mind — you'll want to get foods with longer shelf lives, preferably at least two or three years. This is also an area where the "healthy" foods with no preservatives are not necessarily the best choice. Preservatives extend shelf life and are, unfortunately, desired.

You still want to try to eat and replace most foods every year or two. A good way to remember to do this is to tie it to an important date. For U.S. citizens, you could tie consuming year-old food to April 15th, which is the U.S. federal tax filing deadline. If you'll be getting a tax refund, you can use it to replace the old stockpile. Or, if you must pay additional taxes, it's a disaster . . . and eating disaster preparation food is appropriate.

Minimum preparation

If stored properly, foods like flour, rice, dried beans, and pasta can last for a very long time. However, they require water, heat, and time to prepare. Additionally, they're almost pure carbohydrate (except for beans).

For Level 1 preparation, there will likely be limited or no power or water, making these foods very difficult and time-consuming to prepare. Stick with foods that can be eaten right out of the package or can or require minimal preparation. Yes, chili tastes better when heated, but odds are that sometime in your life, maybe as a teenager — or maybe yesterday — you ate right out of a can. If not, try it; it's not as bad as you think. Even with Level 2 preparation, when power and water are available, ready-to-eat meals are still important because they require less time and effort and are portable in case you have to evacuate.

Calorie-dense foods with protein and fat

You're not on a diet, and you don't have infinite shelf space. Getting by without grocery stores is all about maximum calories in minimum space. As mentioned, a gram of fat carries nine calories versus four grams for protein and carbohydrates. Protein is critical for maintaining your organs and muscles. Carbohydrates are not as important and having a large percentage of the calories coming from fat and protein rather than carbohydrates also helps reduce the required water for toilet flushing.

To identify foods that are high in protein and fat, not surprisingly it's important to read content labels. Another way to quickly identify some of these foods is if the package reads, "low-carb," "keto," or "keto-friendly." However, marketers can be quite loose in their definitions of these terms, so you'll still want to check the label for the breakdown of calories by protein, fat, and carbohydrates. You'll also want to get as wide a variety of foods as possible so you're not eating the same thing every day.

For Level 2 preparation, where you're able to sustain an ongoing source of potable water, reduced carbohydrate intake is a little less important but still has advantages.

Choosing optimum foods to fill your pantry

The best scenario is to stockpile foods that meet the criteria above and that you already eat. With that said, if you regularly eat fresh foods, bread, and pasta, you may have to step out a bit. Here are some good examples of long shelf life, high-calorie, low-carbohydrate foods.

Canned and processed meats

Foods like the often-maligned SPAM actually shine here. It isn't usually considered the healthiest food to eat on a regular basis, but survival situations dictate different priorities. SPAM has a very high caloric content, containing protein and fat with almost no carbohydrates. Plus, the small rectangular cans are easy to store.

One of the reasons SPAM isn't at the top of most people's healthy food list is its high saturated fat content, but saturated fat actually has an advantage here. Saturated fats are stable at room temperature (meaning they're solid, not liquid). Because of this, they don't oxidize and go rancid as fast as fats that are liquid at room temperature, increasing their storage life. That's why you can leave butter out on the countertop for a long time without it going bad.

If kept in a cool, dry place, SPAM can usually be stored for three to five years without affecting taste (no cheap shots here) and still remain safe to eat beyond that. For long shelf life foods, it has one of the highest protein contents per cubic inch and per dollar. You may be thinking that you don't like SPAM. That's ok. All of the above advantages apply to most canned meats, including common ones such as chicken and tuna fish.

Also, most people today buy tuna fish in spring water, considering it a healthier option. However, tuna fish in oil provides more calories and higher levels of vitamin D and omega-3s, and the oil slightly extends its shelf life. Figure 7-1 shows the nutritional comparison between a popular brand of tuna fish packed in water versus tuna fish packed in sunflower oil. Note that the sunflower oil is mostly polyunsaturated and monounsaturated fat. In this example, the oil-packed tuna carries twice the calories in the same size container and for about the same cost.

Nutrition Facts

Serving size 1 pouch (74g)	
Amount per serving	
Calories	**70**
	% Daily Value*
Total Fat 0.5g	**1%**
Saturated Fat 0g	**0%**
Trans Fat 0g	
Polyunsaturated Fat 0g	
Monounsaturated Fat 0g	
Cholesterol 35mg	**12%**
Sodium 300mg	**13%**
Total Carbohydrate 0g	**0%**
Dietary Fiber 0g	**0%**
Total Sugars 0g	
Includes 0g Added Sugars	**0%**
Protein 17g	**31%**
Vitamin D 1.5mcg 8%	Calcium 0mg 0%
Iron 0.9mg 6%	Potassium 210mg 4%
Niacin 50%	Vitamin B6 15%
Vitamin B12 90%	Selenium 100%
Phosphorus 10%	

*The % Daily Value (DV) tells you how much a nutrient in a serving of food contributes to a daily diet. 2,000 calories a day is used for general nutrition advice.

Nutrition Facts

Serving size 1 pouch (74g)	
Amount per serving	
Calories	**140**
	% Daily Value*
Total Fat 8g	**10%**
Saturated Fat 1g	**5%**
Trans Fat 0g	
Polyunsaturated Fat 2.5g	
Monounsaturated Fat 4g	
Cholesterol 35mg	**12%**
Sodium 290mg	**13%**
Total Carbohydrate 0g	**0%**
Dietary Fiber 0g	**0%**
Total Sugars 0g	
Includes 0g Added Sugars	**0%**
Protein 17g	**31%**
Vitamin D 1.2mcg 6%	Calcium 0mg 0%
Iron 0.8mg 4%	Potassium 200mg 4%
Niacin 70%	Vitamin B6 12%
Vitamin B12 130%	Selenium 90%
Phosphorus 12%	

*The % Daily Value (DV) tells you how much a nutrient in a serving of food contributes to a daily diet. 2,000 calories a day is used for general nutrition advice.

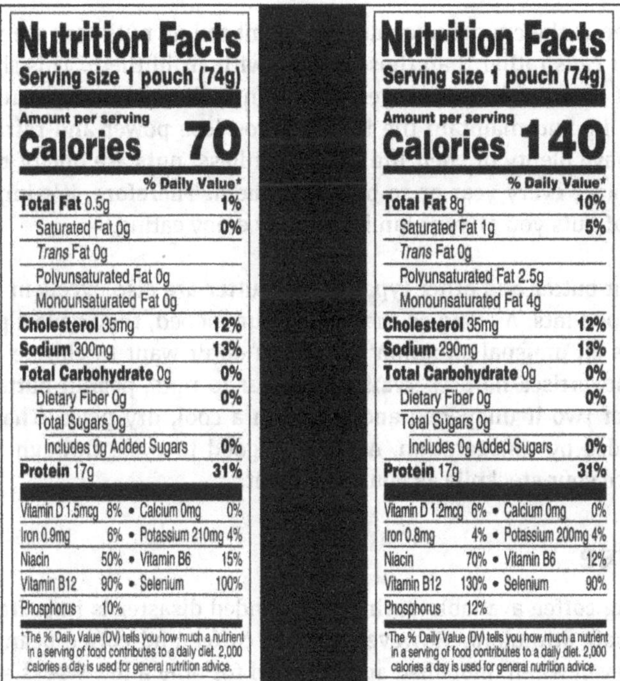

FIGURE 7-1: Nutritional content comparison between tuna packed in water versus sunflower oil.

Of course, you're not limited to tuna and chicken. Canned meats also include ham, corned beef, roast beef, salmon, and sardines. Most of these canned meats also have shelf-lives of three to five years.

Processed meats such as beef jerky and hard salami are also compact and calorie-rich but usually have shorter shelf lives unless they're vacuum-packed. With processed meats, you should also look at the sodium content. They often contain high levels of salt.

Skipping over any health concerns, heavily salted foods tend to make you thirsty and could increase your water consumption. Several canned meats do come with reduced salt, including SPAM.

Pecans, macadamias, and walnuts

If you are vegetarian or vegan, a great source of protein and healthy fats with limited carbohydrates are many types of nuts. Even if you're not vegan, you want to stock up on these because they provide variety and are very portable. The ones with the lowest carbohydrates are pecans, macadamias, and walnuts. The good news is that these nuts contain high levels of healthy fats, such as monounsaturated fats. The bad news is that these unsaturated fats go rancid sooner than saturated fats.

Oxygen is the enemy, meaning you want to buy nuts that are vacuum-packed in jars or cans rather than those in bags with air in them. This should allow a shelf life of about a year. However, storing nuts in your refrigerator will extend that shelf life and maintain the flavor. If you lose power and refrigeration, you will still have plenty of shelf life left. Regardless, nuts are one of the foods you need to replace every year or so by eating them. Therefore, it's important to buy the type of nuts you or your family actually enjoy eating.

Peanut butter and other types of nut butter are also excellent sources of protein and good fats. As long as they remain unopened, they have a good shelf life, but this is an unusual situation where you don't want to choose the "healthy" one that advertises no preservatives. Similar to nuts, peanut butter can last up to a year or two if unopened and stored in a cool, dry place. That shelf life can be extended by refrigeration. Again, it's good to cycle through peanut butter and replace your stockpile as you consume it.

Coffee

Having coffee available during an extended disaster is important for morale and as a safe stimulant. However, ground coffee and coffee beans have short shelf lives even when unopened and are good for only a few weeks after being opened.

If you are a coffee connoisseur, you need to take a couple of deep breaths and try to relax before you continue reading.

Instant coffee has significant advantages in a disaster situation, starting with being "instant" and not requiring any powered machinery to brew. It's easy to store, significantly cheaper than ground coffee, and has a much longer shelf life. When vacuum-packed and stored in a cool, dry place, it can be drinkable for over 10 years.

REMEMBER

You don't have to give up your coffee beans, but it's not a bad idea to stock some instant coffee as a backup.

Dessert

Although I've emphasized reduction in carbohydrates, it's important to have some dessert or sweets to keep up morale. A good example is canned fruit, which has a good shelf life. For sweeteners, high-quality raw honey, if stored properly, has an almost indefinite shelf life. Its combination of low water, high acidity, and natural anti-bacterial properties gives it strong immunity to contamination. In fact, it can even be used as a basic antiseptic.

Although chocolate does not have an indefinite shelf life, if properly stored, dark chocolate can last up to two years. Unfortunately, I've been unable to successfully test the maximum shelf life in our house.

Food rotation systems

It's important to have a system that lets you know which food in your stockpile or pantry is the oldest. There are many ways to do this, and if your background is in accounting or library science, get a magic marker and have at it.

For those, like me, who may not have that level of focus and dedication, here's a simple system: Sometimes called first in, first out (FIFO) management, you eat the oldest food first by keeping the oldest in front. As you add new food, you put it at the back, right behind the old food. Make sure any other household members who prepare food understand and use this system.

Keep in mind that you can increase your stockpile over time, spreading out the cost. This isn't important for foods you use all the time, but it can be important for foods that you use less frequently. With that said, if no one has eaten that can of pickled herring in a couple of years . . . maybe you need to stockpile something else.

REMEMBER

A good general philosophy to remember is, "Store what you eat, and eat what you store." You can use FIFO to help you do this.

Adding food supplements

If you live on a farm and eat a wide variety of fresh vegetables and fruits every day, you probably don't need vitamins. For the other 99 percent of the population, the days of being told that you don't need vitamins if you eat a balanced diet are long gone.

Today's foods are often devoid of much of their nutrients due to processing and transport times. That's not just my opinion. The American Medical Association has officially stated that everyone should be taking at least a basic multivitamin. This is even more important if you're not eating fresh vegetables, which is almost guaranteed in a disaster situation.

MULTIVITAMINS

Fortunately, you can get most of your important vitamins, minerals, and phytonutrients more compactly with nutritional supplements. If you're already taking vitamins you like, stay with them and build up a small stockpile. If not, or if you want to check out your particular brand, there are several independent laboratories, such as Consumer Lab (`consumerlab.com`), that test vitamins.

Consumer Lab has a small subscription fee for detailed reports, but that's how they stay independent without advertising. They test food supplements to make sure that they have what they say they have in them — not too little or not too much. They must dissolve in your stomach, and they can't have any lead or pesticides in them. You'd be surprised how many vitamin brands fail.

Like food, vitamins also have a shelf life. They lose their potency over time due to heat, moisture, and oxidation. This means you want to keep them in a cool, dry place and consume the oldest vitamins first. Since vitamins don't take up much space, keeping a longer-term supply is highly recommended. If possible, buy vacuum-packed vitamins due to their longer shelf lives. Additionally, keeping unopened bottles in the refrigerator or freezer can also increase their shelf life. Don't store vitamin bottles that have been opened in the refrigerator. High humidity can cause condensation (water) to form on the vitamins when they're cooled, causing them to decompose.

ELECTROLYTES

With loss of electrical power, particularly in the summer, there is a potential risk of heat stroke and dehydration. Along with ensuring a supply of fresh water, maintaining your body's electrolyte levels is critical. Sports drinks can provide needed electrolytes, but stockpiling sports drinks takes up valuable space. A better option is to buy electrolytes in powdered form that can be added to water as needed.

Trying a multi-day fast to learn your body's response

If you've ever done a multi-day fast, you can skip this section. By "fast," I mean no food and only water (plus calorie-free electrolytes to prevent dehydration). If you haven't done this before, it might be worth trying. You may be thinking, wait, the whole point of this book is to make sure you don't have to fast.

Although there may be long-term health benefits to fasting, the reason it's suggested is to let you know how your body reacts to caloric restriction. This can prepare you and give you the confidence to know that you can function perfectly well without food for a couple of days. A multi-day fast also gave me appreciation for grocery stores and empathy for the 11 percent of the global population who regularly experience "unintentional fasting."

WARNING

If you want to try fasting, please do your research on the process and risks. People often fail to drink enough water or electrolytes, which can cause dehydration. An excellent reference is *Intermittent Fasting For Dummies*. Also, Dr. Sten Ekberg (a physician and former Olympic athlete) has several excellent podcasts on the topic. As always, if you have any medical conditions or concerns, do not try fasting without talking to your doctor first.

Securing Enough Food for a Month (Level 2)

Level 2 preparation provides a more stable source of potable water and power, allowing food preparation beyond ready-to-eat meals. Stockpiling basic staples will extend and supplement your food supply. If you have limited space, use concentrated foods that have high nutritional content but take up less space in your pantry.

Stocking basic staples

Basic staples for long-term food supplies cover a lot of territory. It includes common dry staples such as flour, rice, beans, and sugar. Using these requires preparation that includes water and a heat source, and most of them are high-carbohydrate foods. However, they do extend supplies and allow variety, particularly when mixed with high-protein/high-fat foods.

For extreme shelf life, hard winter wheat berries win hands down. When stored in a cool, dry place, they can last for 30 years or more. They produce the highest protein and nutrient-rich wheat flour by using the entire berry of the wheat. However, a special wheat grinder is required to turn it into flour. Potato flour is also a good staple for those with gluten intolerance. Textured vegetable protein (TVP) is another rarely considered staple. Made from plants, it has a very high protein content with complete amino acids and a long shelf life without refrigeration. It can be added to most foods and is a great substitute for ground beef. It's particularly useful for those trying to maintain a vegetarian or vegan diet.

Since we all know that butter is the secret to life, ghee is a good replacement. Ghee is basically butter with all the water and milk solids removed. This makes ghee a highly stable fat, very resistant to oxidizing and gives it a much longer shelf life than butter without refrigeration. It can also be used by those who are lactose intolerant. Like butter, ghee adds a lot of flavor to foods and has a published shelf life of two years. However, in Indian culture, ghee that's properly prepared and stored is often used well past that.

It's impossible to cover all the staples, but there are plenty of books, podcasts, and YouTube videos that specialize in disaster preparation foods. If you have any questions regarding the consumption of any of these foods, please read the labels carefully and, if needed, check with your physician.

Using powdered and freeze-dried foods

Most of the food we eat is composed largely of water. Many foods are well over 50 percent water. The beauty of powdered or freeze-dried foods is that while the water is removed, they retain all the calories with half the weight and volume. Most of these foods also have shelf lives of five to ten years if unopened and kept in a cool, dry place.

Freeze-drying, covered in detail later, has the advantage of also retaining the nutrition and can have an even longer shelf life. These types of foods allow a lot more to be stored in a small space. The drawback is that they're expensive, and when reconstituted with water, their texture is a bit different. However, powdered foods can be mixed with other foods, such as soups and stews, to add flavor and additional nutrition.

Ready-made freeze-dried foods are covered later, but here are good examples of powdered staples that have shelf lives of up to 10 years.

- **Powdered whole milk:** This is a good protein/fat blend with calcium and vitamin D, which is also important for infants or young children.
- **Powdered cream:** This is a good source of fat to add calories to many meals.
- **Powdered whole eggs:** This complete protein can be reconstituted and consumed as scrambled eggs or added to other foods.
- **Powdered peanut butter:** This high-protein food can be reconstituted as a topping or mixed with other foods, such as cereal.
- **Powdered butter:** This can be used wherever butter is called for.
- **Bouillon cubes:** These are concentrated meat broths that contain a lot of protein and fat and can add a tremendous amount of flavor to anything.

Expanding your nutritional supplements

Food supplements are even more important in a long-duration survival situation. Canned and prepackaged foods with a long shelf life are usually not the most nutrient-rich. The process used to extend shelf life by ensuring no pathogens often require high temperatures. These temperatures tend to break down vitamins and nutrients. Add a higher level of stress, and you need solid nutrition to maintain health.

EXPANDING NUTRITIONAL AWARENESS

A physician friend told me that with all the things doctors must learn in medical school, they receive very little nutritional education. Physicians are required to do Continuing Medical Education (CME) every year to maintain their license. When asked how much that cost, my friend said a pharmaceutical company paid for it.

Understandably, pharmaceutical companies want to make sure physicians are aware of the latest drugs, but the net result is that not all physicians are up to date on the latest research in nutrition. With that said, there are many that are. However, if you want to know more about nutrition, diets, or fasting, do your own research. Pick up well-reviewed books or watch podcasts by highly credentialed experts. Dr. Sten Ekberg, mentioned earlier in this chapter, covers a wide variety of nutrition and health topics in his podcasts.

Stockpiling your supplements

As covered previously, if you're currently taking food supplements and are happy with them, just build up your reserve to at least a six-month supply. Vitamins do degrade over time, particularly over six months, so storage becomes more important. As covered in the Level 1 section, vacuum-packed vitamins maintain their potency longer, and you can increase that by keeping them in the refrigerator or freezer.

I try to avoid recommending any specific brands of any product and strongly encourage doing your own research with any supplement using independent labs such as `consumerlab.com`. However, with the importance of nutrition, Nutrilite and Life Extension are two food supplement makers that I've had good experiences with for many years. Both companies do third-party independent testing and apply the latest clinical studies for their formulations. Nutrilite is also the only global vitamin and dietary supplement maker that grows, harvests, and processes plants on its own organic farms, and the founder of Nutrilite is credited with inventing the multivitamin in 1934. Regardless, choose a reputable food supplement maker with supplements that have all successfully passed independent lab tests. Of course, there is a *Nutrition For Dummies*.

Adding protein powder

Everyone should also have a supply of high-quality protein powder. Good quality protein powder is expensive, but it is the most compact and concentrated nutrition you can get. The advantage of protein powder is that unflavored proteins can be added to other foods, or the flavored proteins can be mixed with water or milk (even powdered milk) and usually taste a lot like a milkshake. If you're not vegan, Nutrilite Whey Protein (made from milk) is a complete protein, sugar-free, and comes in vanilla, chocolate, and strawberry. They also make a plant-based complete protein. As long as protein powder remains sealed and stored in a cool, dry place, its shelf life should exceed two years.

Plenty of podcasts highlight foods you can buy to create your own survival pantry. Though you want variety, remember that the best survival foods are calorie-dense, have a long shelf life, satiate appetites, and minimize waste. I've heard that Twinkies can last for centuries.

Choosing to maintain a vegetarian or vegan diet

If you are determined to maintain a vegetarian or vegan lifestyle in a survival situation, there are ways to prepare that will allow this, but it will require more time and work to store and prepare and may cost more. A number of vegetables, such as beans and legumes, contain complex carbohydrates and low amounts of simple sugars and are high in protein. Beans and legumes can last a couple of years in cans, and dried beans in airtight containers have an almost unlimited shelf life. However, dried beans do require more preparation to eat. My favorite "bean" is the cacao bean, but for some reason, chocolate isn't classified as a vegetable. What a travesty!

Evaluating ready-made survival foods

The best way to stockpile food for an extended period, a month or more, is to build your own survival pantry tailored to your diet and tastes. A faster and simpler option is to purchase ready-to-eat meals designed specifically for disaster situations. A major advantage of prepackaged survival food is that it has extremely long shelf life and usually comes in easily storable, compact, stackable containers. A variety of survival foods are available, preventing the monotony of eating the same thing. With that said, many of these meals get most of their calories from simple carbohydrates, such as pasta and rice. These ingredients are much less expensive to source, allowing the manufacturers to offer them for lower prices, but they aren't necessarily optimal for disaster situation diets.

Emphasize fat and protein over carbohydrates

You don't need to eliminate carbohydrates, but most of your calories should come from proteins and fat. Some prepackaged food companies allow you to select specific entrees to customize your ratio of protein, fat, and carbohydrates. You'll also want to try different prepackaged foods to see how easy it is to store and prepare them; of course, you'll also want to find out how they taste. Buying a small initial sample is a great way to test them.

Freeze-dried foods perfect for stocking and evacuation

Prepackaged freeze-dried foods have extremely long shelf lives, often more than 25 years. The process of freezing and then sublimating the ice in a vacuum removes almost all the water, resulting in the same food having about one-third the weight and half the volume, while retaining all the nutrition. Unlike canned foods, which lose a lot of vitamin value due to the high temperatures required in the canning process, freeze-dried foods retain 97 percent of their nutritional value. Freeze-dried foods are reconstituted by adding water. In most cases, the taste is the same, although the consistency can be a little different.

Almost any food can be freeze-dried, from cooked chicken to uncooked steaks to vegetables and fruit. Freeze-dried meats include chicken, steak, ground beef, and pork. This makes freeze-dried food perfect for stockpiling and evacuation. The only downside is that due to the extensive process, freeze-dried foods are expensive.

If you have a permanent source of water, such as a well, restricting carbohydrates is less of an issue. However, lower-carb diets still have advantages, such as greater calories per cubic inch, reduced total food required, and, yes, less toilet paper to stock. A good option is to both build your own nutritionally optimized pantry and supplement it with freeze-dried foods as well as prepackaged survival foods that include pasta and rice. This gives you greater variety and a backup supply of survival-specific foods that are easy to store and have a long shelf life.

Fishing and hunting

Unless you're already a skilled fisherman or hunter, it's much more cost-effective, safer, and less time-consuming to simply stockpile food. Even if you are a skilled hunter, it makes sense to stockpile food because you don't know if the disaster will impact fish or game in your area or if you'll evacuate to an area where there is no fish or game. You also must be healthy and mobile to fish or hunt, and that might not be the case depending on the disaster.

Finally, fish and game have to be eaten quickly, refrigerated, or put through a preservation process to store long-term. For these reasons, fishing and hunting should be a backup plan. On the other hand, there's always a possibility that you have to evacuate and are unable to take your stockpiled food with you, and fishing or hunting may be a primary source of food.

Fishing

If you already know how to fish, enough said. If you don't know how but have patience, meaning you don't mind staring at a fishing line for hours (clearly not my favorite activity), connect with a friend who enjoys it. They're usually happy to share their love of fishing and teach you all you need to know. Yes, there is a *Fishing For Dummies*.

Hunting

Hunting is usually associated with firearms such as rifles or shotguns, which are covered in Chapter 14. However, there are other ways to catch small prey that can be effective and don't require a firearm. This includes bow hunting that doesn't require ammunition and can be done quietly without drawing attention or setting traps. *Wilderness Survival For Dummies* is an excellent reference.

Hunting, like anything else, is a learned skill, and if you've never hunted before and wish to have it as a future skill, read up on it. Then, find an experienced friend or family member who is a skilled hunter and learn from them. They can give you valuable advice on techniques and which firearms are optimal for different types of game. They can also teach you how to process the game, as well as firearm safety.

In most populated parts of the world, access to large game is limited compared to areas with small game. Even in the suburbs, there are small animals like rabbits and squirrels. Urban environments are much more limited but do have edible birds.

By the way, avoid hunting with that friend who says, "Hold my beer, and watch this."

Grilling

Most apartments or condominiums don't allow gas or charcoal grills, but if you have one, you could certainly use it to cook. However, your grill may be of limited use since it's usually used to cook meat that has a short shelf life, even when refrigerated. Unless you're hunting or fishing, you will quickly use up your store-bought meats. Additionally, for gas grills, the propane may be more valuable for fueling a heater or powering a generator. Options to maintain power, heat, and refrigeration are covered in Chapter 12.

Gardening, canning, dehydrating, pickling, and freeze-drying

Being able to can, dehydrate, pickle, or freeze-dry food is a great capability, particularly if you grow some of your own food. These processes require specialized equipment, supplies, and knowledge. If this is something you already do or if these are skills you would enjoy learning and can afford the equipment and time, go for it. This is a productive hobby regardless of disasters and allows you to grow your own healthy foods and preserve them. If this is of interest, *Backyard Homesteading For Dummies* provides information on how to accomplish this.

If gardening isn't an option due to your location or you're a serial houseplant killer, and canning, dehydrating, pickling, or freeze-drying isn't something you'd enjoy learning, it's probably not worth the significant investment in equipment and time. These skills are great to have, but there's no question that stockpiling food — even for a year — is much more cost-effective and requires a fraction of the time.

The same applies to raising livestock. Raising livestock is a great option if you happen to live in a rural area that doesn't restrict land use — and you have the time and interest to raise animals such as chickens for eggs. However, most people have neither the space nor the desire to raise livestock, and, again, it's easier and more cost-effective to stockpile food. (If raising livestock interests you, see *Raising Chickens For Dummies*.)

Sealing food with vacuum

If you wish to try some food preserving technology, vacuum packing or vacuum sealing may provide the most benefit for the cost. Many of the foods that have been highlighted have good shelf life only if they're unopened. As soon as their package is opened, the shelf life often drops to weeks or days. Vacuum sealing allows some foods to be resealed, slowing the oxidation process and preventing fats from growing rancid as quickly. Vacuum sealing can also prevent or slow the growth of some types of bacteria.

WARNING

Some potentially dangerous bacteria are anerobic meaning they don't need oxygen to grow. They can do just fine in a vacuum. Don't depend on vacuum packing to prevent bacterial growth. The primary cause of bacterial contamination is handling the food in nonsterile conditions before resealing.

IN THIS CHAPTER

» Determining the risk of a sewer backup

» Considering portable toilets

Chapter 8

Pooping When the Sewer Stops Working

This isn't one of those topics anyone wants to think about, but what goes in must come out. The vast majority of households are connected to a municipal sewage system. Like municipal water plants, sewage treatment plants require electricity to pump and treat sewage.

Sewage systems will function for a while without power since the initial leg of the trip usually uses gravity to get to the main sewer lines. The main sewer lines eventually require lift pumps to keep the sewage moving toward the treatment plant. Generators usually back up the primary sewage pumps. In major urban or suburban areas, these pumps and generators are numerous and must be constantly refueled to keep them running. For long-term power outages, this becomes a challenge. Additionally, not all neighborhoods have generator-powered pumps. Once the pumps stop, sewage will eventually have no place to go, and backups will occur. I'll go easy on the illustrations in this chapter.

If you live in a rural or suburban area and have your own septic system, you shouldn't have to worry about sewage backup issues when the power grid goes down. One exception to this is if you have an aerobic septic system, as I do. These septic tanks require electricity to power air pumps in order to function properly. Regardless, all septic systems need some maintenance. Over time, sludge builds up in the bottom of the tanks, and depending on use, may need to be pumped out every three to five years. Advanced and aerobic septic systems need annual maintenance and often require more frequent pumping out.

Additionally, tree roots can block drain lines and drainage fields. You want to have your system checked out every few years and, if needed, pumped out. A disaster is a terrible time to discover your septic tank has issues. Even if you have a septic tank, we recommend a quick review of this chapter, including the section on portable toilets, in case you need to evacuate and take your "toilet" with you.

Creating a Backup Plan for When Things Back Up (Level 1)

If the power grid is down for an extended period, it isn't a question of if the municipal sewer and trash collection will stop working; it's simply when. There are several steps you can take to reduce that risk or mitigate it. The first priority is protecting yourself and your family from disease or infection. Garbage and human waste are common sources of these, whether you have to deal with a clogged sewage system, portable toilet, or just garbage.

Gloves

Gloves are obviously important for protecting your hands, but can be critical when dealing with medical situations, human waste, or garbage. There are two categories: disposable gloves and work gloves. You need both. Work gloves are designed to protect your hands from things like sharp metal edges, wood splinters, and blisters. They're reusable but usually don't provide a watertight barrier.

Watertight disposable gloves are made of thin latex or nitrile plastic and designed to prevent liquids or biological material from coming in contact with your skin. A good supply of these is important. I recommend the stronger 8-millimeter-thick nitrile gloves. They're a little more expensive but reduce your risk of exposure. You want to have a good supply on hand, and it's not a bad idea to keep an extra box in your vehicle.

Trash

If you have municipal trash pickup, it's easy to take it for granted. In almost any disaster situation, this luxury will cease, and it could be for an extended period.

Although not as big a threat as sewage, trash can become a health hazard over time, as decaying food scraps can be a breeding ground for disease, insects, and rodents. The simplest solution is to have large trash bags and lots of them. They're inexpensive and don't take up much space. Don't go cheap here. Get the heavy-duty, contractor-grade trash bags that are at least three millimeters thick. Fifty-gallon (1,000-liter) bags are a good size, but don't buy a size you can't comfortably handle when they're full.

All trash eventually has to go outside. Where it goes depends on your location. If municipal trash pickup is suspended, you would like to put the trash bags downwind and in an area that provides a barrier from foraging animals who can rip the bags open. If you live in an urban area, there may be a designated or generally agreed-upon area to put them.

TIP

Trash bags have many uses beyond trash. They can be used to protect items from water at home or during an evacuation. They can be used to cover windows. They can be turned into makeshift raincoats and used in many other ways. Having plenty of extra bags available is always a good idea.

Municipal or city sewer system failure

In the U.S., 83 percent of households are connected to a public sewage treatment system. As mentioned, most public sewage treatment plants have backup power. This means the disaster would have to be severe enough to damage the sewage collection or treatment infrastructure, or there would have to be an extended power loss before backup occurs. However, some situations could cause an immediate stoppage, such as massive flooding or earthquakes that rupture sewage lines.

If you live in an apartment or condominium and your home isn't on the top floor, a sewage backup could affect you. This could also apply to a house if your elevation is lower than the other houses on your neighborhood sewage branch. Modern apartments and condos have backwater valves to prevent sewage from backing up from the street lines into the buildings. Houses don't normally have these, and most apartments or condos don't have backwater valves between building floors.

A dangerous situation can occur when there's water pressure, but the sewage pumps quit. With the continued use of water and toilets in the apartments or condos above you or the houses on a higher elevation, the sewage has no place to go. Eventually, it will start backing up and coming out of your toilets and drains. Once it starts, it may not stop and can completely inundate a house or apartment. This is very dangerous and can expose you and your family to deadly bacteria and viruses that cause diseases like dysentery or cholera. The only solution is to evacuate immediately.

If you own a house that is one of the lowest elevations in the neighborhood, you could have a backflow valve installed on the sewer line that comes out of your house Figure 8-1. Residential backflow valves require regular maintenance, and a plumber friend tells me that they're notorious for getting clogged. If you have access to a sewage cleanout fitting outside, you could also try opening the fitting in an emergency. However, this just moves the sewage out of your house and into your yard.

Even if backup doesn't occur, you will eventually reach a point where the toilets and drains no longer work. Before that happens, you need a "backup" backup plan.

FIGURE 8-1: Sewer backwater valve.

Stopboxstudio/Getty Images

Toilets to go

The simplest and least expensive option is to buy a portable toilet. These toilets use buckets or similarly shaped containers filled with bags that allow for easier disposal, as shown in Figure 8-2. These can be purchased online for less than $100. Some of them are even collapsible for easy storage and transport.

Or, you can make your own. With a five-gallon (20-liter) plastic bucket from Home Depot or Lowe's, you can buy a cushioned toilet seat designed specifically to fit on top of these buckets from companies like TripTips. Lined with biodegradable bags, you can use kitty litter or buy powders such as Wenge Degradable Gel to solidify the liquids for easier disposal. These types of toilets are portable and can be taken with you in a vehicle. They're useful for evacuation, as well as for camping.

FIGURE 8-2: Portable toilet.

Ivan Traimak/Adobe Stock Photos

A more comfortable but more expensive electric portable toilet is covered in the Level 2 section. Additionally, Chapter 7 covers dietary changes that will help reduce the amount of solid waste you or your family generates.

Finishing up the paperwork

Another not very popular but important topic is toilet paper. Explaining what happens when you run out isn't required. Unfortunately, the simplest solution is to stockpile enough to get you through a couple of weeks. It's not expensive, but toilet paper does take up a lot of space. One potential location is to stack it above your water stockpile. It uses up the unused space above the water containers without adding any significant weight. In an emergency, cloth such as old socks or washcloths can be used if you're able to wash and sterilize them immediately after use. They could be tossed into a bucket that already has water and a strong bleach solution. Better options are covered in the Level 2 section.

Using Technology to Improve the "Backup" Plan (Level 2)

If you happen to have a recreational vehicle such as a camping trailer or motor-coach with a toilet, you have a backup. If you don't have an RV, there are high-tech portable systems you can purchase separately that are often used in RVs or during camping.

There are several types to choose from. They go from simple composting toilets through cassettes up to electric toilets that seal waste in bags at the push of a button. Figure 8-3 shows the Laveo, which is portable, self-contained, and doesn't require adding composting material, making the waste disposal process simple and sanitary.

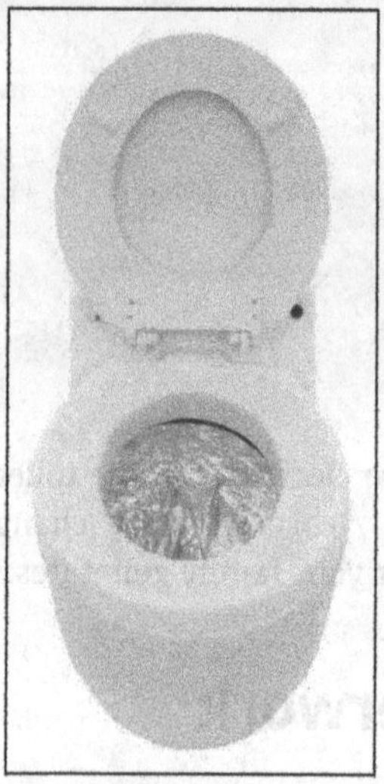

FIGURE 8-3: Laveo electric portable toilet. Courtesy of Laveo.

When the "flushing" button is pushed, a small motor spins the waste into a sealed bag. Each bag cartridge can handle multiple "flushes" before needing to be replaced. The downsides are the higher cost of the unit, the required cartridges, and the small amount of electricity required to operate.

This is the toilet that I use in my camper van design in Chapter 21, but new products and technologies are constantly emerging. Always do your own research to determine what best suits your situation.

IN THIS CHAPTER

- » Evaluating your physical and medical condition
- » Choosing or building first aid kits
- » Stockpiling medications
- » Emergency prescription medications

Chapter 9
Treating Injuries and Illness without Emergency Medical Services

In a disaster, emergency services such as ambulances and hospitals may be limited, while the odds of injury or sickness are higher. With or without a disaster, basic first aid training is a good idea, as well as keeping a reasonable supply of first aid kits, medical supplies, and equipment. Additionally, you want to evaluate the physical and medical condition of you and your family. It's particularly important to identify special needs if emergency services or treatment aren't available, or you have to evacuate.

I need to repeat my disclaimer from Chapter 7: Marrying a medical professional does not make *me* one. Therefore, you should carefully research any suggestions that involve medicine or medical treatment. If you have any medical conditions or questions, consult a physician before applying anything I suggest . . . because my mom's medical advice — "Don't go swimming for 20 minutes after eating or you'll get a cramp and drown!" — might not have been entirely accurate.

Understanding Your Personal Health

The first step is to evaluate your and, if you have a family, their physical and medical condition. That covers everything from vision, hearing, and mobility issues to medications and medical equipment.

Evaluating your medical condition and medication requirements

Chronic illnesses that require ongoing treatment or medication will have a major impact on your decision to stay or evacuate, as well as what supplies you need to stockpile. Serious illnesses may drive you to evacuate early to ensure access to medical facilities. Additionally, if medical equipment like oxygen bottles or an oxygen concentrator is needed, this can also drive your evacuation decision or determine the level of preparation required to stay. For example, if you need electricity for medical devices, Level 2 or 3 will be required to stay in your home if a disaster takes out the power grid.

Even if you or your family members don't have any chronic medical conditions, you need to honestly evaluate your and their physical condition. This is particularly important for those of us who are no longer in our twenties. It's easy to overestimate capabilities and important to be honest with yourself about your actual abilities. I try to maintain my health and fitness, but no matter what I do, I'll never get a call during the NFL Draft.

An honest evaluation helps you identify a health and fitness baseline and hopefully improve it with diet and exercise. It also lets you know what you may struggle with in an emergency. For example, could you or other members of your home climb down a rope ladder from a second-story window during a fire? Once you know your limitations, you can look for alternatives or tools that might assist.

Consulting with your doctor to consolidate or eliminate medications

Take stock of all the medications that you or your family need. This may sound obvious, but if at all possible, you want to consolidate or eliminate any medications that aren't absolutely necessary. Western medicine focuses heavily on specialties, which is great, but a physician friend of mine told me that sometimes, the right hand doesn't talk to the left hand. A general practitioner can often see the big picture and may help you evaluate and consolidate treatments and medications. Pharmacists can also provide important information.

Acquiring First Aid Kits and Supplies (Level 1)

Every home should have basic medications and medical supplies, and every home and car should have a first aid kit. There are some items that should be in every kit, and there are others that may be more important based on your situation or location. A first aid kit is of limited use if you don't know how to use it. It's important, as a minimum, to get basic first aid training.

Getting first aid training and having a medical guide

You can take first aid courses onsite or online with nonprofit organizations like the American Red Cross for less than $40. The American Red Cross's Cardiopulmonary Resuscitation (CPR) class also teaches an important skill, even if no one in your party has a cardiac condition, because trauma can require resuscitation. Another good class is Stop the Bleed. A more advanced option is to take a full EMT (Emergency Medical Technician) course.

You should also have a medical app on your phone. There are many to choose from, but a good example is the American Red Cross's free First Aid app (see Figure 9-1). It not only provides quick reference for emergency information and first aid but also allows you to schedule training.

In addition to the phone apps, you also want to have a hard copy as a backup. A good example that's small enough to fit in a pocket is the *EMS Field Guide*, which is available on Amazon.

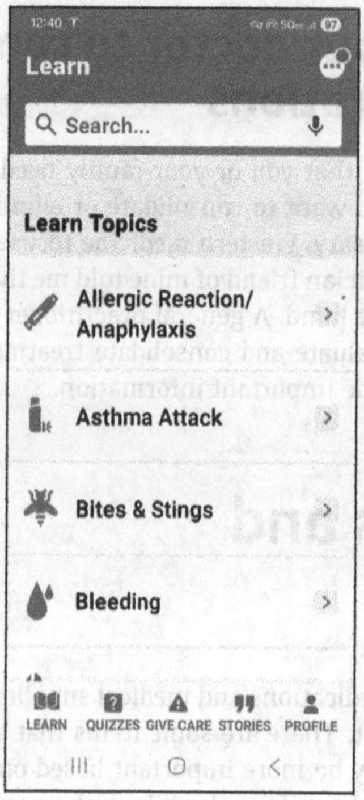

FIGURE 9-1: The free American Red Cross First Aid app.

Stocking over-the-counter medications

During a disaster, not only could emergency services be unavailable, but stores and pharmacies that carry basic over-the-counter medications may be out of commission. Even if they are available, a disaster might prevent you from getting to them. Every home should have over-the-counter medications to handle basic pain, inflammation, allergic reactions, vomiting, diarrhea, indigestion, and constipation. All drugs have a shelf life, so make sure you update them regularly and keep them in a cool, dry place. You may want to do your medicine freshness check at the same time you check your pantry. Below is a basic list of common over-the-counter medications you should have on hand. Popular brands of the medications are used for easy identification, but all of these medications can be found in other brands or in generic form.

- **Pain relievers:** These include aspirin, ibuprofen (Advil, Motrin IB), or naproxen (Aleve) and acetaminophen (Tylenol). All these, but acetaminophen, have anti-inflammatory properties.
- **Antihistamines:** These include diphenhydramine (Benadryl Allergy) or loratadine (Claritin) for allergic reactions.

- **Stomach and antidiarrheal:** These include loperamide (Imodium) and bismuth subsalicylate (Kaopectate or Pepto-Bismol).
- **Antacids:** These include Maalox, Mylanta, Rolaids, or Tums for heartburn and Pepcid (reduces stomach acid production).
- **Antiseptic wipes and antibiotic ointments:** These are alcohol wipes and antibiotics that include Neosporin and Bacitracin Plus.
- **Cold/Flu relief:** These include decongestants (Sudafed), cough suppressants (Robitussin), and expectorants (Mucinex).
- **Aloe gel, hydrocortisone cream, or calamine lotion:** These soothe bites, sunburns, and skin irritation.
- **Eyewash solution:** This is useful for flushing out eye irritants.
- **Insect repellent**: This prevents insect bites.
- **Hydrogen peroxide:** This can be used as an antiseptic for wounds, but also to disinfect surfaces; it is milder than bleach.

TIP

For severe allergic reactions, emergency rooms often prescribe a combination of Claritin (H1 antihistamine blocker) and Pepcid (H2 antihistamine blocker). Always consult with a physician or pharmacist before combining any medications.

Stocking your prescription medications

If you take medications for a long-term or chronic condition, it's critical to have a reasonable supply in case you can't get to a pharmacy. With the possible exception of pain medications, most physicians are usually ok prescribing a 90-day refill. You may also be able to ask your health insurance company to assist you in obtaining enough medication and supplies to have on hand. Keep in mind that drugs have a shelf life. They should be kept in a cool, dry place, and of course, use the oldest first. You can usually extend the shelf life of most non-liquid drugs by refrigerating them, but make sure they're unopened and kept in an airtight container.

TIP

Always fill prescriptions on the first day you become eligible for a refill, rather than waiting until the day you run out. A 90-day refill doesn't help if the disaster happens on day 89. If you are able to obtain an emergency supply, establish a plan for rotating your supply so that it remains up to date, and check medication expiration dates.

Choosing or Building First Aid Kits

You need to buy or build a couple of first aid kits (see Figure 9-2). You want your primary one in your home and more compact ones in your Bug-out bag and vehicles. For your primary first aid kit you keep at home, you may want to use a large, clear plastic bin for visibility and access. You may also want a supplemental kit that includes additional trauma treatment items such as splints and tourniquets.

TIP

If you or your family have special medical needs, build a more sophisticated first aid kit that might include hearing aid batteries, extra glasses, inhalers, and syringes. However, all first aid kits should contain the basics.

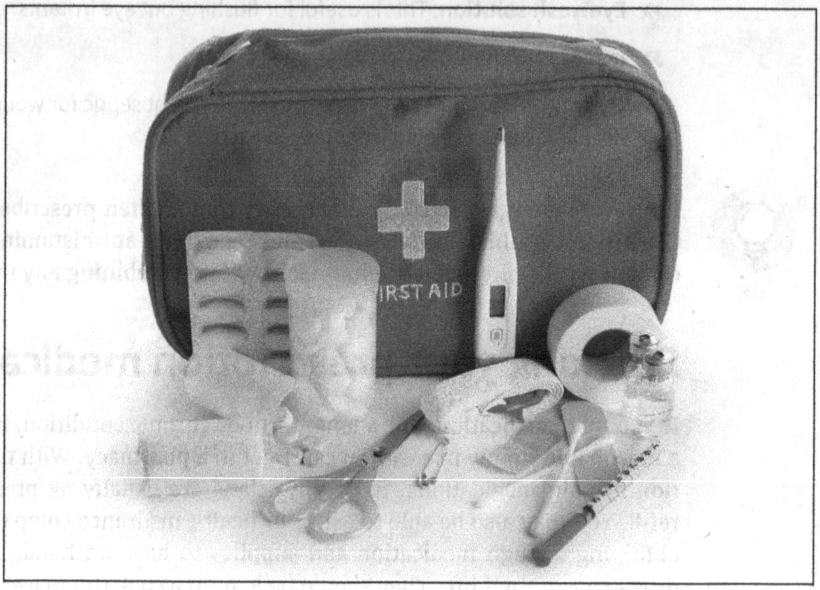

FIGURE 9-2: First aid kit.

Pixel-Shot/Adobe Stock Photos

According to the American Red Cross and medical experts, a good first aid kit should contain the following:

- Disposable gloves (see the "Nitrile gloves" below)
- Antiseptic pads (sterile alcohol)
- Antibiotic ointment
- Pain reliever (aspirin or acetaminophen)
- Anti-inflammatory (ibuprofen)
- Antihistamine for allergic reactions

- Antidiarrheal
- Sting relief
- Adhesive bandages and gauze
- Ace bandage
- Scissors
- Tweezers
- Duct tape
- Syringe for irrigation
- Thermometer
- Compact heat-retaining blanket
- Hemostatic spray or bandage (stops bleeding)

Additional items for trauma and other injuries (requires training)

- Pulse oximeter (measures pulse and blood oxygen level)
- Blood pressure monitor
- Stethoscope
- Splint
- Tourniquet
- Chest seal
- Wound packing gauze
- Hemostat
- Burn dressing
- Nasopharyngeal airway (NPA)

In addition to the above, there are several items that you may want to upgrade or add, depending on your medical history or location.

Nitrile gloves

It's important to avoid skin contact with toxic, corrosive, or biologically dangerous material. Infectious material is rarely transmitted through skin contact unless there's an open wound. However, even the smallest cut or abrasion can give viruses or bacteria access to you or someone you're treating. The most common infection scenario occurs after contact with an infectious agent and then touching your face before washing your hands. The nose and mouth are the primary entry points for bugs.

Disposable gloves in first aid kits are designed to prevent biological material from coming in contact with your skin or *your* skin coming into contact with someone you're treating. They're made of latex or nitrile (see Figure 9-3).

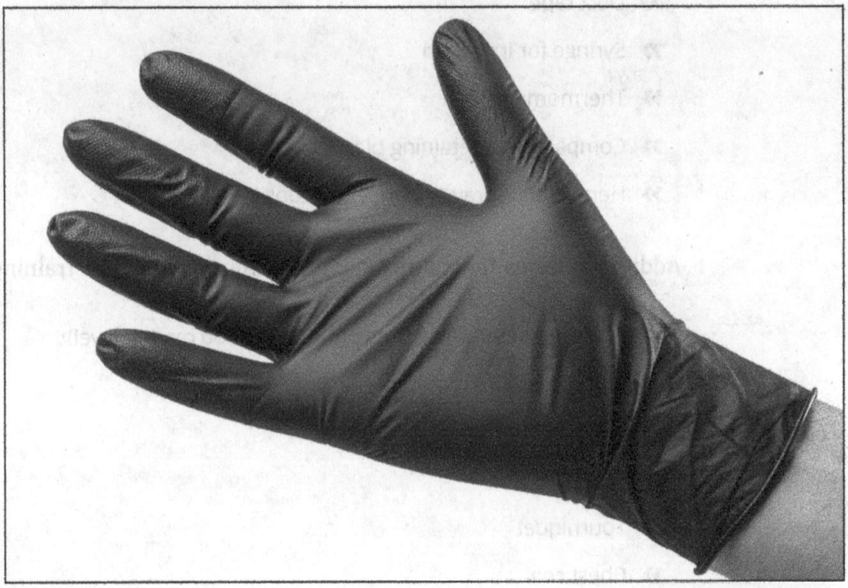

FIGURE 9-3: Disposable 8mm-thick nitrile gloves.

PhotoHUB/Adobe Stock Photos

Latex is based on natural rubber, but some people are allergic to it. Even if you're not allergic to latex, someone you treat could be. Nitrile is a synthetic rubber and is less prone to tearing. It's also more resistant to chemicals and only a little more expensive. Both latex and nitrile gloves come in standard four-millimeter thickness, which is very thin and fragile. These gloves can be torn just by putting them on your hands too quickly, which is likely to happen during an emergency.

I recommend replacing the four-millimeter gloves that come in your first aid kit with better ones. Stronger nitrile gloves (eight millimeters) are twice as thick and can reduce the risk of tearing and, therefore, infection.

TIP

In addition to buying eight-millimeter nitrile gloves for your first aid kit and bug-out bag, get a large box for the house and car. They have multiple uses, including handling sewage, leaking trash, changing a tire, dicing jalapeños, and preventing you from supergluing your fingers together while fixing that toy.

Epinephrine Autoinjector

If you don't know what an EpiPen (Epinephrine Autoinjector) is, you probably don't need to stock one. An EpiPen is used for anaphylaxis, a serious and potentially fatal allergic reaction. As the "autoinjector" part of the name implies, they are powered syringes that inject epinephrine to counter the symptoms of a severe allergic reaction that includes an inability to breathe.

Epinephrine Autoinjectors require a prescription, lose their effectiveness after a year, and must be replaced annually. Epinephrine is also sensitive to temperature extremes, so refrigerating it won't extend its shelf life and may damage the drug.

However, a new nasal spray epinephrine was just released. It still requires a prescription but replaces an injection with a simple nasal spray, is more compact, and has a shelf life of up to 2½ years.

Venomous snake or insect bite medication

A snake or insect bite from a venomous species usually requires immediate transport to a medical facility to receive anti-venom as soon as possible. Despite marketing, medical professionals say snakebite kits are not effective and may actually cause additional tissue damage. Treatment requires a medical professional to identify the correct anti-venom and administer it while monitoring for anaphylaxis. Anti-venoms cannot be purchased even with a prescription. They're expensive with short shelf lives.

However, one of the immediate risks of a venomous bite is an immune reaction that causes rapid swelling. This could constrict airways and prevent breathing. One recommendation by medical professionals is to include a bottle of Benadryl in your first aid kit. Benadryl is an antihistamine that can help counter allergic symptoms like swelling.

For fast action, children's chewable Benadryl is recommended because it can be chewed quickly and held in the mouth for faster absorption. The dosage is correct for children and can be easily increased with more tablets for adults. In the event that the antihistamine doesn't help and an Epinephrine Autoinjector is available, it can be used as a last resort. The antihistamine or epinephrine is only intended to buy time to get the victim to an emergency room for treatment.

Mosquitoes and ticks are not only irritating, but they can also carry serious infections. Mosquitoes can carry malaria, Zika virus, and West Nile virus. My father was a veterinarian and research scientist and contracted malaria. Ticks can cause many different types of infections, including Lyme disease, Rocky Mountain spotted fever, and Alpha-gal syndrome (AGS). You can buy an inexpensive tick removal tool that helps pull ticks off without leaving part of it embedded in the skin.

To help reduce the chance of having to remove ticks, make sure you have insect repellent wipes or spray. Deet is the most effective active ingredient. A highly rated repellent for both ticks and mosquitoes is Ben's, which contains 30 percent DEET (diethyltoluamide). See `https://bens30.com/`.

Radiation exposure measures

This may seem a bit extreme, but exposure to radioactive particles can come not just from nuclear war but from a nuclear power plant accident. Prevailing winds can carry radioactive particles far from the source.

A common radioactive element released during a nuclear accident is Iodine-131. Following the Chernobyl disaster, a significant increase in thyroid cancer cases was observed in the surrounding area for the decades that followed. If you live near or downwind of a nuclear power plant, adding Potassium Iodide tablets to your first aid kit can help during a nuclear accident by saturating your thyroid. This reduces its ability to absorb the radioactive Iodine-131. To be effective, it must be taken no earlier than 24 hours prior to or no later than 4 hours after exposure and provides protection for 24 hours.

RADIOACTIVE FALLOUT MIGRATION

Many years ago, I was in Finland to flight test the first F-18 Hornet to be built there. Since I like trying local food, I found a little hole-in-the-wall restaurant. The waiter recommended their reindeer stew. I tried it, and it was one of the best stews I've ever had. After the meal, I thanked her for the recommendation and said I'd be back for more. She paused and then said quietly that she didn't recommend eating the stew on a regular basis. When I asked why, she said that the reindeer had been exposed to fallout from the nuclear power plant disaster at Chernobyl.

Chernobyl was 450 miles (730 km) from where we were, and the disaster occurred over a decade before my visit. In addition to questioning my ability to select restaurants, it demonstrates that wind can carry radioactive contamination far from the source. Radioactive material that is inhaled or ingested, whether by reindeer or humans, can remain in the body indefinitely. Apparently, *Rudolf the Red-Nosed Reindeer* was based on a true story.

WARNING

Potassium iodine blocks the most common radioisotopes from nuclear accidents, but does not block all radioisotopes. It's not effective against most of the radioactive elements found in the fallout from nuclear weapons. Potassium iodide does carry some health risks. Before purchasing, go to the CDC website to learn when and how to take it and the risks: `https://www.cdc.gov/radiation-emergencies/treatment/potassium-iodide.html`.

Expanding Your Medications and Supplies for Longer-Term Disasters (Level 2)

In addition to first aid kits, training, and over-the-counter medications, if possible, you would like to extend any prescription medications to a six-month supply.

Requesting important emergency medications

Along with prescription medications, it would also be good to have oral antibiotics for emergencies. Talk to your physician and explain that you're trying to build up a small supply of key medicines for an emergency situation where you might not have access to them or a hospital. Explain that you would only use them as a last resort when medical infrastructure is inaccessible. There are very good reasons why they will be hesitant to give you an antibiotic prescription without an illness. You can loan them this book and highlight the warnings below.

WARNING

Antibiotics should never be used outside a physician's direction except in an extreme emergency. This isn't just a legal disclaimer. There are critical reasons for this.

- All antibiotics have side effects and can also cause significant reactions. Depending on your health, other medications you're taking, or your genetics, some of these reactions can be dangerous or cause permanent damage.
- One size does not fit all. Different antibiotics are effective for specific infections and not useful for others. The dosage also varies. There's a reason physicians go through many years of medical school versus someone making suggestions in a disaster preparation book.

» If antibiotics are taken for the wrong infection, in the wrong dosage, or for not long enough, it can cause the infection you're trying to combat to become immune to that antibiotic. This means that if the infection returns, you've rendered the antibiotic useless. If you spread that bug to others, you've also rendered it ineffective for everyone else.

It's estimated that there may be millions of deaths across the world because of antibiotics that are no longer effective due to over- or misuse. For these reasons, they should be held in reserve as a treatment of last resort and ONLY when a physician or hospital isn't available. If your physician is willing to help, ask them which antibiotics they recommend. If they don't understand or are unwilling to help, there are online clinics with licensed physicians who can recommend and prescribe them.

In some countries, such as Mexico, many antibiotics can be purchased over the counter. If you are able to obtain antibiotics, it's critical that in an emergency, you know where to find information on what type of infection an antibiotic is effective against, the dosage, how long it should be taken, as well as the side effects. If the disaster prevents you from reaching any medical facility, the best strategy is to call a medical office, a medical professional that you know personally, or a telehealth professional. As a backup, the *Nursing Drug Handbook* and *Physician's Desk Reference* are excellent resources.

Most oral antibiotics have a shelf life of two to three years if kept in a dark, cool, dry place. This means you shouldn't keep them in your bathroom due to the high humidity. Keeping them in your refrigerator can significantly increase their shelf life.

Creating a shelter agreement with medical personnel

To go to Level 3 preparation for medical treatment, you will need to marry a physician or give birth to one. Since that might not be possible for everyone, there is another option. If you know a good physician or physician's assistant (PA), you might consider working out a mutually beneficial arrangement.

If you have Level 2 or above disaster preparation at your home or a vacation home that can accommodate others, you might offer to share it with a medical professional and their family during a disaster. Although that represents a major commitment and more mouths to feed, it also gives you medical support and additional people for security. Obviously, you want to choose any potential survival partners very carefully since you might be living with them for a while.

3

Sheltering

IN THIS PART . . .

Learn when and how to shelter in place versus evacuating

Stay connected when the cell and Internet networks fail

Keep phones, lights, and heating or cooling powered when the power grid goes down

How to protect yourself and your family when law enforcement isn't available

Know the basic skills for troubleshooting and fixing critical equipment

IN THIS CHAPTER

» Finding immediate emergency shelter

» Fortifying your home from storms or intruders

» Creating safe spaces inside your home

» Using RVs as a shelter option

Chapter 10
Sheltering in Place

After air, shelter is the number one priority if you don't have it. The strategy is to stay in your current residence if possible. If the disaster prevents that, relocating to another home or securing accommodations is the priority. Chapters 11–15 cover connecting, powering, protecting, and fixing; Chapters 16–18 cover evacuation strategies.

The first step is to decide in advance under what circumstances you will evacuate. Of course, every situation is unique, but having a go/no-go criterion is critical.

Preparing to Stay (Level 1)

Preparing to stay in your home during an emergency doesn't mean riding out all possible threats. Some emergencies, like earthquakes or hurricanes, may require you to temporarily seek shelter elsewhere and then return when the immediate danger is passed.

Finding immediate shelter for time-critical disasters

In the middle of a time-critical disaster such as a tornado, earthquake, or fire, adrenaline is flowing, putting you in "fight or flight" mode. Adrenaline speeds up your reaction time, increases your energy reserves, and raises your pain threshold, all of which are important when immediate action is required. What adrenaline doesn't do is facilitate in-depth logical thought.

As a pilot, I discovered that during in-flight emergencies, my IQ usually dropped. Things like the simple math needed to calculate flight time with fuel remaining became more challenging. The majority of tactical jet fatalities occur when the aircraft is beyond saving, but the pilot waits too long to eject. As an F-18 instructor, I taught my students to decide when to pull the ejection handle before they ever set foot in the jet. It's essential to know under what circumstances you will evacuate to prevent *analysis paralysis*. Make as many critical decisions as possible in advance without the adrenaline.

The first step is to identify the most likely threat for your particular situation and location. Regardless of the cause of the disaster, immediate threats usually involve things like floods, fires, or attacks. Once you determine the most likely threat or threats, you can calmly and carefully make a plan for that scenario.

Determining a tornado shelter location in advance

If you live in an area prone to tornadoes and don't have a tornado shelter or basement, you need a plan that you can execute quickly. Canvass the area you live in and determine the closest tornado shelter. Public buildings such as schools often have shelters that can survive a tornado. If there isn't one or it isn't close enough to get to during a storm, find a neighbor who has a tornado shelter or basement. Ask them if you can join them during a major storm.

REMEMBER

Most neighbors are happy to share their shelter in a tornado. If not, find another neighbor. If no neighbor is willing, maybe you need to move to a neighborhood . . . with nicer people.

If you live in an area with a high tornado threat and have no basement and there are no public buildings or neighbors close enough, you may want to seriously consider creating your own tornado shelter, which is covered in the Level 2 section. Here are the recommended immediate steps to take if you have no tornado shelter.

1. **Stay away from any windows, doors, and outside walls, as these are the most vulnerable areas during a tornado.**
2. **If there's no basement, go to an interior room on the lowest level of the house. Bathrooms, closets, and hallways are often good choices.** If the bathroom has a tub, get in it and stay as low as possible.

3. **Once in an interior room, get under something sturdy like a heavy table for added protection.** If there is no heavy furniture to get under, pull a mattress over you.
4. **Cover your head and neck with a mattress, cushions, a blanket, and your arms, or anything available to shield against flying debris.**
5. **If you're in a mobile home, find shelter elsewhere.** Mobile homes offer little to no protection against tornadoes.

Finding the safest location during an earthquake

The best place to be during an earthquake is outside and away from any buildings or structures that could fall on you, but that's not usually possible due to the sudden onset. Barring that, when the ground moves, get under or below heavy furniture that might protect you if the ceiling collapses.

If that's not possible, move close to an inside wall or door frame and protect your head with your arms. If you live in the city and are not home when an earthquake occurs, you want to get as far away from buildings as possible. Instead of looking down at the ground, looking up for falling debris could save your life.

You may be surprised to learn that underground areas such as subways are actually one of the safest places to be. The impulse is to get out from underground, but the risk of falling debris is significant in a city. Subways and other similar underground structures experience less movement during an earthquake, kind of like being underwater during a tidal wave. They're also built to handle heavy overhead loads, by definition, and most are also designed with earthquakes in mind.

Protecting against fire

Many different types of disasters can cause fires. Beyond wildfires, they can be initiated by lightning or power lines blown down during a hurricane or tornado. They can also be started from a ruptured gas line during an earthquake, or . . . a 9-year-old scraping the propellant out of a model rocket engine into a paper cup and lighting it on fire. I got the fire out, but it did singe my eyebrows.

EXTINGUISHING FIRES

Everyone should have at least one good fire extinguisher at home and another in their car. It's also important to know the different classes of fires and choose extinguishers that are effective on all of them. See Table 10-1.

As a minimum, you should have a 2.5-pound (1 kg) extinguisher for your home, usually kept near the kitchen.

TABLE 10-1 Classes of fires by burning material

Class of Fire	Description
Class A	Fires in ordinary combustible materials, such as wood, cloth, paper, rubber, and many plastics
Class B	Fires in flammable liquids, petroleum greases, tars, oils, oil-based paints, solvents, lacquers, alcohols, and flammable gases
Class C	Fires that involve energized electrical equipment
Class D	Fires in combustible metals, such as magnesium, titanium, zirconium, sodium, lithium, and potassium

However, if you have a large home, like to deep-fat fry turkeys, enjoy shooting off mortar fireworks, or have a child like I was, a couple of larger extinguishers are appropriate.

A fire extinguisher is useless if you can't get to it when you need it. You can now purchase compact fire extinguishers that are about the size of a can of spray paint. They're effective on almost any type of fire, and they're small and inexpensive enough that you can buy a batch of them and stash them around the house. Good places to put them are near every entrance to the kitchen, in the garage, utility room, and each bedroom, as well as in your car. Because of their small size, they should be in addition to the larger 2.5-pound (1 kg) extinguisher.

Finally, check your smoke detectors and make sure they're working. If your home doesn't have carbon monoxide detectors, get some. In the U.S., about 400 people a year die in their homes from carbon monoxide poisoning. During disasters, the use of gas-powered heaters and generators increases the risk.

Most smoke, fire, and carbon dioxide detectors use the little, boxy 9-volt batteries, which have a shelf life of about five years. Even if they're not beeping, replace them every few years. If you think you're likely to forget, you can buy the more expensive lithium versions with a 10-year life.

ESCAPING FIRES

Regardless of whether you're dealing with a wildfire, a house fire, or your brother-in-law's attempt at barbecuing, an immediate escape plan is essential. It may sound silly to have an escape plan in a house that you're totally familiar with, but things can be very different during an emergency.

When you hear about an entire family perishing in a house fire, it's normal to wonder why they didn't just leave the house. What is often missed is that fires can happen at night while you're sleeping. Fires can kill the electrical power and lights, and quickly fill the house with blinding smoke, making it impossible to see. They can incapacitate you with the inhalation of carbon monoxide or toxic gases within a couple of minutes.

It's also easy to forget about all the flammable items in most households, including your car's gas tank in your garage, cans of spray paint in a closet, rubbing alcohol or hair spray in a bathroom, or a grill's propane tank on your patio. Additionally, some houses have natural gas appliances such as furnaces, water heaters, and stoves. When a fire ignites any of these, the entire house can be engulfed in flames in seconds.

It's also easy to imagine you could hold your breath long enough to get out of the house. Try it. From your bedroom, try holding your breath and getting out of your home as fast as you can. Now try it blindfolded on your hands and knees. You have to assume that it will be at night with no electrical power, or your vision will be completely obscured with smoke.

Chapter 5 highlighted the use of little cans of pure oxygen. A good example is Boost Oxygen, which comes in 10-, 5-, and 3-liter sizes (see Figure 10-1). The 5-liter size is only about the size of a soft drink can, but it can give you the precious minutes needed to escape and help others. This means they need to be within easy reach, such as in a nightstand drawer or under the bed. You want to have as many of these little oxygen cans as there are people in your home. Buy an extra can and try it to get comfortable with its operation.

FIGURE 10-1: Five-liter Boost Oxygen can.

WARNING

These bottles are filled with almost pure oxygen. Fires love oxygen, and it will make a fire burn much more intensely. Make sure you only pull the air release trigger when it's held tightly over your nose and mouth, and don't let the oxygen flow anywhere near a fire.

Another important item to have nearby is a flashlight that can be strapped around your head. A headlamp allows you to illuminate your path while keeping your hands free. The light will help you see, and a can of oxygen will give you time, but you still need an escape plan.

Flames, hot air, and smoke rise. Staying close to the floor, even if you have to crawl, may give you the best chance to see and navigate through an area filled with fire and smoke. Keep one of these flashlights and the oxygen close to your bed.

If you live in a two or three-story home or apartment without an outside fire escape, consider buying an emergency escape rope ladder, as shown in Figure 10-2. They can be used to evacuate from a second or third-story window. These rope ladders are fairly inexpensive and can be stored under a bed.

FIGURE 10-2: Emergency escape rope ladder.

Generated with AI using ChatGPT-OpenAI

WARNING

Make sure the ladder is rated for the maximum weight of whoever might have to use it and that everyone in your home knows how to safely deploy it from a window or balcony.

I remember thinking school fire drills were good because they got us out of class for a while. In fact, fire and emergency drills are important and not just for schools. You should run an emergency drill with your family at least every year and cover several scenarios with emphasis on the ones you're most likely to see.

PROTECTING YOUR HOME FROM WILDFIRES

As mentioned in Chapter 3, if you live in the Western U.S., make sure you have the Watch Duty app. This nonprofit organization of wildland firefighters, first responders, and dispatchers accurately displays up-to-date maps of all major fires from the Pacific to the Mississippi River. If you live outside the Western U.S., there may be similar apps in your area or emergency service notifications. Although there are steps you can take to help protect your home, if you're notified of an approaching fire or identify one that could be a threat, evacuate. Don't wait. Wildfires driven by wind can expand rapidly and cut off escape routes.

If you live in an area prone to wildfires, there are some basic steps you can take to improve your home's survivability, but don't stick around to test it. Create a clear zone around your entire house that has no flammable material and extends 30 feet (10 meters) away:

- Remove dead vegetation and thin the surrounding vegetation in order to break up the fire's path to your home. Keep the grass cut to reduce fuel.
- If you can't remove nearby trees, cut the lower branches up to 10 feet (3 meters) off the ground. This prevents "ladder fuel" from climbing up into the tree canopy.
- Cover roof soffits with metal screens to prevent burning ash from entering your attic and seal any gaps in your foundation with fire-resistant caulk.

Additional measures are covered in the Level 2 section.

REMEMBER

If this all seems extreme, try watching video of wildfires driven by high winds.

Fortifying your home from storms and intruders

Here's a simple, inexpensive way to improve your home's security in extreme weather or from an intruder, even if you live in a rented house or apartment. Most exterior doors fail where the deadbolt meets the doorframe or at the hinges. Or the doorframe gives way after being ripped out of the house's framing structure.

To prevent this, simply replace the screws that hold the door hinges and deadbolt striker plate with longer screws. Instead of just anchoring the hinges and striker plates to the door frame, the longer screws go through the thin door frame and anchor it into the house's framing structure, as shown in Figure 10-3. This simple step significantly increases the impact force the door can withstand before breaking.

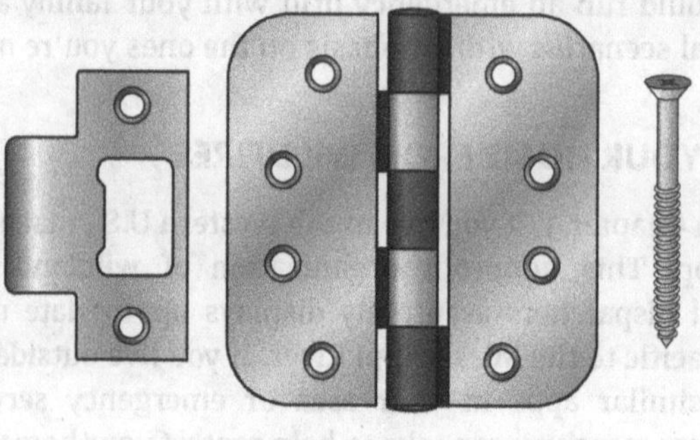

FIGURE 10-3: Strengthening exterior door hinges and locks with larger wood screws.

The easiest way to do this is take out just one screw from one of the door hinges. Don't worry, there are enough screws left to prevent the door from falling off. Take that screw to a hardware or home improvement store and find screws that look the same but are about three inches long (75mm). Get enough to replace all the screws in each hinge and the striker plates on the other side of the door, where the doorknob and deadbolt are. Do this on all exterior doors. It can also be done to any important interior doors, such as your bedroom. A power screwdriver or drill makes this much easier.

WARNING

Be careful about using screws longer than three inches (75mm) to avoid going through the framing member and hitting electrical wiring.

Introducing the bug-out bag

The term "bug-out bag" is commonly used when talking about disaster preparation. It's usually a large backpack with things that are useful in a disaster or evacuation situation. It can hold everything from a first aid kit to your laptop. It will be covered in Chapter 16, but I'm introducing it here because it can also be a "bug-in bag." As such, it's a central spot to keep important items in one location for easy access.

Improving Your Home's Security (Level 2)

There are steps you can take to fortify your home, enhance its security, and create safe spaces inside. In 2021, Texas experienced a record-breaking subzero freeze that lasted for a week. It overloaded the grid and froze natural gas lines. This took down half of the Texas power grid for four days, rupturing water lines everywhere. During this period, many desperate people broke into homes for heat and water.

Fortifying your home from storms and intruders

There are several reasonable cost upgrades that can improve the ability of your home to withstand natural disasters and intruders. This is Level 2 preparation, but I'll start with the least expensive options first, some of which are dependent on your location and type of home.

Barricading exterior doors

For about $100, you can take it to the next level by adding a removable door barricade. You may be picturing a giant wood or steel bar with huge brackets on each side. However, there are now barricades that are extremely unobtrusive when not in use. As simple as they are, they can dramatically improve the ability of any door to withstand a major impact. This will reduce the chance of the door failing during extreme weather and prevent or delay forced entry by an intruder. A good example is the Doorricade, as shown in Figure 10-4. You may be able to install it even if you're renting, but check with the landlord.

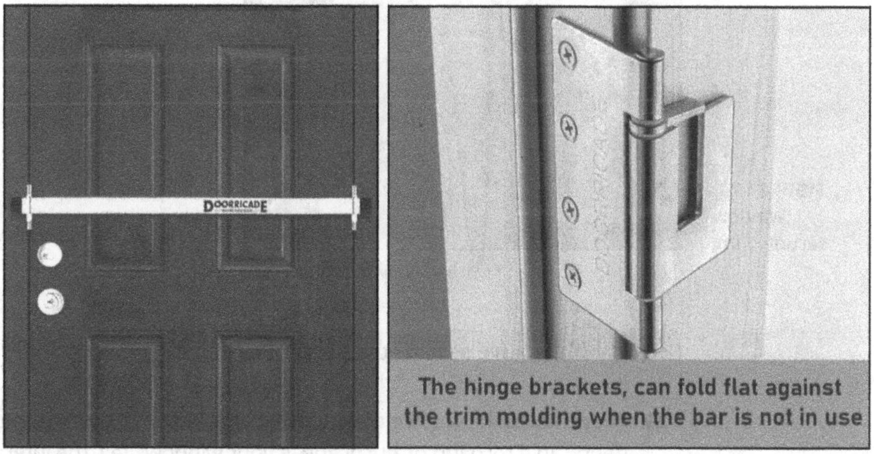

FIGURE 10-4: Installing a Doorricade removable door barricade to strengthen exterior doors.

Adding security film to windows and glass doors

Assuming you own your home, replacing windows with hurricane or impact windows provides a much higher level of protection from storms and intruders. Our home is oceanfront and was built with impact-resistant windows designed to survive extreme wind and flying debris from hurricanes. However, these "hurricane" windows are expensive. The cost of replacing all your existing windows would probably fall under Level 3 preparation.

A much less expensive option that provides many of the benefits of hurricane windows is the application of security film to the window. This can be applied to any window or glass door, even if you are in a rented apartment, since it can be removed. Security film is usually about eight millimeters thick with an adhesive that sticks to the glass. When properly applied, the film is invisible. The glass will still shatter, but it will stay in place and won't easily break out of the frame, as shown in Figure 10-5. You can see online videos of attempts to break through these security film-modified windows.

FIGURE 10-5: Window security film.

frankoppermann/iStock/Getty Images

Security films have several uses and benefits:

- They reduce the chance of windows being blown in by extreme wind or flying debris. In a tornado or hurricane, if your windows fail, the internal pressure created by the extreme wind can literally lift the roof off.
- Security film also provides protection from forced entry. An attacker can eventually break through, but it takes more work and time. An opportunist burglar or looter will likely move on to an easier target. It also gives you time to respond or escape.

» These films usually provide additional protection from UV and provide some heat rejection. They can be clear or tinted for reduced light or increased privacy.

WARNING

Security film won't make your windows bulletproof. They cannot protect you if someone outside shoots through your window . . . on the other hand, an attacker trying to break through your window or glass door is equally vulnerable. Just saying . . .

Professionally installed, security films usually cost about $6–8 per square foot of glass, which is much less than the cost of impact windows and doors. You can also buy the film and install it yourself if you're good at DIY projects. Security film is arguably the simplest and most cost-effective way to increase your home's resistance to storms and intruders.

Premade plywood "hurricane shutters"

Covering windows with plywood is critical during hurricanes, but can also be useful for helping keep your home warmer in the winter or cooler in the summer when heating or air conditioning is limited or not available. During long-duration disasters, covering ground-floor windows can also help secure your home from intruders, whether you're home or you've evacuated.

The key is to precut plywood pieces to fit over each window and exterior door in advance. Don't wait until a hurricane or other disaster to buy and cut plywood. These plywood "shutters" can be nailed or screwed into the window/door trim, but there are better, faster options. Several systems can attach the plywood panels faster. I use a system called PlyFASTner, as shown in Figure 10-6. Installing PlyFASTner requires preinstalling long bolts into the window/door trim.

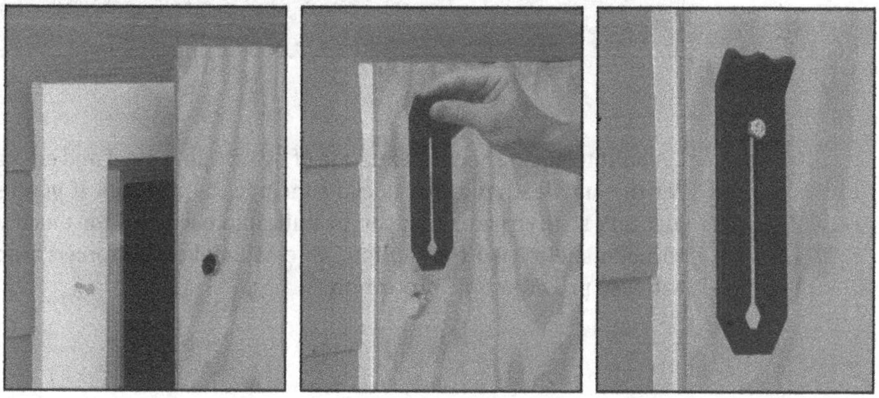

FIGURE 10-6: PlyFASTner installation of temporary plywood "hurricane" shutters.

When not in use, the bolts are tightened so that they're flush with the window and door trim and painted to match, making them almost invisible. Holes are drilled through the plywood to line up with the bolts. Before a storm, the bolts are backed partway out of the trim. The plywood is installed so that the bolts stick out of the holes, and then a patented clip is slipped over the bolt heads. The bolts are then retightened, fastening the plywood to the window or door trim.

Buying or building a tornado shelter

If you live in a tornado-prone area and there are no neighbors or municipal tornado shelters near enough to reach in time, installing your own tornado shelter may be required. The simplest path is to build or buy a prebuilt one, as shown in Figure 10-7.

FIGURE 10-7: Tornado shelter.

William McDill/Shutterstock

Prebuilt tornado shelters are made of heavy-duty steel and are usually over $4,000 for the smallest, and that doesn't include installation. If you're handy, there are also DIY shelter plans that can be built in a backyard for much less. If installing a tornado shelter isn't an option, an earthquake-reinforced room, covered below, can also provide some protection.

Creating an earthquake sanctuary inside your home

During earthquakes, take cover where you are rather than trying to get outside because you're vulnerable while trying to escape. The primary risk is a collapsing wall or ceiling.

Taking cover under strong furniture

If you live in an earthquake-prone area and your residence is such that you cannot get outside quickly, the simplest and least expensive solution is to buy or build a very strong piece of furniture that you can get under. It should be big enough and strong enough to protect you from a collapsing wall or ceiling. This could be an exceptionally strong dining room table or a high platform bed with massive supporting legs that you can fit under. If you have large top-heavy furniture such as dressers or china cabinets, you should attach them to wall studs with brackets to prevent them from falling over during a quake.

Reinforcing a room

If you own your residence, you can modify one room to increase its structural strength and ability to survive a collapsing ceiling or wall. The easiest way to do this is to choose a small interior room. A closet is perfect if you and your family can squeeze into it during an earthquake. If it's not big enough, you can apply this to more than one closet.

Creating a reinforced room in your home requires cladding the walls and ceiling of the room with plywood. Using ¾-inch (18mm) plywood provides excellent strength without losing a lot of interior space, and plywood comes in a variety of finishes. When installed properly, this simple modification dramatically increases the structural strength of the room, creating a fortified capsule to help protect from collapsing walls or ceilings. It's a simple job for a contractor, though if you're good with DIY carpentry, follow these basic steps:

1. **Temporarily remove shelves, hanging rods, baseboards, and crown molding.**
2. **Using large sheets of ¾-inch (18mm) plywood, cut pieces big enough to cover each wall and the ceiling.** Install the ceiling plywood first so it will rest on top of the wall plywood.
3. **Using a stud finder, locate the studs behind the drywall.** Screw the plywood into the ceiling and then the walls with screws long enough to go through the plywood, drywall, and most of the framing members. Space the

screws six inches apart (150mm). Add steel L- brackets at the corners and where the wall plywood meets the ceiling plywood.

4. **You can place drywall over the plywood, or if you can live with a slightly rougher appearance inside your closet, use plywood with a finished surface.** Countersink the screws, caulk them and the joints, and paint the plywood. Reinstall shelves and hangers.

5. **If the closet has a hollow-core door, replace it with a solid-core door.** Reinforce all the hinges and striker plates with longer screws, as covered in the previous section.

You can still use it as a closet as long as you can quickly toss the clothes out and squeeze inside. This would also be a good place to stash your Bug-out bag with cans of oxygen. Even if you fortify a room, strong furniture that you can get under is still a good idea in case you can't get to the room in time.

Improving your home's resistance to wildfires

The most important step you can take is creating a clear zone around your home, as covered in the Level 1 section.

Hardening your home against wildfires

In addition to the Level 1 steps covered earlier in this chapter, the following steps are more extensive and expensive:

- Replace decking and fences with fire-resistant or composite materials.
- When your roof needs to be replaced, upgrade to a metal roof or use clay or tile shingles.
- Upgrade your home's siding to non-combustible materials such as fiber cement board, brick, or stucco.

Protecting your home with sprinkler systems

A sprinkler system is not going to stop a wildfire. At best, it will provide a short period of protection. A wind-driven wildfire will rapidly evaporate any water. The best results require saturating the ground and vegetation around your home before evacuating. There are a couple of challenges with operating a sprinkler system during a wildfire:

- Water pressure will likely be lost either due to damage or to authorities turning it off to conserve water pressure for firefighters. That means having a water reservoir available, such as a swimming pool, hot tub, or water tanks.
- If the system needs power to operate, and the power grid fails or is shut down, you need either a battery backup or a generator to power the system.

There are basic DIY systems that can be installed as well as advanced commercial fire suppression systems. The most effective commercial systems are automated and use a special fire suppression foam. However, you have to weigh the high cost of one of these commercial systems versus the limited protection they provide.

Regardless, never depend on any system or stick around to see if it works. Chapter 5 covers critical items such as masks and supplemental oxygen that can protect you during an evacuation. Chapter 23 covers vehicles that are particularly effective in these situations.

Using an RV for a Backup Shelter

If you already own a recreational vehicle (RV) like a motorcoach, camping trailer, or even a tent, it can provide an emergency shelter option. Even your car can provide temporary shelter, and some SUVs have the ability to fold the seats and add an inflatable mattress. For example, you can buy a custom-made inflatable mattress that fits a Tesla Model Y and, when combined with the EV heat pump, can provide a heated or cooled place for two to sleep during an emergency, an evacuation, or just for camping.

I live on the Texas coast, which is prone to hurricanes. Because there are usually several days of warning before landfall, there's time to pack up an RV and relocate with important possessions and supplies. This would also apply to areas at risk for wildfires or volcanic activity where there's prior warning.

However, with widespread or global disasters, most RVs suffer from the same limitations as a house. They can only be used as long as their batteries, propane, or water lasts. There are additions and modifications, however, that can significantly extend an RV's ability to operate off-grid. Chapter 21 will cover these, as well as Level 3 RV designs.

IN THIS CHAPTER

» Staying aware with apps

» Maintaining a connection when the cell phone/Internet network is down

» Using radios and satellites

» Protecting your devices from an EMP

Chapter 11

Connecting without the Networks

This chapter covers staying aware of what's happening and being able to communicate with family, friends, and emergency services when the cell phone network and Internet go down. It also covers accessing information via radio and protecting your cell phone and other devices. Chapter 12 covers powering and recharging these devices when the power grid goes down.

Using Apps That Provide Advanced Warning

Before covering strategies for staying connected when the cell network and Internet fail, it's important to have apps that provide advanced warnings *before* the networks go down.

Wireless Emergency Alerts

The first and simplest in the U.S. is the national Wireless Emergency Alert system. All phones made after 2012 have the ability to receive these alerts. In the U.S., they're sent out by national and local governments and tied to your location. Alerts include warnings about severe or catastrophic events such as tornadoes, floods, tsunamis, earthquakes, volcanic eruptions, and terrorist attacks. They can also notify you of law enforcement events in your area, such as kidnappings (Amber alerts) or an active shooter situation near you. Most countries have similar systems.

When you get a new phone, it comes with Wireless Emergency Alerts turned on. Some people turn it off due to a concern that the government can use it to track their location. However, this system doesn't use your phone's location; instead, it broadcasts to all cell phones that happen to be in a particular area by sending the alert to those cell towers. Even if you turn location data off, this alert system will still work. It's the same technology that your navigation app uses to warn you of traffic jams in your area.

I recommend leaving the Wireless Emergency Alert system active. You can tailor the settings to control notifications by event type and how it will notify you:

- On Android phones, go to Notifications and select Advanced > Wireless Emergency Alerts.
- On iPhones, select Notifications, scroll down to Government Alerts, and select the options you want.

On both types of phones, you can select specific alerts and how they're presented.

Weather apps

Most people have a weather app on their phone. If you don't have one, it's a good idea to get one. There are many to choose from, and you may have to try out several to find one that best covers your local threats. To reduce being bombarded by too many notifications, only select the truly dangerous events that apply to your area. Most of these weather apps get their information directly from government services such as the National Oceanic and Atmospheric Administration (NOAA) in the U.S. It's not a bad idea to have their website on your phone as well. This is particularly important for extreme weather events such as hurricane development and tracking.

Space weather apps

Several apps monitor and warn about solar flares and coronal mass ejection events. These apps can warn you using NOAA's Geomagnetic Storms Impact Scale, which goes from G1 to G5, as shown earlier in Chapter 2 (see Figure 2-7).

TIP

Download the Space Weather Live app to notify you of impending solar flares or CMEs. You can also subscribe to the Space Weather Prediction Center at `www.swpc.noaa.gov/content/subscription-services`.

Wildfire apps

For wildfires, as covered in Chapter 10, if you live in the Western U.S., download the Watch Duty app. If you live in another fire-prone area, do an Internet search for any notification apps for your area. Many weather apps will also provide fire notifications. Most of these apps are free, and if notification is turned on, they can provide the extra time to protect your home or evacuate.

General warning apps

There are dozens of commercial "safety" apps with subscription fees. Some simply have you hold down a button on your screen when you're in a dangerous area, and if you let go and don't enter a pin, it will send the police. Others use community or user input to provide information on emergencies or unusual events in your local area, from fires to protests.

One of these apps may be good to have, particularly if you live in a high-risk, urban environment, but do your research by checking out safety app reviews. Some have mixed reviews for over-notification or issues with false or biased reports.

Staying Connected When the Cell Phone Network Fails (Level 1)

One of the top priorities is having situational awareness; in other words, you need to know what's happening. This is critical because it will help you decide whether you can stay where you are or need to evacuate. You also want the ability to reach emergency services and to reach family and friends to determine if they're OK. This can be important for deciding whether you need to go to where they are or if they need to come to you.

Understanding cell phone network and Internet vulnerability

Most people now get their local, national, and global information from a news or social media app or a TV network. These sources won't be available if the cell network and Internet go down.

Cell phone networks

Cell phones are really just small, short-range, two-way radios. They connect across the globe by using relay stations. These relay stations receive and retransmit calls and data. They use antennae that are mounted on elevated structures such as cell phone towers, but also water tanks and buildings.

These cell phone relay stations require electrical power to operate, and even the tallest towers only have a maximum usable range of about 25 miles (40 km). The antennae, transmitter, receiver, and power source can all be damaged or incapacitated by extreme wind, floods, wildfires, earthquakes, volcanic ash, EMPs, or cyberattacks. In other words, practically any disaster can take out your ability to connect using the regular cell phone network. Maintaining connectivity when the cell network is down, without training carrier pigeons, will be covered in this chapter.

Internet

Your Internet connection may be similarly vulnerable. If it comes in through a 4G or 5G system or hotspot, it uses the same system as cell phones and will fail when your cell phone connection is lost. Even if your Internet connection comes in through a conventional or fiber-optic cable, that cable (whether on power poles or buried) is susceptible to disasters that include storms, floods, wildfires, and earthquakes. Additionally, the nodes that connect those cables to the Internet backbone require electrical power and are also vulnerable.

If your Internet uses a satellite system, you're much more likely to maintain connectivity through a disaster. While satellite systems do have ground stations that could be affected by disasters, there are many of them, and they're geographically distributed, making it unlikely that all of them will be affected. Tapping satellite networks can be done under Level 1 preparation and will be covered later under "Texting via satellite."

Wi-Fi

Most homes use Wi-Fi to connect all their devices to the Internet. Your Internet comes into your home through a modem. From there, the Internet connects to your Wi-Fi router, usually via an Ethernet cable, which broadcasts that signal throughout your home and beyond, as shown in Figure 11-1. Wi-Fi routers must be powered along with your cell phone and computer. Keeping them powered and charged is covered in the next chapter.

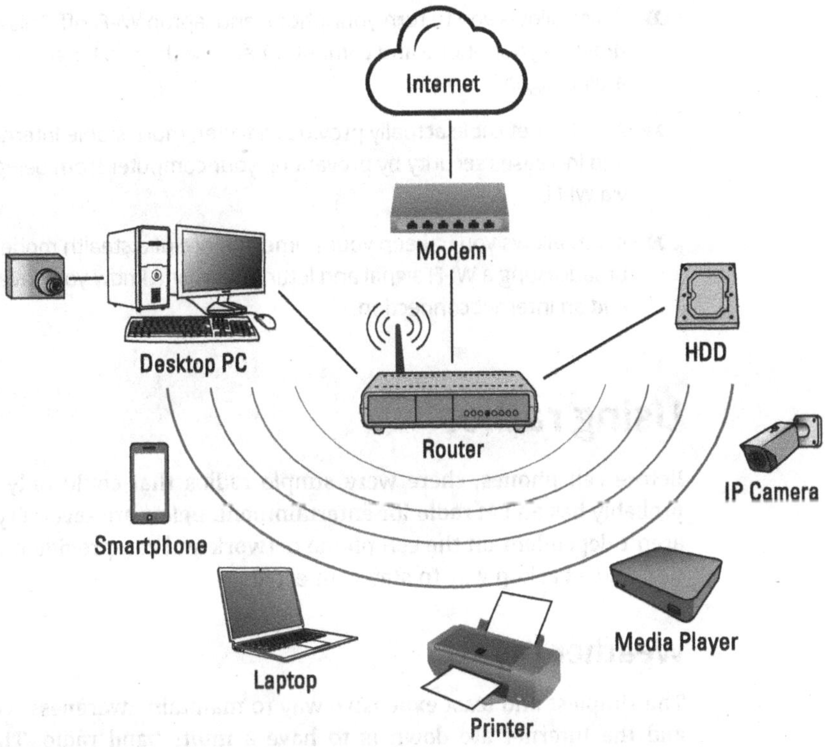

FIGURE 11-1: Residential Internet via modem and router.

You can bypass your router and connect your computer — and even your cell phone — directly to the modem using an adapter cable. You can purchase an adapter cable that has an Ethernet port on one end and a USB cable that's compatible with your cell phone on the other.

You plug the Ethernet cable that comes out of your modem (the one that normally goes to your Wi-Fi) into the adapter. On the other end, it has multiple USB ports and a phone-compatible USB cable. The USB ports can be used to connect to a desktop or laptop computer. The USB cable can connect directly to most cell phones.

If you have a modem and Wi-Fi router combined into one unit, it will still have an Ethernet port and should have the ability to turn off the Wi-Fi transmitter via a hardware switch or software control.

Although connecting your computer and phones with long Ethernet cables may create a tripping hazard, there are some potential advantages during a disaster:

- If you're running on battery or generator power, this eliminates the power needed to run your Wi-Fi.
- It also allows you to turn your phone and laptop Wi-Fi off. This reduces battery drain on your phone and computer because they no longer have to broadcast a Wi-Fi signal.
- An Ethernet cable actually provides a faster, more stable Internet connection and increases security by preventing your computer from being hacked via Wi-Fi.
- It also allows you to keep your home in more of a stealth mode by not broadcasting a Wi-Fi signal and letting everyone know you have power and an Internet connection.

Using radios

Before cell phones, there were simple radios that could only receive. Your car probably has an FM radio for entertainment. Below are several types of radios that aren't dependent on the cell phone network and can provide important information and a backup way to stay connected.

Weather radios

The simplest and least expensive way to maintain awareness when cell networks and the Internet are down is to have a multi-band radio. They're specifically designed to receive weather alerts and emergency broadcasts, and some have additional shortwave frequencies. The best of these also include a small solar panel or even a manual crank to recharge the batteries and even your phone, as shown in Figure 11-2.

Scanners, CBs, and ham radios

Scanners are radio receivers that can rapidly scan frequencies, particularly those that emergency responders use, such as police and fire. They stop scanning when they come across a frequency that's in use. Often referred to as "police scanners," they're usually more expensive than a pair of handheld radios that can monitor and even scan many of the same frequencies. Additionally, emergency services are moving to encrypted radios to prevent the release of personal information.

FIGURE 11-2: Handheld weather and shortwave radio with solar and hand-crank charging.

Birgit Reitz-Hofmann/Adobe Stock Photos

Citizen band or CB radios are radios that can access a special set of channels that handheld and ham radios cannot use. Although not as popular as in the past, they're still used in the U.S. and Canada primarily by commercial truck drivers for short-range communication about traffic, weather, or for emergency assistance. Because of their lower frequency, they require an antenna to get their maximum range, which is around seven miles. Most other countries have similar systems but use different frequencies.

Ham, or amateur radio, covers a wide set of frequencies from low to very high. With powerful enough transmitters and an exceptionally large antenna, some of these frequencies allow communication for thousands of miles. However, in the U.S. and most countries, you must have a license, which requires taking an exam to demonstrate technical proficiency and an understanding of the regulations. If this is of interest, becoming a ham radio operator is an excellent hobby, and ham radios provide a powerful national or international emergency network during large-scale disasters. For most, however, a simpler option may be the more advanced version of two-way, handheld radios covered below.

Handheld radios

These small portable radios, often called "walkie-talkies," can cost less than $40. Although they have a very short range, usually less than a mile (1.6 kilometers), they can be useful if you're traveling or evacuating in two or more vehicles. The next step up from these basic walkie-talkies are more powerful models that have a longer range. Many of these can also access frequencies such as the weather band, police, fire, and some even have amateur radio frequencies. These radios are worth the extra cost because the range is extended to several miles, and they can monitor and even broadcast on emergency frequencies. A pair of these, as shown in Figure 11-3, runs about $70 and up.

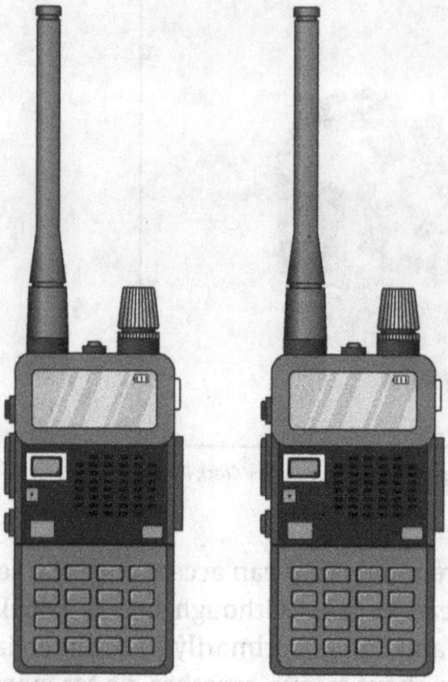

FIGURE 11-3: Handheld two-way radios with weather, emergency, and shortwave frequencies.

Grassetto/Getty Images

Outside of emergencies, they're also great for staying in touch with friends or family while hiking, or at large events like concerts or the beach, when cell towers are often overloaded.

WARNING

Although you can monitor any of the frequencies that these more advanced handheld radios provide, be careful. Transmitting on some of the frequencies requires an amateur radio license to avoid Federal Communications Commission (FCC) fines.

Using your cell phone without cell phone towers

You may be thinking that if the cell network and the Internet go down, your cell phone is useless. However, your phone can do many things.

GPS navigation

Your phone doesn't need a cell tower to use basic GPS navigation. Cell phones receive signals directly from the GPS satellites to triangulate their position.

However, apps like Google Maps and Apple Maps do use your cell phone's Internet connection to plot trips, which limits their usefulness when the cell network is down. Fortunately, there is a way around this.

TIP

To use Google Maps or Apple Maps to plot a trip when the cell network is down, you need to have offline maps downloaded. To download these, select either of the map apps, then tap your profile picture or initial in the corner, then select "Offline Maps." You can't download a map that covers the entire country, but you can download regional maps that are relevant to you. These maps take up a bit of memory and won't provide traffic information without an Internet connection. They also won't show recent changes due to construction, but they will allow full navigation capabilities without the Internet. It's good to update them every year.

Survival and medical apps

An excellent use of your phone when it's offline is for first aid and other survival apps, including medical reference guides covered in Chapter 9. Ensure that these apps are specifically designed to operate without an Internet connection. They can also hold digital copies of books for reference. These could include, oh, I don't know, maybe the digital version of an amazingly good disaster-prepping book.

Storing important information

Your cell phone can also store documents. These can be copies or photographs of critical items such as driver's licenses, passports, insurance documents, property titles, and bank information. However, if you decide to do this, carefully consider the warning below.

WARNING

Phones can be lost or stolen. Storing personal or financial data on your phone can be very risky unless you use a strong file encryption method. Most phones offer this capability, but make sure you understand how to use it and the risks. Another option for storing personal digital data is covered in Chapter 16.

Texting via satellite

The simplest, most cost-effective way to maintain connectivity when the cell phone towers are down is the recent introduction of satellite direct-to-cell (DTC), which allows you to use a satellite network to send and receive text and basic data when the cell phone network is down, or you're in a cell signal dead spot.

DTC works on any modern phone but incurs an additional subscription cost. It also requires a partial view of the sky (so your phone can see the satellites). However, I've found that DTC works well inside cars and may work through thin roofs or near windows. It's currently available in the U.S. and most countries through Starlink. Prices vary by carrier, but the monthly cost should be somewhere around an additional $15 on your current phone plan. Amazon Leo and other direct-to-cell networks should also be available soon.

TIP

Although a $15 a month satellite option pushes the Level 1 budget, satellite networks like Starlink are unaffected by almost all of the covered disasters, with the exception of an EMP. Adding a DTC to your cell phone plan is arguably the least expensive way to stay connected to the outside world, family, friends, and emergency services when the cell network goes down. It also allows several key apps that have low data requirements to function, including GPS and connection apps like Google Maps and WhatsApp.

TECHNICAL STUFF

Cell phone manufacturers are now rushing to design new chips for cell phones that will improve and expand their ability to use the new satellite capability. This will allow voice, high-speed data, and video from almost anywhere in the world via satellite. These new phones should allow greater sensitivity and penetration into ground structures, but they won't work on lower floors, so they'll still need to be paired with terrestrial cell phone towers for complete coverage.

Protecting electronic devices from EMPs

An electromagnetic pulse (EMP) from a massive solar event, such as a coronal mass ejection or a solar flare, can create a huge electrical current spike in the power grid. EMPs can damage or destroy power generation, distribution, and control equipment as well as anything plugged into those circuits. In other words, it can completely take out the power grid and fry whatever is connected to it. Without a surge suppressor between you and the grid, you could lose most of your electrical and electronic devices. However, power surges can also come from more mundane fluctuations in the power grid's voltage, a branch falling across a power line, or a nearby lightning strike.

A nuclear weapon detonation is different. In addition to the EMP that overloads the power grid, it has additional fast-acting pulses specifically designed to fry almost all electronic devices, regardless of whether they're connected to the power grid.

Surge suppressors

The simplest and least expensive way to protect important electronic devices, such as computers, TVs, and cell phones, from solar flares and CMEs is with surge suppressors. They come in a variety of types but usually look like regular power strips. These devices absorb electrical surges and provide protection for the devices plugged into them. This covers anything from a nearby lightning strike to a solar EMP.

Years ago, lightning hit a tree right outside our house. The bolt jumped from the tree to a metal roof covering one of our decks. It took out everything from our TV to the HVAC (heating, ventilation, and air conditioning) and garage door opener. The only thing that survived was our desktop computer, which was plugged into an uninterruptible power supply (UPS) because it had a built-in surge suppressor. It killed the UPS but saved the computer. A whole-house surge suppressor is highly recommended and will be covered in the next Level 2 section.

TIP

Although solar observatories should have about 15 hours of warning before a major Coronal Mass Ejection event arrives, it's best to keep all important electronic devices plugged into surge suppressors all the time.

Faraday bags

Surge suppressors will not protect electronic devices from a nuclear weapon EMP. For that, a Faraday bag is required. Faraday bags are lined with metal fibers, and when closed, they create a conducting metal "cage" that shields the contents from any electromagnetic pulse. Regardless of the frequency or intensity of the pulse, the bag causes the electromagnetic energy to go around the outside, protecting whatever's inside.

A Faraday bag is a good place to keep your emergency electronics, like weather radios and portable handheld radios. They can also protect thumb drives and any other small electronic devices. Faraday bags can also be used to protect your cell phone and laptop, but you can't keep them in there because the same thing that blocks EMPs also blocks your cell signal and Wi-Fi. However, you can keep a bag available at home, work, or in your car.

Aluminum foil

If you don't have a Faraday Bag, heavy-duty aluminum foil is effective, but you have to make sure that you've completely wrapped your phone or other device in the foil so that none of it is exposed. Also, if your device has any exposed metal on it, wrap it in cloth or plastic first, so the metal doesn't touch the foil.

To test your wrapping job, call it from another phone. If it doesn't ring, it's protected, meaning the phone signal is being blocked, which will also block an EMP. You don't have to wrap each item individually; you can bundle them together and then wrap them. For items that are used or recharged occasionally, a Faraday

Bag is better, so you don't have to keep unwrapping and rewrapping them. If someone at work asks you why you have a roll of aluminum foil with you, offer to make them a hat to protect them from aliens. (Yes, I'm kidding.)

Microwaves

As a last resort, if you don't have a Faraday bag or aluminum foil or can't get to them in time, you can try sticking your electronic devices in the nearest microwave oven and closing the door. A microwave oven is designed to keep the microwaves inside the oven so that it doesn't cook you along with your food.

A microwave makes a very basic Faraday cage, but it's neither complete nor optimized to EMP frequencies. If you put your phone inside a microwave and call it, it will probably still ring. However, if you have a cell phone signal strength app on the phone, you should see a five-to-ten-fold drop in the cell signal strength. A Faraday bag or aluminum foil will drop it ten times more.

Also, don't leave your electronics in the microwave, particularly if you have kids. Keep in mind that this level of shielding shouldn't be required for most solar events and really only applies to nuclear detonations. There are more extensive devices specifically designed to absorb EMPs from solar or local events for your entire home or car, which will be covered in "Staying Connected Long-Term from Anywhere (Level 2)."

Setting up non-local emergency points of contact

All the technology is great, but disasters are chaotic, and nothing usually goes as planned. If you or anyone in your party is separated and unable to reach each other, identify, in advance, a non-local contact that everyone can reach. This person should be a responsible friend or family member who lives far enough away so that they won't be affected by your local disaster. They can relay information between those in your party when you can't reach each other directly.

For example, if your preplanned meet-up location needs to be changed or the meet-up time rescheduled, your non-local contact can share this information with everyone. They can also contact local emergency services and pass on your location if you can't reach your local police, fire, or rescue. This is very important if your phone is about to run out of power. In a perfect world, your non-local point of contact would also be your evacuation destination. Additionally, have a backup non-local contact in case your primary isn't available. Make sure everyone in your party has these numbers easily identified in their phones.

Staying Connected Long-Term from Anywhere (Level 2)

Your cell phone service will probably be affected by most major disasters. The towers have limited range, and even if they're not damaged, they need electrical power to operate. A friend of mine is one of the technicians who maintains the backup generators for cell towers. These generators can only run for about 48 hours without being refueled, which can be difficult or impossible in a disaster situation. If your Internet is provided by cable or fiber optics, it's more robust, but disasters can still sever cable connections, and local network nodes require power and are susceptible to disasters.

Iridium satellite network phones

If the cell network is down and you're away from home, currently, the only way to call and talk to anyone anywhere in the world is with a dedicated satellite phone (basic satellite texting was covered in Level 1). The best-known dedicated satellite phone system is the Iridium satellite network. It uses geosynchronous satellites that have almost complete coverage of the Earth's surface, allowing communication from anywhere. They've been around for many years, but don't see widespread use due to their high price. You can buy a satellite phone that uses the Iridium network, as shown in Figure 11-4.

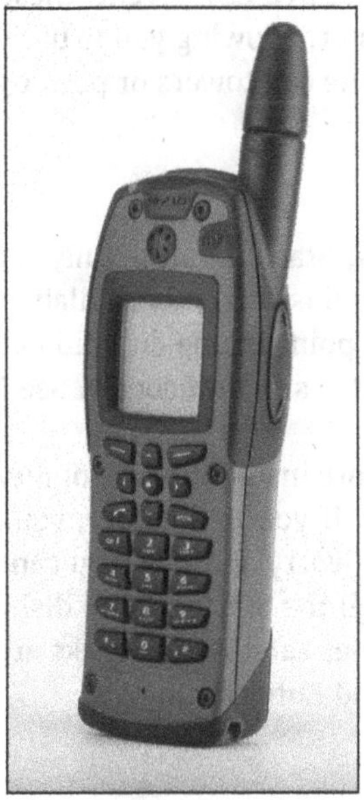

FIGURE 11-4: Iridium network satellite phone.

Navigatorni/Getty Images

These satellite phones are big, have an antenna, cost more than $1,000, and won't replace your regular smartphone. That means this would be carried in addition to your cell phone. The plans are pay-by-the-minute. The least expensive is currently $65 per month for 10 minutes of talk time. Yes, that's not a typo. If you have a job, business, or lifestyle that frequently takes you to areas of the world that have no cell service and you need to talk to people regularly, currently, this is the only solution.

Companies like Garmin offer small devices that don't have voice capability but can send and receive text messages using the Iridium satellite system. The devices cost a lot less than the Iridium phones, and a basic subscription is currently less than $10 per month. As previously mentioned, however, Direct-to-Cell satellite service has more options, is only a little more expensive monthly, and allows you to use your existing phone. As more satellites are added to the global network and other satellite networks are launched, the texting service will expand to voice and data.

Switching your Internet to a satellite network

In addition to adding satellite texting capability to your cell phone plan, another option is switching your Internet service to satellite. These new systems are composed of constellations of thousands of low-earth orbit satellites, improving the connectivity, reliability, and speed. A disaster on the ground is less likely to have any impact. With the exception of a massive EMP event, these satellite systems will survive almost any terrestrial disaster, allowing you to use your Internet connection for phone calls at home when the cell towers or power grid are down.

Starlink

As of the publication date of this book, Starlink is the only high-speed satellite Internet system with global coverage and is currently available in over 100 countries. Unlike satellite TV networks that point in one direction at a single satellite, the Starlink dish tracks multiple satellites simultaneously. See Figure 11-5.

In addition to higher speed, it allows more installation flexibility, reduces weather impacts, and minimizes signal latency. If you're a gamer, you know what signal latency is; if you're not a gamer, don't worry about it. You can also take the dish with you during an evacuation, although the Starlink Mini dish, covered below, is a better option for mobility. Several other satellite networks are in the process of being deployed, such as Amazon Leo and Eutelsat OneWeb.

FIGURE 11-5: Starlink residential dish.

I live on the Bolivar Peninsula in Texas. Currently, Starlink is the only high-speed Internet option in our neighborhood. During a recent hurricane, the cell network went down, but Starlink maintained Internet and phone throughout the nine hours of 60–80 mph wind, with only a few periods of signal loss during ludicrously heavy rain. With that said, the dish must be attached or properly anchored such that it won't blow away.

Because it tracks multiple satellites, it doesn't have to be perfectly pointed at one spot like TV satellites, but it does require a reasonable view of the sky. The multiple satellites also mean that Internet speeds are variable. Depending on the pricing plan chosen, the speed can vary from 50 to 400 Mbps. The cost is generally a bit higher than most terrestrial providers, but having the ability to make calls and access the Internet when the cell network and your local Internet are down is a major benefit.

TECHNICAL STUFF

You may be thinking that your 5G cell phone connection can achieve much higher speeds than a satellite system. This may be true, but it's dependent not only on the cell phone network being functional but also on use. We live at the beach. Our 5G connection can go from ludicrously fast off-season to a standstill during summer weekends. During a disaster, even if the network is available, it may become overloaded, and government agencies get priority handling in an emergency. More importantly, when the cell network goes down, so does your Internet.

Starlink Mini

If you already have reasonably priced high-speed Internet, another option is to get the Starlink Mini dish, Figure 11-6. It has several key advantages for disaster situations, including an important option that makes it a powerful and cost-effective backup:

- Starlink Mini is about the same size and weight as a laptop.
- Wi-Fi is built in, and it uses less power, only 25–40 watts.
- It's portable and even works while in motion inside or outside a vehicle.
- Internet speed is slower than the residential dish, but can still reach 100 Mbps speeds.

FIGURE 11-6: Starlink Mini dish.

TIP

If you have high-speed home Internet, here's an option that's perfect for disaster backup. If you purchase a Starlink Mini, you can select the Standby Mode. Currently, Standby Mode drops the subscription fee to $5 a month, but still provides low-speed internet access (500 kbps) with no data limits. Although those speeds are very slow, you can still make cell phone calls, send and receive emails, and browse the Internet. When the cell network and grid go down, Starlink Mini provides satellite-based, cell, and Internet access that you can throw in a backpack for $60 a year.

Protecting your entire home from an EMP

While you can't plug your HVAC system into a surge suppressor, some devices can help protect your entire home from large power surges, including EMPs and much more common surges caused by power grid issues, power line damage, or nearby lightning strikes.

We live on the Texas coast, where hurricanes, tropical storms, and the salt air play havoc on the local power grid. The first thing our builder recommended was the installation of a whole-house surge protector. This small box sits between the power grid and your home's power distribution panel, absorbing small fluctuations, as well as large surges by shunting them to the ground. They cost around $200 and must be installed by a licensed electrician. A whole-house surge protector protects your home in a disaster and can save you a lot of money on damaged equipment and insurance claims from lightning strikes.

TIP

These devices usually have small indicator lights. When the light goes out, it's time to replace the surge protector. It should be checked regularly, particularly after storms. Even with a whole-house surge suppressor, you still want to plug your sensitive electronics into regular surge suppressors to protect from internal surges or lightning strikes that actually hit your house and don't come in through the power grid.

There are also specialized surge suppressors designed specifically to protect exterior air conditioners and heat pumps, whole-house generators, and even your automobiles, but a whole-house surge suppressor is the most important step.

Storing and accessing digital information

In addition to thumb drives, e-readers are particularly good for disaster situations. These inexpensive and exceptionally thin and light tablets use e-ink technology to create black-and-white displays. Since they only use power to refresh the screen, their batteries can last for weeks and recharge quickly using very little power. Their size and weight make them very portable and easy to carry or throw in a bug-out bag. They're also easier to read in direct sunlight (like reading print on paper) than regular tablets. The downside is that you can't read them in the dark without a light (although some have a backlit option).

There are color e-ink tablets, but they're more expensive and use more power. Most of these e-ink tablets can display almost any document or picture format, and you can upload apps to them. They can also be used like a USB drive to hold gigabytes of important documents and whole books, like — oh, I don't know — maybe *Disaster Prepping For Dummies*.

IN THIS CHAPTER

» Understanding the power grid

» Powering medical devices, communication, and lighting

» Powering refrigeration and heating

» Selecting backup power sources

» Using generators with portable power stations

» Adding portable solar panels

Chapter 12 Powering without the Power Grid

Our technological society is dependent on electricity for almost everything. Beyond immediate safety or medical concerns, the primary reason people cannot stay in their homes during or after a disaster is loss of power and water. Unfortunately, every global or local disaster covered can cause both. It can be a brief loss of power or a longer-term failure of the power grid. Without the ability to keep a cell phone charged, it's impossible to stay aware of what's happening or connect to emergency services, family, and friends. Power is also important for lighting, refrigeration, and heating or cooling. For some, there may be a need to power a medical device such as a CPAP (continuous positive airway pressure) machine or an oxygen concentrator.

Maintaining some level of power is central to being able to stay in your home during a disaster. With so many different technologies and misconceptions about power creation and storage, this is the longest and most technical chapter, but it's important. Please hang in there. If you have a roof covered with solar panels and a battery backup, congratulations! You can skip this chapter.

Understanding and Prioritizing Power

The first task is to understand how power is created, stored, and distributed, as well as its vulnerabilities.

Defining power grid limitations

The power grid is a complex network of power generation, storage, and distribution. Power generation includes fossil fuel-burning plants, nuclear reactors, hydroelectric dams, solar farms, and wind turbines. The challenge is that power demand is variable, changing significantly by season, weather, and time-of-day. Power generation must be able to handle the highest load but also scale down and store power when demand is low.

Most areas of the world have redundancy in the form of backup generation. If a power production source is lost, such as solar panels at night or a casualty to a power plant, there's usually a secondary source that can be engaged. These secondary sources may include gas turbines that can be quickly spun up, water reservoirs that can power hydroelectric generators, or battery farms. That's the good news. The bad news is that the growth of electric vehicles and, even more so, the energy required to power the massive new AI data centers is significantly increasing demand.

What all this means is that even without disasters, the power grid will become more stressed. On top of this, the grid is susceptible to almost any disaster, from a solar superstorm to an ice storm that drops a tree branch on the power line to your home.

Prioritizing power

Determining the priorities for power depends on your location, medical condition, and your budget. Unless you need electrical power for a medical device, Level 1 preparation will cover basic lights and communication. That may sound strange with the need to keep food in your refrigerator from going bad and heat in the winter, but it's critical to know what's happening in order to decide whether you should stay or evacuate. You may also need to call emergency services and know the location and status of other members of your family.

Robust satellite communication strategies can be achieved with Level 1 preparation and were covered in Chapter 11. Powering refrigeration, heating, or air conditioning won't be achieved on a Level 1 budget. If you live in an area with extreme summer or winter temperatures that could be life-threatening, Level 2 preparation will be required. Below are the top requirements for electrical power, listed roughly in order of priority:

1. **Medical equipment (if applicable):** This covers electrically powered medical equipment and critical medicines that require refrigeration. The level of priority depends on how dependent you, or a family member, are on the device. A CPAP (continuous positive airway pressure) machine to treat sleep apnea is important, but an oxygen concentrator for COPD (chronic obstructive pulmonary disease) may be essential for survival.
2. **Communication:** This is primarily your cell phones, but can include computers and radios. This keeps you informed of the status of any emergency or disaster, which will drive your decision to evacuate or stay. Cell phones allow you to reach emergency services such as police, fire, and medical, and stay in touch with family and friends.
3. **Lighting:** This includes not only lights inside and outside your home, but also maintaining power for rechargeable or battery-powered flashlights.
4. **Refrigeration:** This is simply to prevent food in your refrigerator from spoiling. However, as covered in Chapter 7, your goal is to have a pantry full of foods that don't require refrigeration.
5. **Heating and cooling:** Depending on your location's climate, this could be the number 2 priority. This not only prevents you and your family from freezing or heat stroke, but can also avoid bursting a water pipe during a deep freeze.

Understanding how much power you need

You don't have to be an electrical engineer to determine how much power you need to keep critical devices and appliances running, but it does take some thought. Before we can determine the best way to provide backup power for your situation, you need to know what you want to back up. This depends on several things, including your preparation budget.

Not surprisingly, the more things you want to keep powered, the bigger and more expensive the backup system needs to be. Fortunately, the backup strategy is scalable, so you can build it to your budget and then expand it in the future. Before you choose which appliances and devices you want to power and which you can live without, you need to know how much power they use. To help you do that, some basic electrical concepts need to be highlighted, but don't worry; we also have a backup way to figure out how much power is needed using a table of common appliances.

Defining watts versus watt-hours

A *watt* is just a measure of the power a device needs to operate. For example, most hair dryers require about 1,200 watts to run. If you run a second hair dryer, you'd be pulling a total of 2,400 watts. Since most household circuits can only handle 1,800 watts, it might trip the circuit breaker. The same applies to generators and backup batteries.

When you're evaluating what size you need, the first step is to add up the watts of all the devices you want to run at the same time. That total tells you how much the generator or battery must be able to supply at any instant. Watts are a measure of the immediate power required, kind of like how much horsepower your car has.

On the other hand, *watt-hours* are a measure of capacity over time, kind of like how much fuel you have in your car's tank. For example, a backup battery might be able to supply enough watts to run that hair dryer, but its capacity of watt-hours will tell you how long it can run that hair dryer before running out of power.

Motors matter

Everything that uses electricity can be broken into two basic categories: things with motors and things without them. This is important because things with motors need extra power to start — sometimes a lot of extra power. Once their motors are running, the power demand drops.

Items with motors include everything from your air conditioner and refrigerator to your blender and vacuum cleaner. Devices with compressors, like air conditioners, often need three times as much electricity to start as to run. If you want to run these devices, you have to size your alternate power supply to cover these huge start-up power spikes.

Heaters have huge appetites

Although things that heat up, like water heaters, stoves, and ovens, don't need extra power to start, they can suck a lot of power. Even with a Level 2 investment, unless you have a large budget for your backup power, it's best to plan on getting by during a disaster without the big power hogs like stoves and electric clothes dryers.

In Chapter 7, we emphasized stockpiling food that doesn't require cooking. As for electric clothes dryers, yes, it is possible to dry clothes by hanging them up on a line, as your great-great-grandparents did. The one appliance that would be nice to have for cleaning and showers is a water heater, despite its large electricity appetite. Water heaters will be covered in "Exploring Power Options" later in this chapter, but it may not be an option due to loss of water pressure.

Determining the power required for appliances

To build the right-sized backup power system, we need to know the maximum or peak power it will have to supply. That consists of adding up the watts of all the appliances and devices you want available during a disaster. To do this, we need to know what each appliance and device needs. There are several ways to do this. Starting from the easiest:

- Some devices have their power requirements listed on an attached label or plate. You may need to do a conversion, which is covered in the Technical Stuff below.
- If you know or can find the manufacturer and model number, you may be able to look online and find its power specifications.
- If you really want to geek out, you can buy a little device called a "Kill A Watt." Plug any appliances into it, and it tells you exactly what it draws.

For air conditioners or heat pumps, in addition to the running watts, you need the starting watts. This is important because their compressors can pull triple their running power. Unfortunately, they list their starting power in amps rather than watts. Look for either "starting current," "inrush current," or "locked rotor current (LRC)." Then use the Technical Stuff below to convert to watts.

TECHNICAL STUFF

If the appliance only shows amps, you can easily convert to watts by multiplying the amps by the volts. For a hair dryer that draws 10 amps and uses the U.S. standard 120 volts, the calculation is 10 amps × 120 volts = 1,200 watts. A heat pump that draws 30 amps on a 240-volt circuit would be 30 × 240 = 7,200 watts. If none of this makes sense, don't worry; we'll cover an easier way to figure out the power your appliances use in the next section.

Using a table to estimate the power required

If electricity isn't your thing, no worries. Use Table 12-1 to estimate the power required.

If you have an exceptionally large appliance, like a giant subzero refrigerator, double the watts listed. Or if you have an old refrigerator or air conditioner, they'll be less efficient, and you'll want to increase the watts by about 30 percent. Even if you can calculate all the watts required, use the table to check your numbers and to make sure you don't miss any devices. This table will be used in the Level 1 and Level 2 preparation sections to determine generator and/or battery backup size.

TABLE 12-1 Average running watts, starting watts, and 24-hour power required for common appliances

Generator or Portable Power Station (Battery Backup) Required Capacity				Appliance or Device	Running Watts	Starting Watts	Use per Day	Watts / 24 Hrs
5,500–12,000 Watt Capacity	**2,500–5,000 Watt Capacity**	**1,000–2,000 Watt Capacity**	**UPS**	Phone charging	15	N/A	24 hrs	30
				Security camera	4	N/A	24 hrs	96
				Toaster	1,200	N/A	5 min	100
				Coffee maker	1,200	N/A	15 min	300
				Microwave	1,200	N/A	15 min	300
				CPAP machine	45	N/A	8 hrs	360
				Ceiling/box fan (low)	30	N/A	12 hrs	360
				Hairdryer	1,500	N/A	15 min	375
				Laptop computer	70	N/A	6 hrs	420
				Starlink Mini with Wi-Fi	35	N/A	24 hrs	840
				LED/LCD TV (65-inch)	150	N/A	6 hrs	900
				Washing machine	1,200	2,300	1 hr	1,200
				Dishwasher	1,800	2,000	Varies	2,000
				Desktop computer	250		8 hrs	2,000
				Sump pump ⅓ HP	800	1,300	3 hrs	2,400
				Well water pump	1,000	2,100	3 hrs	3,000
				Clothes dryer	3,000	3,500	1 hr	3,000
				Large refrigerator	600	2,200	4 hrs	2,400

Generator or Portable Power Station (Battery Backup) Required Capacity	Appliance or Device	Running Watts	Starting Watts	Use per Day	Watts / 24 Hrs
	Small AC inverter (8,000 BTU)	700	1,000	8 hrs	5,600
	Window AC (13,000 BTU)	1,400	2,800	8 hrs	11,200
	Furnace/HVAC (fan only)	550	1,000	24 hrs	13,200
	Water heater (50-gallon)	4,000	N/A	4 hrs	16,000
	AC/heat pump (3-ton)	3,000	16,000	6 hrs	18,000
	AC/heat pump (4-ton)	4,000	21,000	6 hrs	24,000
	AC/heat pump (5-ton)	5,000	27,000	6 hrs	30,000

Powering Communication, Lights, and Medical Equipment (Level 1)

Level 1 focuses on maintaining communication, basic lighting, and any needed medical devices that require electricity. This level cannot be maintained indefinitely or keep you and your family comfortable. The Level 2 section will cover options that can significantly extend your time and comfort.

Powering critical medical equipment

If you or a member of your household has a life-threatening medical condition that requires a powered device, you probably already have a backup power supply. Other medical devices require power, but their loss isn't immediately life-threatening, such as a CPAP machine for sleep apnea.

Because of CPAP's widespread use, I'll use it as an example. CPAP machines draw 30–100 watts, depending on whether the air humidifier function is used. (The humidifier heats water in a tank to increase the air's humidity.) A CPAP machine could draw a total of 600 watts over an 8-hour night. This means that a very small generator or a larger battery backup can supply enough power. However, some strategies can reduce the power required. The first is to turn the humidifier down or off, which can reduce the total power consumed per night to 300 watts or less.

Another option is to purchase a travel CPAP. These smaller machines usually draw less than 20 watts, and some offer optional battery packs. With 20 amps over 8 hours, that's only 160 total watts needed. It's easy to find an inexpensive uninterruptible power supply (UPS), covered below, that can keep a CPAP running all night. The challenge is being able to do this for multiple nights during an extended power loss; doing so requires Level 2 strategies.

Powering communication and lighting

If no medical devices are needed, the first priority is keeping your cell phone alive. The term "phone" is obsolete. Smartphones are everyone's link to the world, providing news, critical notifications, navigation, medical information, and much more.

All phones have a power-saving mode. When activated, this mode reduces processing speed, dims the display, and shuts down any non-essential apps. The power saving mode can double or even triple the time between charges. Phones can also be used as flashlights, but using them that way will drain their battery quickly. Always use dedicated flashlights.

Supplying power with an old school UPS

The simplest and cheapest way to keep your phone charged during a power outage is to use an uninterruptible power supply. A UPS is just a big, cheap rechargeable battery designed to run a desktop computer for a half hour or so to allow time to backup data and shut it down during a power outage. They've been around for many years and are inexpensive because they use the older sealed lead acid batteries, as shown in Figure 12-1.

A basic UPS costs around $65 but can keep two phones charged for a couple of weeks (if you don't use it to back up your computer). The batteries need to be replaced every five years, but they're inexpensive. They can also recharge your laptop for an extra day or two, but it's best to reserve it for phones.

FIGURE 12-1: An inexpensive uninterruptible power supply powered by an old tech sealed lead acid battery.

charnsitr/Adobe Stock Photos

Supplying power with small lithium power banks

It's also good to have a couple of pocket-sized lithium power banks you can take with you, as shown in Figure 12-2. A 20,000 mAh (milliampere-hour) power bank costs about $30 and should give two phones a couple of full charges. For a little more, you can get a power bank that has solar cells. The small solar panel will only trickle charge the power bank, but with the sun, it might keep one phone charged if it's in power-saving mode.

Supplying power with your vehicle

Yes, you can use your automobile as a backup battery and even as a generator. You can charge phones, and you can even power household appliances by buying an inverter that converts 12 volts to household voltage. However, there are critical limitations to consider.

- The 12-volt socket on modern vehicles has a 15-amp fuse. That means powering anything that pulls more than 180 watts (15 amps × 12 volts = 180 watts) may blow the car fuse that powers the 12-volt socket.
- Most automotive batteries have at least 500 watt-hours of capacity. However, drawing down 40 percent of that capacity (about 300 total watt-hours) may prevent the battery from starting your car.

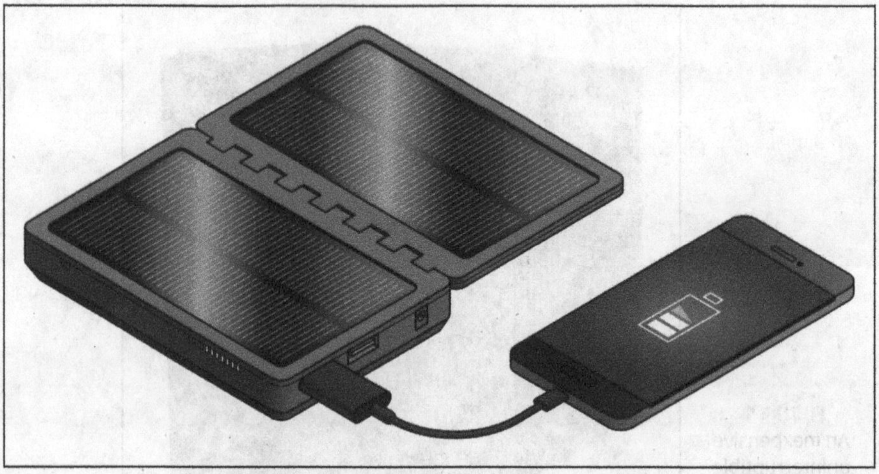

FIGURE 12-2: Portable power bank with solar cells for charging cell phones.

Zern Liew/Shutterstock

Without the engine running, you could power a 50-watt CPAP machine for five or six hours before running the battery too low to start the vehicle. You can also run higher-watt devices like a small refrigerator by buying an inverter that connects directly to the vehicle's battery terminals (bypassing the fuse), but the engine must run continuously.

Most car alternators can produce 80 amps, but at idle, that drops to about 30 amps (12 volts × 30 amps = 360 watts). Pulling more than 360 watts will drain the battery even with the engine running. Unless you have a second vehicle for evacuation, it's best to limit vehicle power to recharging phones to avoid running down the vehicle's battery or using up evacuation fuel.

Flashlights

Although you can use your phone to provide basic light, a dedicated flashlight will save your phone's battery. It's important to have several types of LED flashlights, including handheld, lantern, and head-mounted flashlights. These head-mounted lights can free up your hands, which can be a lifesaver during a fire.

TIP

A good idea for an emergency backup light is to buy several cheap solar yard lights. Charge them up in the day and bring them inside at night for basic low-level lighting.

Small batteries

It's best to try to stay with one or two types of batteries for simplicity and storage. The older C- and D-type batteries contain a lot of energy, but they're becoming less common. The most common battery sizes today for flashlights and most devices are AA and AAA. Avoid the cheap so-called "heavy-duty" batteries. They're made of zinc-carbon, last about ¼ as long as alkaline batteries, have a shelf life of only three years, and are prone to leakage. Alkaline batteries are not only more powerful, but they also have a shelf life of 10 years and are a bit less prone to leaking. Alkaline batteries also come in a rechargeable format with a similar 10-year shelf life.

Lithium batteries are a step up from alkaline batteries and also come in AA and AAA sizes. Lithium batteries hold about 40 percent more power than alkaline batteries; they don't leak, and they have a 20-year shelf life. The downside is they're about three times more expensive.

WARNING

Make sure to check the batteries in your important devices at least once a year, not only to make sure they have power but to prevent them from leaking and destroying your equipment.

TIP

Buy a little plastic battery case that holds at least two dozen AA and AAA batteries and comes with a tester. Using the oldest first and continually replacing them ensures the shelf life remains about 10 years. Choose a time each year to check all your devices' batteries. Tie it to a date you'll remember, like your birthday or the day after your tax filing deadline. As mentioned previously, you'll either be getting money back to buy new batteries or you'll be experiencing a real disaster by paying additional taxes. Additionally, buy a few rechargeable lithium batteries. With a 20-year shelf life, you can keep them in reserve. If you run through all of your alkaline batteries, you can recharge them.

Jump-starting your car and phones with one device

It's important to carry jumper cables in case your auto battery dies. This is even more likely in a disaster where you may be using your car's 12-volt accessory socket to charge phones. The problem with jumper cables is that you need another car.

There are small lithium battery banks that can jump-start a car and recharge your phone, as shown in Figure 12-3. These small portable devices carry a surprising amount of power. I was able to jump-start a car twice and still recharge a phone. You can also begin recharging them as soon as the engine is running. Depending on their size, they start around $60. The key is to remember to recharge them occasionally since all batteries lose charge over time. Even electric vehicles have accessory batteries required to "start" them, and they can also be jumped.

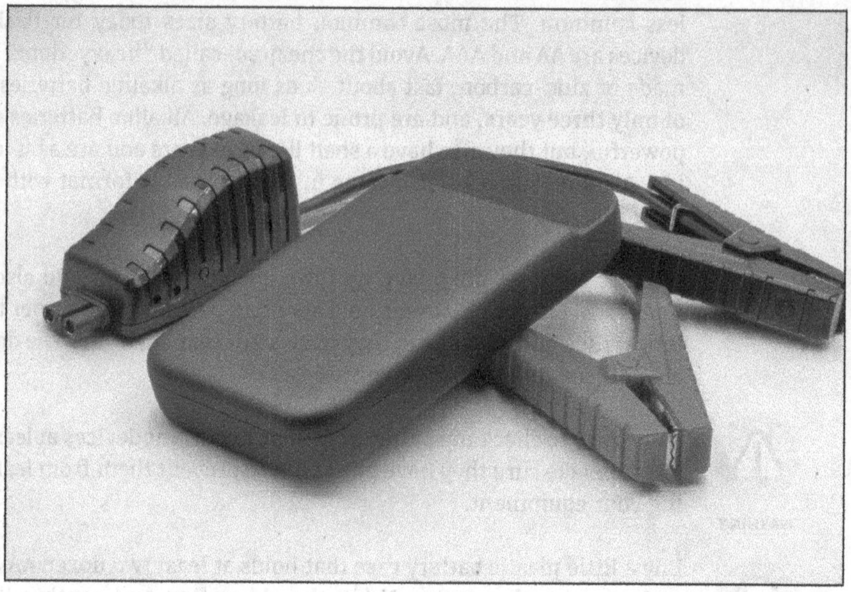

FIGURE 12-3: Combination car battery jumper and backup cell phone charger.

Panama/Adobe Stock Photos

Using cheap portable solar panels to recharge

Eventually, the UPS and lithium power banks will be drained. An inexpensive way to recharge them is with a small portable solar panel. The one shown in Figure 12-4 is only about 10 inches (25 cm) wide and produces nine watts in direct sunlight.

That's not much, but it should provide enough power to charge a phone in three to four hours. These run around $40. Or if you have multiple phones or limited sun, you can buy larger foldable panels up to 100 watts for around $100. We'll cover even larger portable panels and ways to store that power in the Level 2 preparation section.

Pedal power

Portable solar panels are great if you have access to the sun or even a reasonable amount of daylight. This may not be the case if you're caught in a long period of extreme weather, or if there's no place to deploy even a small solar panel at your residence. Portable generators are covered in the Level 2 section, but if you don't have access to sunlight, a last-ditch option might be a small hand crank or pedal generator. They convert calories into current, requiring a significant amount of work to create a small amount of power.

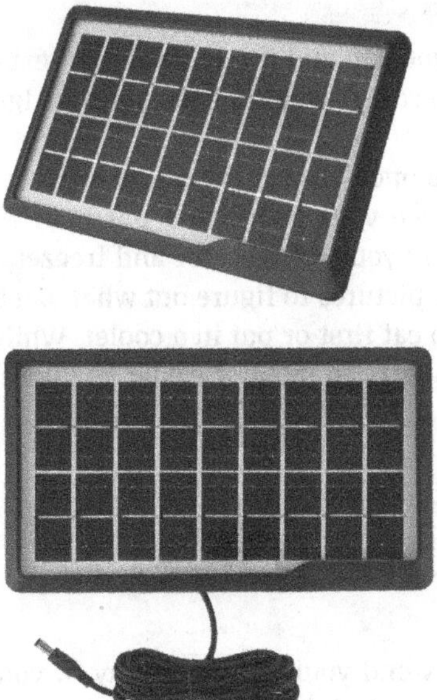

FIGURE 12-4: Small portable solar panels for recharging phones and small power banks.

A_A88/Adobe Stock Photos

The hand crank devices are usually part of a flashlight or radio and include a small lithium-ion battery to hold the charge. Larger pedal-powered devices can produce about 20 to 30 watts, which is enough to recharge a power bank or phone. These pedal generators, however, push the boundary of the Level 1 budget, normally exceeding $100. However, DIY systems allow you to convert your existing bicycle into a stationary bike with a bike stand and a small bicycle generator for less.

Dealing with the loss of refrigeration, heating, or air conditioning

Level 1 preparation provides a way to have light and keep your cell phones charged, but won't provide heating, cooling, or refrigeration. However, there are basic steps that can help to deal with the loss of refrigeration, air conditioning, or heating.

Refrigeration

If you don't open the refrigerator, the temperature should remain low enough to keep food safe to eat for up to four hours. For freezers, if you don't open the door, food is usually good for 24 hours (up to 48 hours if the freezer is completely full). However, to determine if your food is safe to eat, it's important to keep a thermometer inside your refrigerator. If the temperature hits 40°F (4°C), the food enters the danger zone where bacteria will begin to grow. If power doesn't return within four hours or the temperature hits 40 degrees and you can't move the food to a cooler with ice, eat what you can and throw away the rest. The same applies to the freezer. The next section covers ways to keep your refrigerator running.

TIP

With no power, every time you open your refrigerator or freezer, you lose about 10 minutes of refrigeration. Take your phone and put it in wide-angle camera mode with the flash active. Open your refrigerator and freezer and quickly take a picture of the contents. Use the pictures to figure out what you have, what'll spoil quickest, and what you want to eat first or put in a cooler. While you're at it, take a picture of the food in your pantry to make it easier to take stock of your total food reserves.

Exploring Power Options (Level 2)

To provide enough power to extend your ability to stay in your home and do it more comfortably, you need to go to Level 2 preparation. Level 2 is broken into three sublevels of increasing cost and effort.

- The first sublevel adds the ability to power medical devices continuously and keep your refrigerator running for a week or more.
- The next sublevel adds the ability to heat or cool at least one room of your home.
- The third sublevel allows heating or cooling your entire home and powering other key appliances for a week or more.

Powering everything indefinitely usually entails a solar roof and a large battery backup system, which costs tens of thousands and falls under Level 3 preparation in Part 5.

The first step is to determine exactly what you want to power and how many days you want to be able to do that. For blackouts lasting a day or two, if your residence allows, a small portable gas-powered generator will keep the refrigerator cold, your electronics powered, and run a fan in the summer. You'll need a couple of five-gallon containers of gasoline or extra propane tanks.

The challenge comes when you go beyond a couple of days. Even small generators can run through five gallons of gas or a grill-sized propane tank in 12 hours if they're run continuously. With a creative combination of new and old technology, you can maintain refrigeration, heating, or cooling for an extended period without breaking the bank. Doing so requires some basic knowledge of ways to generate and store residential power.

Powering with gas generators

Gas-powered generators are loud and thirsty but provide excellent backup power. They come in a variety of sizes, from small portable generators that can be carried to large whole-house backup generators, as shown in Figure 12-5.

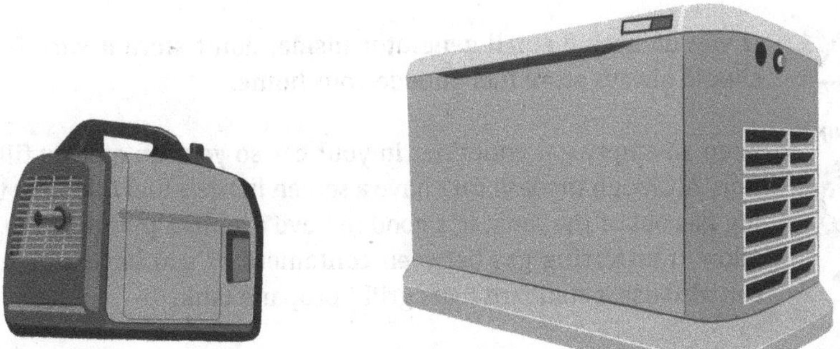

FIGURE 12-5: A small portable gas generator (left) and a whole-house automatic backup generator.

These generators use a variety of fuels such as gasoline, diesel, propane, and nat ural gas. For simplicity, I'll use the term "generator" to cover all of these. You want to choose the smallest generator that will cover your needs. Not only is a bigger generator more expensive, but it also consumes more fuel to produce the same amount of electricity. When fuel supplies may be limited in a long-duration disaster, every gallon counts.

WARNING

No matter what fuel a generator uses, it produces carbon monoxide, which is a colorless, odorless gas that will kill you. Carbon monoxide binds with your hemoglobin, preventing oxygen from being absorbed, meaning that you basically suffocate. Never run a generator in your house or any enclosed space, such as a garage or shed, or even close to a window or door. It's also critical to have a carbon monoxide detector in your home.

Gas generators and apartments/condominiums

You may be thinking that a gas generator is out of the question because you live in a townhouse, condominium, apartment, or a community with strict homeowner association rules. To be fair, gas-powered generators are noisy, produce toxic exhaust, and can be a fire hazard. However, apartment, condominium, and homeowner association (HOA) bylaws usually state that you cannot *use* a portable gas-powered generator. They don't say you can't own one.

In a true emergency, when the power grid is lost for many days, your neighbors probably aren't going to complain if you help them keep their phones charged. They may even be willing to supply fuel in exchange for power. Many of the small, gas-powered generators now use inverter technology. In addition to reducing fuel consumption and producing "cleaner" power for sensitive electronics, inverter generators run quieter.

WARNING

If you do keep a small generator inside, don't store it with fuel in its tank. You should always store fuel outside your home.

TIP

Keep an empty gas container in your car so you can quickly fill it at any gas station. Although modern cars have a screen in their fuel filler line to prevent siphoning gas out of the tank, it's good to have a siphon pump. These little hand pumps allow transferring gas between containers. If you have a bi-fuel generator, you can also use a standard "gas grill" propane tank.

Inverter technology

Many small to medium-sized gas generators are now available with inverter technology. Instead of the generator running at a constant speed, this technology allows the generator to throttle the motor and run at the most efficient speed. This saves fuel and reduces noise, but it also produces cleaner power for electronics and for charging portable power stations covered later. The small additional cost is usually worth these advantages.

TECHNICAL STUFF

Non-inverter gas generators run at a constant speed. When a heavy power demand hits, like starting an air conditioner, the engine briefly bogs down, causing the voltage and frequency of the alternating current to sag. This isn't good for sensitive electronics like computers or portable power stations. Inverter technology eliminates this by converting the alternating current to direct current. Then it uses a microprocessor to convert it back into alternating current with stable voltage and frequency, producing "clean" power. This microprocessor also continuously evaluates the electricity demand and throttles the engine to run at the most efficient speed, reducing fuel consumption and noise.

Fueling gas generators

Unfortunately, most gas generators can only run a maximum of eight to twelve hours on a tank of gas. If you reduce their load and only run them for limited periods, you can extend that time to a day or two. Of course, you can keep refilling them, but long-duration disasters may make gasoline and other fuels harder to obtain. The longer the disaster lasts, the more difficult it becomes. You also have to leave your home to replace the fuel, which may not be possible or safe. However, combining these gas-powered generators with portable power stations can significantly increase their ability to power for longer periods.

Gasoline generators

Gasoline-powered generators come in all sizes. The smallest ones can be easily carried and can put out 1,000–2,000 watts. These small inverter generators cost between $300-600. The next most common size is in the 5,000-watt range and costs $700–1,000. See Figure 12-6.

FIGURE 12-6: Midsized portable gas generator.

DonNichols/Getty Images

Generators large enough to power a small home's central air conditioning or heating system put out about 12,000 watts and can be found for about $2,000. Residential generators that produce over 15,000 watts are usually permanently installed and run on propane or natural gas, as pictured back in Figure 12-5. They start at about $5,000 and go higher depending on output. This doesn't include the cost of permanent installation and connection to your power panel.

TIP

Generators are usually advertised by their maximum "starting" power. They can't sustain that power level, so be sure to use their lower "running" power when determining the size.

Advantages that gasoline generators have over propane or natural gas are that they produce more power (electricity) per gallon, and gasoline is easier to store and purchase. A disadvantage is that, unlike propane, gasoline starts to oxidize and break down into gums and varnish within three months. This will quickly clog an engine and even prevent it from starting. This is a real problem for generators that run rarely.

TIP

Although Premium (93 octane) won't improve the performance of an engine designed to run on regular gas, it will extend the gasoline's life. High-octane gas contains fewer unstable hydrocarbons, extending the gasoline's life from three months to nine months. Adding a high-quality stabilizer additive like Sta-Bil can add another year to that. Even with additives, gasoline should never be stored beyond two years. If that's likely, having a generator that runs on propane may be the best option.

Diesel generators

Diesel generators are similar to gasoline generators but are known for their higher efficiency and durability. They can run thousands of hours and will produce more power per gallon than gasoline generators. Diesel fuel is less flammable and more stable than gasoline, but it will still start oxidizing after nine months without an additive. Diesel generators are usually used in commercial applications due to their greater weight and cost. For example, a 5,000-watt diesel generator can weigh almost 100 pounds more than a gas generator and cost three times as much.

Natural gas and propane generators

Many large whole-house generators are powered by natural gas and don't need to be refueled. The natural gas is piped directly to your house and may also power your furnace or water heater. These generators aren't affected by a simple blackout, but they are dependent on the municipal natural gas system. Disasters such as earthquakes and wildfires can stop the flow directly, or the gas distribution pipelines may be shut off by authorities due to the fire risk. Additionally, natural gas distribution systems require electrical power to monitor and control the gas supply, so long-term loss of the power grid will eventually shut down your natural gas.

Most natural gas-powered whole-house generators can also run on propane. This may be done by flipping a lever, or it could require switching out a small orifice. Regardless, you will need to install and connect a large propane tank or have fittings that allow you to connect the generator to smaller replaceable tanks. Keep in mind that standard 20-gallon (75-liter) "gas grill" tanks can only be filled with about 15 gallons (60 liters) due to gas expansion limits. A large whole-house generator can consume that in a few hours and can cause the gas regulator to freeze up on small propane tanks.

TIP

If you have a natural gas whole-house generator, make sure you know how to switch it over or get the propane orifice from the manufacturer, along with instructions on how to change it. You'll also need a fitting that allows you to bypass the natural gas and connect it to a propane tank. An option to avoid installing a conversion valve, connection lines, and a propane tank is to buy a small gasoline-powered generator as a backup to your backup. That may sound absurd, but a small gasoline generator is less expensive than installing a large propane tank and easier than switching out multiple small propane tanks.

WARNING

Dealing with natural gas or propane connections can be dangerous. An ignited leak can create a disaster worse than what you're preparing for. Unless you know how to do this safely, have a qualified plumber install the connection hardware.

Most propane-powered whole-house generators are installed with large propane tanks, usually 250 to 1,000 gallons. Depending on the generator and tank size, they can provide constant electrical power for a week or more, and longer if used judiciously. However, residential regulations in your area may prevent the installation of the propane tank or require that it be buried underground, and the cost of the generator and propane tank usually exceeds $10,000. This will be revisited in the Level 3 part of Chapter 20.

Bi-fuel and tri-fuel generators

Another option is a generator that can run on two or three different fuels. The most common type of bi-fuel generators runs on gasoline and propane, with tri-fuel generators able to run on gasoline, propane, and natural gas. Switching fuel types is usually as simple as flipping a lever. It should be noted that these generators produce less power on propane and natural gas than they do on gasoline.

For example, a tri-fuel generator running on gasoline that produces 10,000 watts will only produce about 9,000 watts on propane and 8,000 watts on natural gas. The good news is that these bi-fuel and tri-fuel generators usually cost only a little more than single-fuel units and are often worth the extra cost if you have access to the other fuels.

TIP

Regardless of fuel, all generators need to be "exercised." Manufacturers usually recommend running them for at least 15 minutes at least twice a month to keep their batteries charged and ensure they're fully operational. Portable generators are designed to run outside, but leaving them outside and constantly exposed to sunlight and rain will shorten their life.

All gas-powered generators suffer from one major drawback: They need to be supplied with fuel to keep running. Portable power stations, covered next, are basically large batteries and don't need to be fueled. However, they do need to be charged and recharged.

Portable power stations

Portable power stations are also called "solar generators." These are large lithium-ion battery packs with built-in chargers and inverters that can charge quickly and hold that power until needed, as shown in Figure 12-7.

The "solar" prefix is marketing and simply means they can be recharged with solar panels, even though they don't come with them. Like gas-powered generators, they come in a variety of sizes. The key difference is that gas-powered generators need to be refueled, and portable power stations need to be recharged. A portable power station is the simplest, quietest way to get through a brief blackout. By themselves, however, they're not useful for long-duration blackouts due to their limited capacity.

FIGURE 12-7: Portable power stations that use lithium-ion batteries.

Pixel-Shot/Adobe Stock Photos

A gas generator's run time is measured by the size of its fuel tank, measured in gallons or liters. A portable power station's run time is measured by its battery capacity, measured in watt-hours. A small power station can hold 2,000-watt-hours, which will run a CPAP machine for a couple of days or a large refrigerator or small window air conditioner for half a day and costs about $1,000.

However, even doubling a portable power station's capacity still won't get you past a couple of days of refrigeration or cooling. By themselves, portable power stations provide limited backup time at a high cost. When combined with gas-powered generators, however, portable power stations complement each other, providing more options and extended run times.

TIP

You can build a large DIY portable power station by buying and connecting a large lithium-ion battery, a battery charger, and an inverter for half the price of most portable power stations. However, you must be knowledgeable about electrical systems and batteries, and it helps if you're unafraid of electrocution or fire.

WARNING

Portable power stations use lithium iron phosphate ($LiFePO_4$) batteries, which are safer and less likely to catch on fire than the lithium nickel manganese cobalt batteries used in many EVs. With that said, any damaged or overcharged battery can create a fire hazard. Additionally, building your own portable power station with high amperage batteries can represent a shock and fire hazard if not done properly.

Portable solar panels and wind turbines

Outside of gas-powered generators, solar panels and wind turbines are the primary ways to generate residential electricity to charge portable power stations.

Solar panels

Solar panels have many positives. They have no moving parts, almost no maintenance, last for decades, and provide free power as long as the sun shines. That last benefit is its biggest drawback — no sun, no power. That may be an issue if you live in a condominium or apartment, but you may still be able to use portable solar panels to supplement your power. Combining portable solar panels, a gas-powered inverter generator, and a portable power station can be the perfect trifecta.

Wind turbines

Wind turbines have an advantage over solar power; they can create power day or night as long as there's wind. The drawback is that they need strong, constant wind, and the wind turbine needs to be really big to generate significant power. Unless you live in a rural area, installation of a wind turbine might not even be allowed.

For the vast majority of locations, installing a wind turbine to provide Level 2 power isn't economically practical compared to other options. There are, however, exceptions. Wind turbines will be readdressed in Chapter 20 as Level 3 preparation.

Powering Basic Heating and Cooling (Level 2)

If you have a roof full of solar panels with backup batteries that allow your home to operate independent of the power grid, you're probably not reading this chapter. Fortunately, with some MacGyvering, you can achieve many of the benefits of a whole-house solar system by leveraging old and new technology, and you can do it without taking out a second mortgage. This technique is scalable from powering a refrigerator to handling your home's central air conditioner.

Combining a gas-powered generator with a portable power station

The most cost-effective strategy to extend your ability to stay powered during a long power outage is to pair a gas-powered generator with a portable power station (battery backup). This leverages the strengths of both. To do this, you need an inverter gas generator that can power all your chosen appliances with enough additional power to charge the portable power station at the same time. When the power station battery is full, you shut down the gas generator and run everything off the power station.

When the power station's battery gets low, you fire up the gas generator again, recharge, and repeat. By alternating between the generator and the power station, you significantly increase the time you can power your home with the same fuel. It also allows you to run the portable power station at night when the demand is the lowest, and the noise of a gas-powered generator won't disturb others or attract unwanted attention. This allows you to sleep at night without worrying about running out of gas, and since portable power stations are silent, you will be able to hear any alarms or unexpected sounds, such as an intruder.

WARNING

Most portable power stations WILL NOT accept power from non-inverter generators (inverters are explained earlier under "Technical Stuff"). These small non-inverter generators don't produce clean enough power for these battery systems. Large whole-house generators usually provide clean enough power even without inverters, but make sure you check their specifications.

Choosing a gas-powered generator

The foundation of this type of system is the gas-powered generator. It provides the most power and bang for the buck. Choosing the right size is covered below.

TIP

Gas-powered generators are the most efficient when they run at 80 percent of their published power output. This also improves their long-term reliability. Therefore, choose a generator that can power all of your chosen appliances AND charge your power station at the same time while running at about 80 percent of its published "running" power output.

Choosing a portable power station

The portable power station needs to have a lithium-ion battery big enough to power all the same appliances that the generator does, and do it for a reasonable amount of time. Eight hours would be the minimum to keep your chosen appliances powered overnight without running the generator. The power station also needs to be able to recharge quickly by accepting as much power as the generator can feed it.

TIP

Portable power stations are only about 85 percent efficient at converting their battery's stored DC power to the household AC power. They also consume power when their inverter is on, even if nothing is plugged into them. That means you want a portable power station that has a watt-hour capacity at least 120 percent above your maximum required. Also, be sure to always turn the portable power station's inverter off when it's not being used.

WARNING

When the generator is recharging the portable power station, you don't want it to pull more power than the gas generator can produce, especially when the generator is also powering your appliances. If the power station pulls power beyond the generator's maximum output, the generator will stall and shut down. Make sure your portable power station allows you to adjust maximum input power to match your generator's output capability.

As of the publication date of this book, a portable power station sized to complement a gas generator is about twice the price of the generator, but battery prices continue to drop.

Illustrating a basic Level 2 backup system

Using the information in Table 12-2, five items have been selected that would be important to have powered during an extended blackout. In this example, you want to provide power for phone charging, surveillance cameras, a coffee maker, a laptop, satellite internet, and a small high-efficiency window air conditioner/heat pump, as shown in Table 12-2. This assumes heating or cooling a room is a top priority, and you're going to eat what's in your refrigerator and freezer quickly, and then transition to your disaster preparation pantry.

Heat stroke or freezing is a higher priority than keeping food cold. However, if the location or the season doesn't require heating or cooling a room, you can easily power a refrigerator instead of the air conditioner/heat pump.

TABLE 12-2 **Total watt-hours needed for a basic Level 2 backup scenario**

Generator Capacity	Appliance or Device	Running Watts	Starting Watts
5,000 watts of continuous output required	Phone charging (15 watts × 2)	30	N/A
	Security camera (5 watts × 2)	10	N/A
	Coffee maker	1,200	N/A
	Laptop computer	70	N/A
	Starlink Mini with Wi-Fi	40	N/A
	Window AC (6,000 BTU)	600	1,200
	Recharge power station	2,000	N/A
Total running/starting power required (watts)		**3,950**	**4,550**

REMEMBER

Your priorities may be different, but in general, you always want to at least cover the three Cs: communication, connection, and cooling (or heating).

You may be thinking that you don't have or want a window air conditioner. This example assumes you're not yet ready to invest in a power backup system big enough to power your central air, which will more than double the cost. Instead, you can use a window air conditioner/heat pump to cool or heat just one room. Figure 12-8 diagrams this example; the generator is supplying power to the listed appliances and charging a portable power station. This design can be scaled up to provide enough power to run your central air and most appliances.

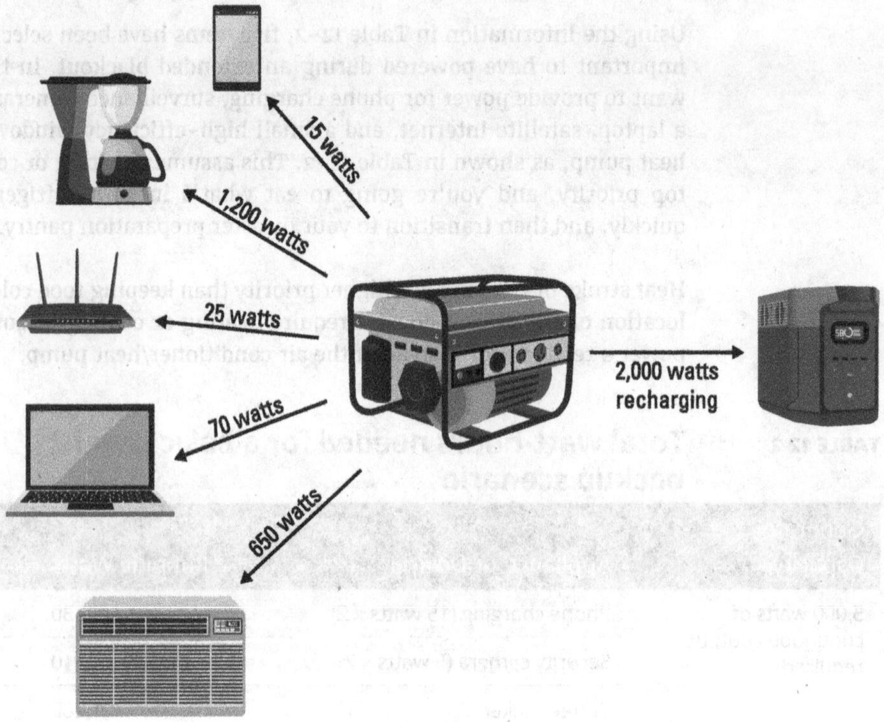

FIGURE 12-8: Diagram of a gas generator powering basic appliances and charging a portable power station.

5,000-WATT GAS-POWERED GENERATOR

From Table 12-2, you need 3,950 running watts and the ability to surge to 4,550 starting watts. With their small fuel tanks (usually about 4 gallons), most gas generators can run 10–12 hours at 60 percent power output before refueling. As of the publication date of this book, a 5,000-watt gas generator with inverter technology can be purchased for about $800. A dual or triple fuel generator costs a bit more.

3,500-WATT-HOUR PORTABLE POWER STATION

To store the power supplied by the gas generator, you need a portable power station. The power station should be able to run all your chosen appliances for at least 10 hours without running the gas generator, as shown in Figure 12-9.

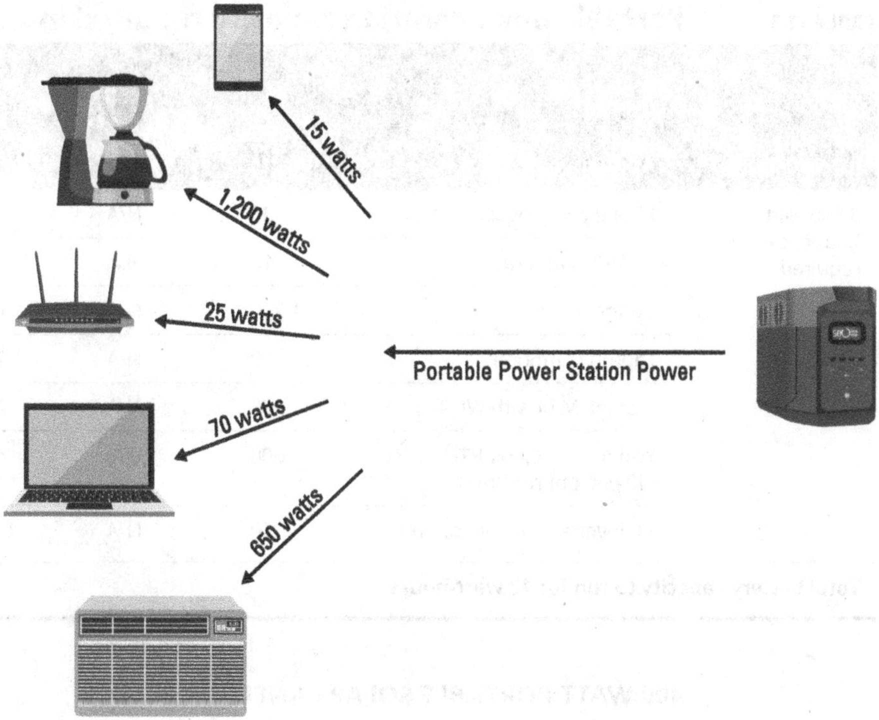

FIGURE 12-9: Diagram of portable power station supplying power when the gas generator is off.

Like the generator, you need to select a power station that can handle the maximum starting watts. Unlike the generator, however, you also need to decide how long you need it to supply that power before the battery is drained. An optimum situation would be to run the generator in the day and the portable power station at night. That means the power station should be able to handle all the loads for at least 10 hours, and preferably 12 to give a margin.

You must also include the parasitic drain of the power station's inverter when it converts the battery's DC power to AC, usually about 20 watts per hour. This required capacity is illustrated in the last two columns of Table 12-3.

In Table 12-3, the portable power station has to have enough output power to handle the maximum starting load and the watt-hour capacity to run for 12 hours. Keep in mind, some devices, such as phone chargers, coffee makers, and air conditioners, don't run at full power all the time. Air conditioners cycle on and off to maintain temperature, which reduces the total power required. From the right-hand column of Table 12-3, you need about 3,290-watt-hours of battery capacity to run everything for 12 hours. A 3,500-watt-hour portable power station should work. A power station of this capacity currently costs about $1,500, but lithium-ion batteries continue to drop in price.

TABLE 12-3 **Portable power station capacity required in watt-hours**

Portable Power Station Battery Capacity to Run for 12 Hours	Appliance or Device	Running Watts	Starting Watts	Use per Day	Watts / 24 Hrs
3,500 watt-hours battery capacity required	Phone charging x 2	30	N/A	4 hrs	120
	Security camera x 2	10	N/A	12 hrs	120
	Coffee maker	1,200	N/A	10 min	200
	Laptop computer	70	N/A	2 hrs	140
	Starlink Mini with Wi-Fi	35	N/A	2 hrs	70
	Window AC 6,000 BTU (40 percent runtime)	600	1,000	4 hrs	2,400
	AC inverter parasite drain	20	N/A	12 hrs	240
Total battery capacity to run for 12 watt-hours					**3,290**

400-WATT PORTABLE SOLAR PANELS

If you have access to any sunlight, deploying portable panels in your yard, deck, or balcony can significantly supplement your generator's ability to recharge your portable power station, as shown in Figure 12-10.

A set of foldable portable solar panels that would fit on a deck or balcony, under ideal conditions, can produce 400 watts of power per hour for about four to five hours, depending on your location and season. That could add 1,600-watt-hours to your portable power station, which would reduce the gas generator's running time and fuel consumption even further.

This example also provides a backup if you run out of fuel for the gas generator. A 400-watt foldable portable solar panel runs about $500 (see Figure 12-11). The more portable solar panels you have, the less time your generator needs to run. This combination of gas generator, portable power station, and portable solar panels provides the longest duration of power support for the least amount of fuel.

The example used was a minimalist system designed to provide the basics of communication, connection, and cooling or heating for one room for an extended period. Table 12-4 is a rough breakdown of the cost. Before purchasing a gas generator, portable power station, or portable solar panels, do your homework and make sure they're compatible with each other. Additionally, read reviews and check ratings by independent reviewers such as the nonprofit Consumer Reports or other independent labs.

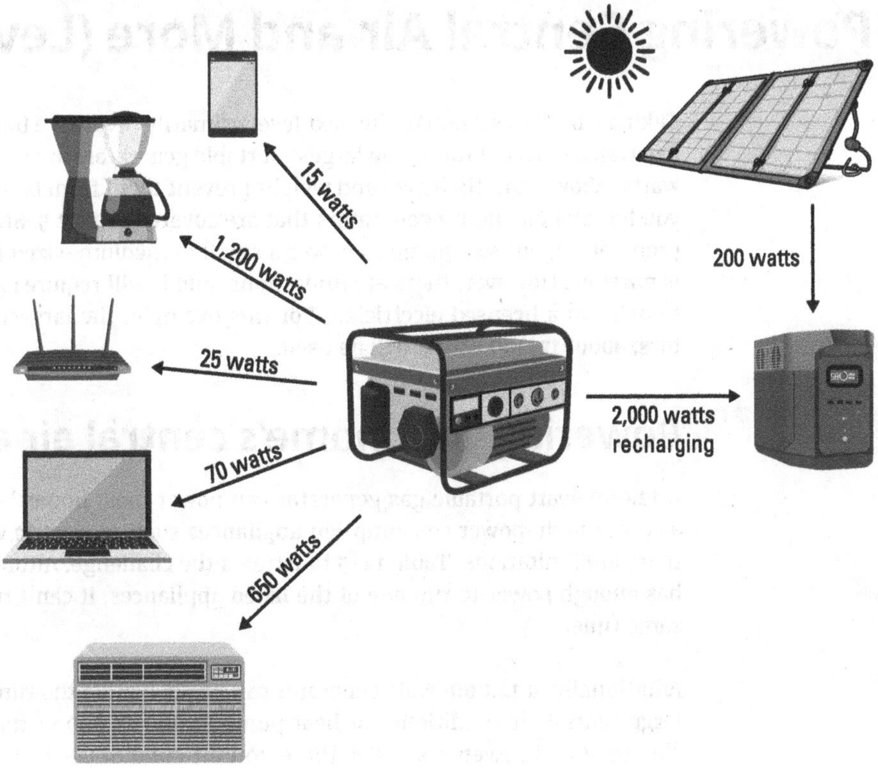

FIGURE 12-10: Diagram of a portable power station supplemented with a portable solar panel.

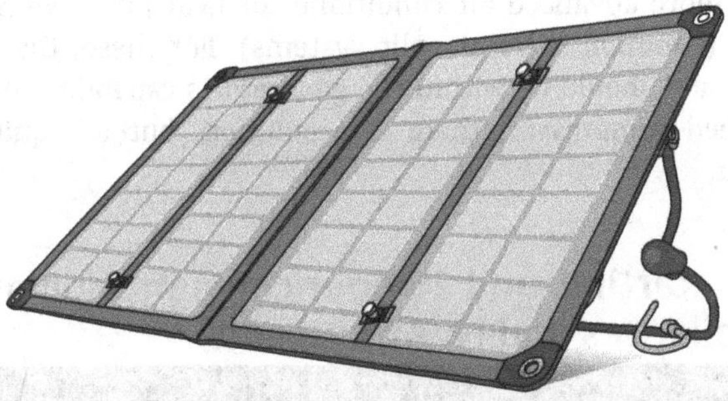

Premium Illustration/Adobe Stock Photos

FIGURE 12-11: Foldable portable solar panels.

TABLE 12-4 **Estimated price for the example system**

Dual-fuel 5,000-watt gas generator	$800
3,500-watt-hour portable power station	$1,500
400-watt portable foldable solar panels	$500
Cables and plugs	$100
Total	**$2,900**

Powering Central Air and More (Level 2+)

Taking a backup system to the next level primarily involves a bigger generator and a portable power station. The largest portable generators are usually under 14,000 watts. Above that, their size and weight prevent them from being "portable," and you have whole-house generators that are covered in Part 5. Staying with Level 2 preparation, but scaling up to power a small to medium-sized home's central air is possible. However, there are limitations, and it will require electrical modifications from a licensed electrician. For this example, the largest portable generators, about 12,000 watts, will be used.

Powering your home's central air and heat

A 12,000-watt portable gas generator can power most homes' central air as well as other high-power consumption appliances such as electric water heaters, but there are limitations. Table 12-5 illustrates the challenge. Although the generator has enough power to run any of the listed appliances, it can't run them all at the same time.

Additionally, a 12,000-watt generator can easily handle the running wattage of a large central air conditioner or heat pump (3,000–8,000 watts), but may not be able to start it. Even a smaller three-ton air conditioner compressor could pull more power to start than a 12,000-watt generator can produce. The exception is if you have a more advanced air conditioner or heat pump with a variable speed compressor (common in mini-split systems). For these, the starting power is much lower and should be within the generator's capability. If you don't have a variable speed compressor, there is a solution, but it requires modifications covered next.

TABLE 12-5 Running, starting, and 24-hour consumption of common large appliances and HVAC systems

Portable Power Station Required Capacity	Appliance or Device	Running Watts	Starting Watts	Use per Day	Watts / 24 Hrs
	Well water pump	1,000	2,100	6 hrs	3,000
	Refrigerator	600	2,200	8 hrs	4,800
	Furnace/HVAC (fan only)	550	1,000	24 hrs	13,200
	Water heater 50-gallon	4,000		4 hrs	16,000
	AC/heat pump (3-ton)	3,000	16,000	6 hrs	18,000

Installing a soft starter to slash HVAC's starting power

Installing a Soft Starter on your HVAC compressor ramps it up to speed gently, reducing starting amperage by up to 60 percent. As a side benefit, it should extend the life of the compressor. A good example is the Micro-air EasyStart in Figure 12-12. This allows a 12,000-watt portable generator to start a standard air conditioner or heat pump up to about 5 tons. Soft Starters cost around $300 plus the cost of installation.

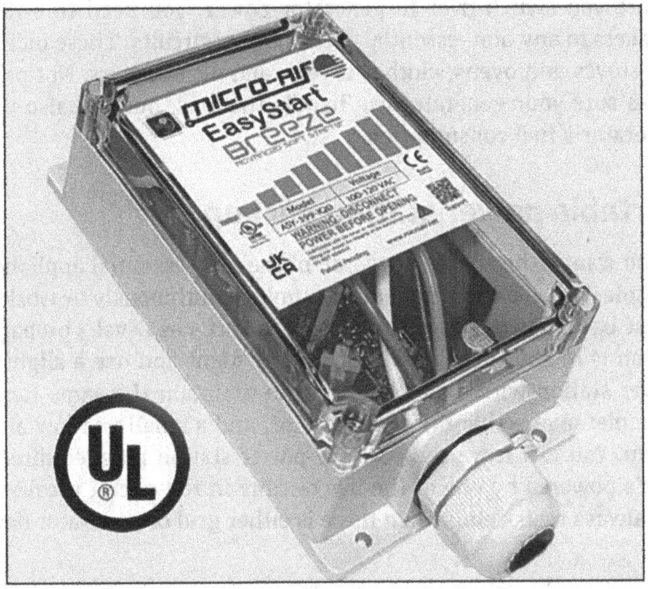

FIGURE 12-12: A soft starter such as Micro Air's EasyStart can be wired into your HVAC compressor.

Although this will allow you to start and run your home's central air, you can't just plug your central air system into a generator, and there are limits on how many additional appliances can be powered.

Installing a generator transfer switch

To power your central air and any other appliances or outlets in your home requires wiring the generator directly into your home's main circuit breaker panel. When the power grid is active, power goes to the circuit breaker panel. When the power grid goes down, before the generator can supply power, the circuit breaker panel must be isolated from the power grid. Isolating the circuit breaker panel requires the installation of a transfer switch on the main panel breaker that ensures the house can only be powered by either the grid or the generator. Doing so does two things:

- It allows the generator to power all the circuits in your home.
- It prevents your generator's power from going back into the power grid and electrocuting the line worker trying to fix the power outage. This is why you need a qualified electrician to install the generator connection and transfer switch.

Before you switch over to generator power, you need to switch off the circuit breakers to any non-essential appliances or circuits. These include hot tubs, electric stoves and ovens, clothes dryers, and dishwashers. Not only do you want to make sure your generator can handle the load, but you also want to reduce the generator's fuel consumption.

Portable power station backup

If you want to be able to power all of the non-essential appliances, it will require a whole-house backup generator running continuously or working with a whole-house backup battery system covered in Part 5 as Level 3 preparation. The Level 2 option is to shut down the generator at night and use a slightly bigger portable power station with extension cords to maintain the same items in the original example: phone charging, refrigerator, and a small window air conditioner/heat pump. You can leave the portable power station plugged directly into an outlet that's powered by one of the live circuits in the circuit breaker panel. That way, it's always recharging when there is either grid or generator power.

Bidirectional charging with an electric vehicle (EV)

Bidirectional charging is simply the ability to not only charge your EV but reverse that and pull that power back out of the battery to run your house using the EV's battery, as shown in Figure 12-13. If you own an EV that has this capability, congratulations, but if you own an EV that doesn't or are thinking of buying an EV, keep reading. It's possible that any EV can be upgraded to bidirectional charging in the future.

Here's why this is important: The biggest portable power stations have about 6,000-watt-hours of capacity. They weigh more than 100 pounds and cost about $3,000. Now, compare that with the battery sitting in an EV. The average EV has at least a 60-kilowatt battery pack — that's 60,000 watts. Now you know why EVs are so expensive.

FIGURE 12-13: Bidirectional charging that allows the EV battery to act as a home backup battery.

Nitiphol/Adobe Stock Photos

Even if you only tap half of that battery capacity to power your home, that's 30,000 watts of backup battery. That's the same as five 6,000-watt-hour portable power stations, which would currently cost more than $15,000. Or you could buy a dedicated whole-house battery backup system, which would cost even more. If you have an EV, you already own a huge potential battery backup, one that spends most of its life sitting idle in your driveway or garage.

Even though most EVs don't yet come with bidirectional charging, there are several companies creating devices that access your EV's battery and allow it to power your home.

WARNING

Unless the system was designed specifically for your vehicle, it may not work or may require MacGyvering. Additionally, without the EV manufacturer's involvement, there is a risk of damage to the EV's charging system, or it might void your EV's warranty. With the power and popularity of bidirectional charging, it's likely that EV makers will offer this as an option in future EVs and may update their systems, or allow third-party companies to access their vehicles. This is a good area to keep an eye on for future developments.

TECHNICAL STUFF

One powerful reason for governments to support bidirectional charging is that all these EV batteries can be used as a giant battery bank to help stabilize the power grid. In several countries and some U.S. states, you can enter into an agreement with your local power provider. When the power grid is experiencing extreme demand, if you're willing to give back some of the power from your EV's battery (you get to decide how much), they pay you a large premium. This prevents blackouts or brownouts, and you get paid for helping to support the grid. This reduces your electric bill and, in some cases, could eliminate it while helping to increase the stability of the power grid.

The best option for maintaining power during an extended disaster is to be independent of the power grid entirely, which is covered in Chapter 20. This isn't just a great disaster preparation strategy. However, depending on your location and electricity cost, it could be a good investment and eventually pay for itself. A great resource is *Solar Powering Your Home For Dummies*.

IN THIS CHAPTER

» Choosing a ninja versus Rambo mindset

» Using surveillance technology

» Evaluating passive defense measures

» Defending with non-lethal means

Chapter 13
Protecting Yourself during Civil Unrest

Security and self-defense can be complex and controversial topics, but they are important. The strategies depend on your location, experience, and philosophy. The first part of self-defense is being aware of your environment. That includes everything from being very observant to security cameras and emergency service broadcasts.

Chapter 10 covered cost-effective measures to secure your home's doors and windows. This chapter also covers defense with non-lethal devices. Firearms are covered in Chapter 14, but depending on where you live, a firearm may not be an option. Even if it is, it's important to look at all the options, not just for you but for family members who do not or, in some cases, should not have a firearm.

The emphasis is on defending you and your family in your home. This is an important distinction because the use of active defense devices outside your home usually falls under different laws. Make sure you understand all local laws regarding self-defense.

Evaluating Your Self-Defense Mindset

Remember that any type of dangerous confrontation reduces your survival odds. There's a famous saying among pilots: "There are old pilots, and there are bold pilots, but there are no old bold pilots." No matter how certain you may be that you have overwhelming firepower, there will always be someone with more. Our philosophy should be more ninja than Rambo. We want to avoid dangerous engagements.

Keeping a low profile

If you are staying in your home during an extended disaster and apply steps from the previous chapters, you should have some level of water, food, and power. However, that preparation may also make you a target during long-duration disasters. Therefore, it's important to keep a low profile. That means not flaunting the fact that you have power, water, and a stockpile of food. That doesn't mean you can't share it with your neighbors, but you don't want an opportunist to use your home as their grocery store. With the utilities down for an extended period, don't advertise by eating and playing music on your deck or balcony. At night, minimize the light coming from your home.

If you have to travel, the strategy should be to see and avoid. We want to be very observant and avoid any situations that could escalate into a conflict. The F-18 is a very capable fighter, but on strike missions, it's often flown to the target at extremely low altitude to avoid detection. The same applies if you are venturing out for supplies.

Listening to your gut feeling

Profiling is bad when used to assume guilt based solely on association, whether that's ethnicity, age, or any other demographic. However, one of the reasons we think this way is because our brains are hardwired to look for patterns as a survival strategy. Imagine your prehistoric ancestor seeing a tiger for the first time. The tiger doesn't look like the lion that ate their cousin the other day, so some ignored it. Your ancestor, however, immediately identified it as a similar threat and ran away. You and I are the great, great, great . . . grandchildren of the person who correctly "profiled" it, rather than the tiger meal. Because of that, your brain is constantly on the lookout for what's going to eat you next.

This usually occurs at the subconscious level, meaning that if you're in a disaster situation or just in a vulnerable position, your subconscious may be picking up cues your conscious mind misses. Trust your instincts, and listen to that inner voice. If you feel uncomfortable, get away as soon as possible. Don't be like the expendable characters in the horror movies that decide to hide behind the chain-saw collection.

WARNING

Because your brain *is* hardwired to look for patterns, it may also see patterns where none exist. This may explain our fascination with conspiracies, but it also means that if you're clearly not in a vulnerable situation, don't let past experiences define relationships with new people. These new people could become important future allies and friends.

Trying to be a lone wolf is dangerous

While being self-reliant is admirable, you can't stay alert or awake 24 hours a day. The technology that follows can help, but in a dangerous situation, there's nothing more important than having another set of eyes on watch and another set of hands to divide up the work. If you have family or friends with you who are old enough, you can divide up the responsibilities and watches. Four-hour watches are optimal if you have enough people. If you don't have anyone else, it's worth inviting a friend or family member to shelter or evacuate with you in a serious disaster.

Regardless, it's important to engage neighbors or fellow condominium/apartment dwellers before disasters occur. Many neighborhoods and apartments have existing watch programs. If there is one, get involved. If there isn't one, start one. At the very least, identify neighbors who appear responsible and who might also have taken disaster preparation steps. Disaster protection and defense are far more effective as a group sport.

Observing Orienting Deciding Acting (OODA)

There's no way to cover every possible disaster scenario or complication created by a disaster. There is a process, however, that can help. It's called the OODA (observe, orient, decide, and act) Loop, created by Colonel John Boyd, a U.S. Air Force fighter pilot and tactician (see Figure 13-1). I won't cover this in detail, but the intent of these steps, in this order, is to act rather than just react. The idea is to figure out what's going on, adapt to the situation, determine the best course of action, and then act. This may sound obvious, but when the adrenaline is flowing, rational thought can be a challenge.

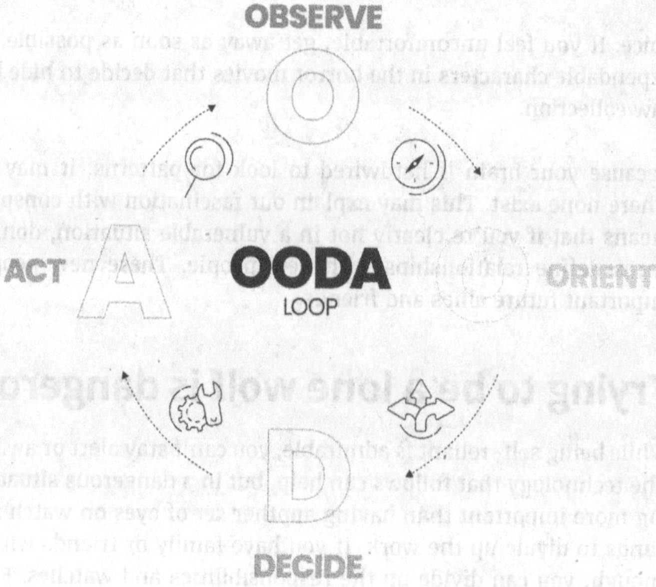

FIGURE 13-1: Colonel John Boyd's OODA Loop.

Whale Design/Adobe Stock Photos

Anytime you're away from your home and in an area where you may be vulnerable, with or without a disaster, focus on the "observe" part of the OODA Loop. Don't wait for that "gut feeling" to make you uncomfortable. Look around and observe. You can't defend against a threat if you don't know it's there. One of the most important warnings a tactical pilot can give their wingman is "check six." This means check your six o'clock position; in other words, "Look behind you." An aircraft behind you is in the best position to use its gun or air-to-air missile to take you out. This applies to disaster situations as well. You must be aware of what's going on in your immediate vicinity, particularly in any blind spots. This includes when you're on foot, in a vehicle, or at home. Here are some things to consider when you're outside your home.

- Don't be buried in your phone or listening to loud music on your ear buds.
- Notice when someone is loitering in an area near you or your vehicle.
- Observe whether you are being watched or followed.

For example, if you're on foot and observe a possible threat, orient by identifying a safer area, such as an area that's more public with people around. Then, make the decision to go there and do it immediately. If that isn't possible or the potential threat is right outside your car or front door, it's important to be ready with a self-defense plan. This will sound strange, but try to think like a bad guy. For example, if someone were desperate and trying to take your supplies, how might they go about it, and what would be your best defensive measure?

Defending with Non-Lethal Devices (Level 1)

This section will cover inexpensive passive technology and active non-lethal devices that improve your ability to defend yourself and your family.

Observing

Situational awareness is critical. Chapter 11 covered the Wireless Emergency Alert system that is built into every cell phone. These warnings are broadcast to your phone by national and local governments based solely on your location. They include warnings about everything from a child kidnapping in your vicinity to tornadoes. This can give you a general warning and important information as long as the cell phone network is operating.

Moving closer to home, inexpensive security (see Figure 13-2) cameras for your home can dramatically improve your immediate situational awareness. Some of these small cameras can be had for $40 and are surprisingly good. Since most of these require power and Wi-Fi, without an operational generator or portable power station, they're not usable, so they'll be covered in detail under the Level 2 preparation section.

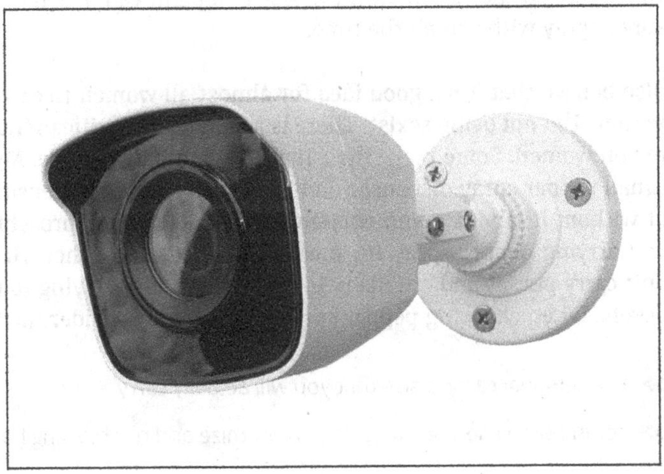

FIGURE 13-2: Small, inexpensive security cameras.

damrong/Adobe Stock Photos

Although technology can help, nothing replaces a set of eyes. If there is a question about the safety or security of your location, whether at home or evacuating, the best strategy is to always have someone on watch. This assumes that there are two or more people in your party and requires setting up specific shifts. The more people you have, the shorter and more comfortable the shifts can be. Once a potential threat is identified, there needs to be a concrete plan for self-defense. This covers a wide category of strategies and devices, but in this Level 1 section, simple and inexpensive options are highlighted.

Defending with pepper spray

One of the simplest and most cost-effective devices for immediate self-defense is pepper spray, also called "mace," which refers to the Mace brand name.

There's a reason law enforcement officers carry it. It doesn't cause permanent injury, but it does cause severe irritation to the nose, throat, and eyes. This pain usually takes the aggressor's mind off any immediate plan to attack and may make it difficult for them to see you.

WARNING

Although pepper spray will cause pain, difficulty breathing, and seeing, it doesn't incapacitate, and the individual you sprayed is not going to be happy, so don't stick around.

There are plenty of different options for pepper spray, from tiny containers that fit in a purse or pocket to ones the size of a paint can. It's not a bad idea to carry pepper spray with you all the time.

I also believe that it's a good idea for almost all women to carry pepper spray all the time. I'm not being sexist. There is a small but significant number of men who prey on women. Some make their living by mugging people. My daughter carries a small pepper spray dispenser on her car key chain. That ensures she doesn't go out without it, and it's immediately accessible when approaching or leaving her car. Carrying pepper spray for men isn't a bad idea either. However, most men don't carry purses and are likely to spray themselves trying to pull it out of their pockets. When choosing pepper spray, you should consider the following:

- For personal carry, a size that you will actually carry
- For in-home use, a gel that doesn't atomize and risk blowing back on you

For home defense, it may be worth investing in a longer-distance, stronger version. The most effective is something often used to protect against bear attacks. I've been told by bear hunters that bear spray is often more effective than firearms. Grizzly bears are big enough that a bullet from a pistol might just irritate them, but bears have sensitive noses, and pepper spray will usually stop them in their tracks.

Bear spray has a range of up to 40 feet and has more than enough for multiple uses. With its longer range and multiple shots, it comes in much larger cans. There are also large pepper spray cans, specifically designed for home defense. They use a gel that sticks to skin and doesn't aerosolize, reducing the risk of peppering yourself.

WARNING

Before purchasing pepper spray, check your local laws. Several U.S. states limit the size, amount, or percentage of active ingredients, and some countries prohibit it entirely or require a permit or background check. Bear spray, with its larger size and more concentrated irritants, may not be legal to carry outside your home, other than in areas where you might encounter bears. Interestingly, the Geneva Convention technically classifies pepper spray as a chemical weapon and prohibits its use by the military. Go figure.

Defending with a stun gun

You don't want to face Freddy Krueger at home in your pajamas with a flashlight. Another option is a stun gun, also called a TASER. Stun guns use extremely high voltage, low amperage electricity to temporarily scramble the human nervous system. Unlike pepper spray, it doesn't matter if you're facing 300 pounds of muscle pumped up on amphetamines.

Tasing can temporarily disorganize their nervous system and cause them to collapse like a rag doll. Since direct contact with an attacker is required, this should be considered as a last line of defense. However, the very loud electrical crackling sound of a stun gun can also be a deterrent. Several small flashlight stun gun combinations sell for around $30 (see Figure 13-3). If you purchase one of these inexpensive stun guns, they tend to have shorter life spans, should be charged regularly, checked, and replaced as needed.

WARNING

A brief touch by a stun gun will cause pain and muscle contractions, but won't disable. To disable an attacker, you must maintain contact for a few seconds. Although the effects of being tased are temporary, there are additional risks of injury when the individual falls to the ground or if they have a cardiac condition.

FIGURE 13-3: Flashlight-stun gun combination.

photographyx/Adobe Stock Photos

TIP

Pepper spray and stun guns are complementary and help offset the limitations of each. One is effective at distance while the other is better for close-in defense. The combination of these two is arguably the most effective, least expensive type of self-defense.

WARNING

Again, know your local laws before purchasing or carrying a stun gun. Similar to pepper spray, some countries, U.S. states, or cities require background checks and a permit, or prohibit them entirely.

Taking self-defense classes

If you have nunchuck skills, you're good to go. For the rest of us, basic self-defense knowledge is always a good idea. If you're a father with a daughter, you'd like her to go on dates carrying an anti-tank weapon, but self-defense knowledge can be as simple as learning how to break out of a hold. It can also include knowing how to effectively use a stun gun or pepper spray . . . maybe by a simple demonstration on your daughter's date.

As with so many other areas, self-defense can have a dual purpose, like getting aerobic exercise by taking a kickboxing class, or it can be fun like playing paintball. If you enjoy competitive sports, many types of martial arts improve physical fitness and teach self-defense and discipline. Examples include Karate, which teaches striking, Judo that specializes in grappling and throwing techniques, Jiu-Jitsu, which centers on ground-based defense and submission holds, and Krav Maga, which focuses on real-world situations.

Defending with Non-Lethal Devices (Level 2)

Chapter 10 covered ways to fortify your home from natural disasters and forced entry. This section covers additional measures and devices to protect you and your family, starting with passive defense and moving on to active non-lethal devices. Again, the focus is on defending you and your family in your home.

Surveilling with security cameras

Security cameras can significantly increase your situational awareness by placing them around your home in areas that can't be easily viewed from inside or from the street. Even condominiums and apartments can use video doorbells.

For houses, you want the entire perimeter of your home covered, which will require more than one camera. It's also important to choose cameras that can see in low light or even total darkness with an infrared capability. This usually consists of a camera with a sensitive sensor, but can also include an active infrared light. The best is a combination of both.

In the areas around your house that have little or no lighting at night, it's best to have a combination camera and floodlight. These can be set to come on automatically when they detect motion and notify you. More advanced cameras can be set to notify and turn on only when a person is detected, reducing false alarms.

Security cameras require power to operate and transmit their picture. There are battery-powered cameras (need to be recharged every couple of months) and solar-powered cameras that eliminate the need to add wiring and allow them to work during a power outage. The bigger issue is that even if the camera doesn't need power, you still need to power your Wi-Fi system so you can receive the videos. On top of that, almost all these systems require the internet to access the video feed.

WARNING

Some systems are advertised as not needing Wi-Fi. That usually means the camera has a built-in cell phone transmitter. Keep in mind that these cameras won't work if the cell towers are out of commission. Sometimes, they advertise no Wi-Fi because the camera can record onto an SD card inside the camera, as if you're going to run outside and pull the SD card to view the video. The only exceptions are camera systems that use old-school hardwired video cables to a central display. These systems are also impervious to Wi-Fi jammers.

TIP

Hardwired video cameras are the most secure, but you can use the less expensive Wi-Fi cameras if you apply the Level 2 backup power and connectivity from Chapters 11 and 12. This combination powers the cameras during an outage, and a satellite connection allows internet access when the cell towers are down, keeping the camera video feed functioning.

WARNING

Security cameras are easy to identify, which can act as a passive deterrent. Studies show that just having them visible reduces burglaries. However, the fact that they're easy to identify also means they're easy to disable. Having multiple cameras around the perimeter of your home is a good idea with or without a disaster, but it's important to understand their limitations.

Protecting with a bulletproof vest

Bulletproof vests may seem a bit extreme because they are. I mention them to provide complete coverage of all major passive defense devices. They are frequently worn by law enforcement and the military for good reason. They work. Bulletproof vests aren't something most people would ever consider wearing on a regular basis. There are, however, locations or situations that might warrant their use.

While doing flight testing of new F-18s at Boeing, I lived in a duplex in downtown St. Louis. Back then, the city had one of the highest murder rates per capita, and my duplex neighbor happened to be a death row inmate lawyer. Hearing frequent gunfire at night, a bullet-resistant vest might have been appropriate jogging attire. Aside from living in an inherently dangerous location, a reasonable application might be putting one on before investigating the sound of someone potentially breaking into your home. If you're in an urban or suburban environment where utilities have ceased for an extended period, it wouldn't be unreasonable to accessorize with one of these before going out.

WARNING

Bulletproof vests don't make you bulletproof. They only protect the vital organs in your chest. Your head still makes a nice target. More importantly, they may make you look fat.

Bulletproof vests come in several levels of bullet resistance:

- **Level 1:** Level 1 vests are not bulletproof and only provide protection from low-energy stabbing with knives or spikes.
- **Level 2:** Level 2 vests stop the most common handgun bullets, cost around $200, and are thin enough that they won't be obvious unless you're wearing a Speedo or bikini.

» **Level 3:** Level 3 vests are heavier and will stop almost all pistol rounds and some rifle bullets.

» **Level 4:** Level 4 vests are effective against rifle and even most armor-piercing rounds. These higher-level vests cost more than $500 and will definitely make you look fat. The vast majority of assaults are from handguns, so unless you're an Oligarch, Level 2 or 3 should be sufficient.

Surveilling with night vision goggles (NVGs)

You have to admit that, as kids, next to X-ray vision, being able to see in the dark would have been the coolest superpower ever. Many years ago, my sister squadron was beta testing new night vision goggles for their night strike missions. They got a batch of brand-new third-generation NVGs. We took them into the locker room and turned out the lights so we could play with them. I remember tossing them to each other in the dark. We had no idea they cost $70,000 each. Fortunately, we didn't drop them. Today, you can buy basic first-generation versions for around $200. The higher generation NVGs can also be purchased, but start at several thousand dollars.

Although there are many variations, most fall into two categories:

» **Wearable:** The first category is the type you can wear while walking around, as shown in Figure 13-4. These usually come with a head strap or helmet mount (the ones you see in the movies). They have no magnification and a wide field of view.

» **Handheld:** The other category of NVGs is used like binoculars. They're handheld with magnification and a narrower field of view.

Night vision goggles can give you an advantage at night, but unless your home is in an unusual location or sits on a lot of land, they probably shouldn't be at the top of your preparation priority list. They're covered here for completeness because they're fun to use, and they have other uses, such as bird watching, hunting, or scaring your neighbors.

WARNING

There may be restrictions on their use in some countries and in California, so make sure you're aware of regulations. There are plenty of NVGs online, but at the couple-hundred-dollar price point, the usability and quality vary. Read the reviews carefully.

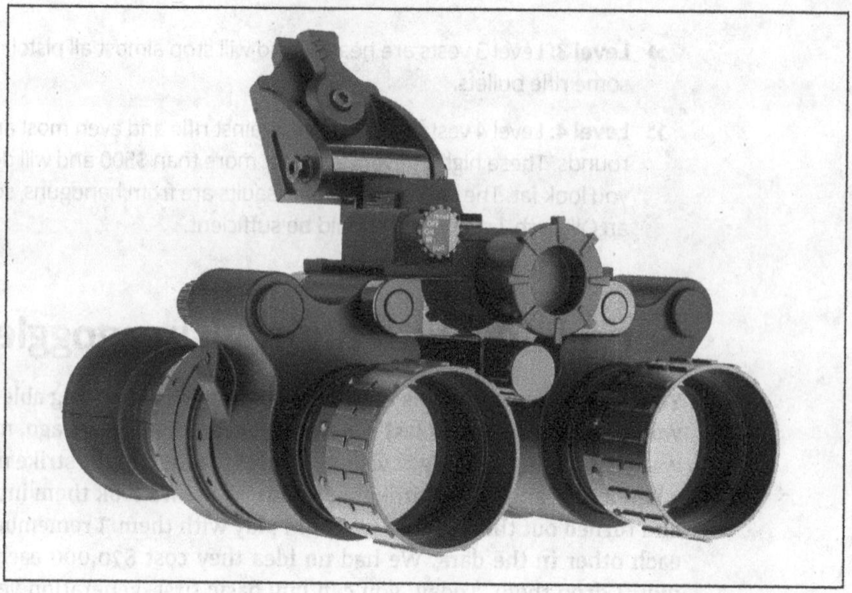

FIGURE 13-4: Night vision goggles.

alexlmx/Adobe Stock Photos

Defending with a gas-propelled stun gun

A more expensive upgrade to a stun gun uses CO_2 cartridges to fire electrode barbs that carry the electrical stun (see Figure 13-5). The barbs remain attached to the stun gun with very fine wires that continue to carry the electricity. Like contact stun guns, the extremely high voltage, low amperage electricity overrides the body's nerve impulses that control the muscles, immobilizing the recipient. These run around $500 and up, but there are now more basic ones on the market for a lot less (make sure you're comfortable with their build quality).

This type of stun gun has the same effectiveness as a regular stun gun but allows engaging an attacker at a realistic distance of about 15 feet (4.5 meters). Their range is limited by the length of the wires and their ability to aim accurately. Choose one with a laser targeting dot to improve accuracy.

The primary drawback is that most of these stun guns have only one shot, after which you have to fall back to using it as a regular contact stun gun until the cartridge is replaced. They can penetrate heavy clothing and even light jackets, but a heavy leather jacket or body armor could block the barbs. That means you'd have to hit them on exposed or lightly clothed skin. Again, a good combination would be one of these, along with pepper spray.

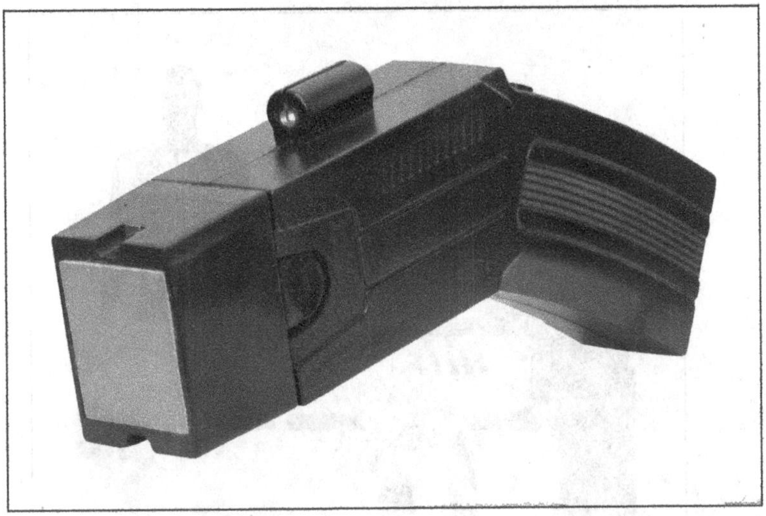

FIGURE 13-5: CO_2 gas-propelled stun gun.

SN VFX/Shutterstock

Defending with gas-propelled pepper

Another option is a CO_2-powered gun that fires balls of pepper dust, similar to paintball guns. An example is the Sabre shown in Figure 13-6.

The balls burst on contact, dispersing a cloud of pepper dust similar to pepper spray. They have a longer range than a stun gun or pepper spray, up to 100 feet (30 meters), and with better accuracy. You don't have to hit the attacker to be effective; hitting the ground near them will disperse the pepper. About the same size as a regular pistol, they hold six or seven rounds per magazine.

Pepper ball guns are large and, like pepper spray, might not stop someone pumped up on drugs, but they have long range, can cover a larger area, and are effective against multiple assailants. Pepper ball guns aren't the best option for close quarters due to the wider dispersal of the pepper powder on impact. The combination of a pepper ball gun for area defense, a gas-fired stun gun for threats within 15 feet (4.5 meters), and pepper spray for very close threats can be effective.

TIP

If you want to get a feel for how these CO_2-powered guns work, go to a paintball park with friends. The accuracy and range are similar to paintball guns, and you get an opportunity to shoot at your most irritating friends.

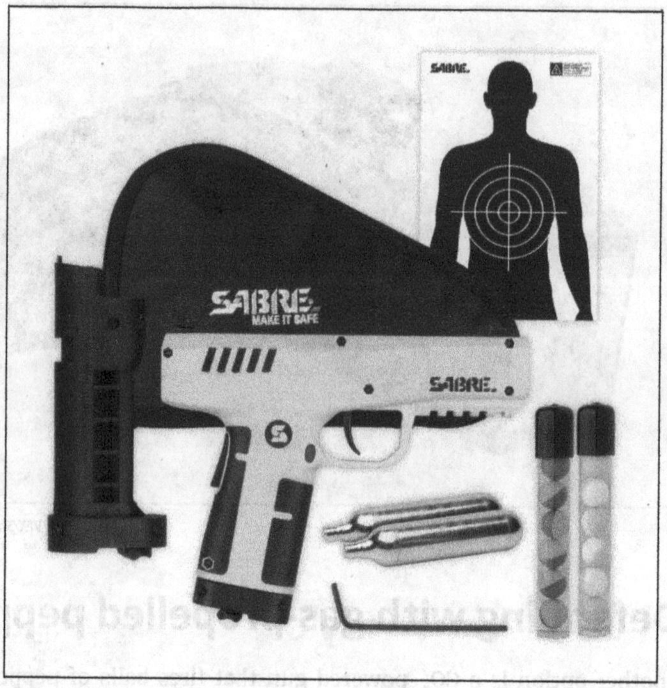

FIGURE 13-6: Sabre CO_2 gas-propelled pepper ball gun.

WARNING As with pepper spray and stun guns, gas-powered pepper ball guns are not legal or may be restricted in several U.S. states, cities, and countries. The regulations can be complex. In some areas, you can own them but cannot carry them outside your home. As always, make sure you understand all laws and regulations before considering them.

Nonlethal versus lethal defensive devices

Those who own firearms sometimes scoff at the use of non-lethal devices such as pepper spray or stun guns. Clearly, if you're facing an aggressor who has a firearm, it's not a fair fight. However, non-lethal and lethal devices are not mutually exclusive and can provide options. Having both allows you to apply the force necessary to handle the situation.

Non-lethal devices have another often-overlooked advantage: In a life and death situation, unless you have combat experience, a law enforcement background, or extensive training, hesitation is a very normal human reaction. A non-lethal weapon is more likely to be used without delay, which could make all the difference in a survival situation.

WARNING

Even if you're experienced in firearms, those in your family or party might not be. I believe every firearm owner would agree that a pistol, rifle, or shotgun in the hands of someone with no experience or training could create a disaster worse than what you're facing.

Defending with what's at hand

Finally, if none of these self-defense devices are available or allowed by local law, use whatever is available. This could include a baseball bat, golf club, walking cane, or a long, heavy flashlight. You never have to worry about whether they were charged or loaded, and they carry their own unique intimidation factor. Keeping one of these items nearby or in a bedroom closet is a good backup plan.

IN THIS CHAPTER

» Considering lethal force for home defense

» Defining your "rules of engagement"

» Evaluating firearms for home defense

Chapter 14
Defending with Firearms

Firearms can be a very controversial topic. Depending on the country you live in, owning a firearm may not be an option. Or your worldview or belief set may prevent you from owning or using a firearm. If any of these apply, you can skip this chapter. Even among those who can own firearms, there are many practical, legal, and moral considerations. One of the reasons this topic is important is that the United States has the largest number of firearms per capita. However, several other major countries also have a large number of privately owned firearms, such as Yemen, Canada, Austria, Switzerland, and Pakistan.

Despite Hollywood, I believe most people are not the type you see in the *Mad Max* movies. Most people are willing to help others if they can. We often see neighbors and communities pulling together during disasters, something they may not do during normal times. The key is "if they can." In a long-term disaster with no power, water, or food . . . fatigue, hunger, and pain can create dangerous desperation in any of us.

Although I achieved the military Expert level in marksmanship and was proficient with the F-18's 20mm cannon, I'm not a firearms expert. There are hundreds of comprehensive books on the choice and the use of firearms for self-defense. This chapter is a high-level overview focused on in-home self-defense. If you have a law enforcement or tactical military background, you can skip this chapter.

Using Lethal Weapons

A lethal weapon doesn't always have to be used to be effective. Its presence can often deter. The best firefight is the firefight avoided. However, a firearm's presence can also provide a false sense of security, and brandishing a firearm too early can create a lethal engagement where none existed.

WARNING

If you decide to own a firearm, it is absolutely critical that you learn how to store, handle, and use it safely. According to the Centers for Disease Control and Prevention (CDC), almost 500 people, mostly children or young adults, are killed every year in accidental shootings in the U.S. It's also important that you decide in advance under what circumstances you will use lethal force.

Understanding Rules of Engagement (ROE)

When engaged in air-to-air combat with an enemy fighter, the decision and ethics are simple: you either shoot them down or they shoot you down. Unfortunately, how the engagement starts often isn't simple. In some cases, the ROE allows firing a missile at an enemy aircraft when they're beyond visual range. In other words, anything coming at you from a certain direction is a bad guy. More often, however, ROE requires identification, usually visual, before engaging. This ensures you don't attack a friendly aircraft, but it is very risky if the enemy aircraft isn't operating under the same ROE.

ROE for ground attack missions is even more restrictive. It's absolutely critical that the right weapon be used, the target correctly identified, and that the weapon delivery be extremely accurate. A mistake can cause collateral damage, which is a euphemism for destroying something you shouldn't or accidentally killing innocent people. The same principle applies to defending yourself, your family, or your home. It's critical to ask yourself these questions in advance:

- Does a potential attacker have to be armed for you to use lethal force?
- If they're not armed, will you use non-lethal force first?
- Does the attacker have to be inside your home?
- What is the risk of collateral damage to others?

WARNING

The walls in most homes are made of sheet rock. Unless a bullet hits a wood stud, it will go right through the wall, but not just one wall. Tests show that a 9mm pistol round can penetrate 12 sheets of sheet rock. That means it could go through six interior rooms, potentially hitting a family member. Buckshot fired from a

12-gauge shotgun is better, but not by much. It can easily pass through four walls, hitting someone three rooms away. Birdshot from a shotgun has the least penetration but can still pass through two walls.

Determining Your Rules of Engagement

It's important to determine in advance your personal rules of engagement by evaluating possible scenarios and how you want to respond. There are many consequences to the application of lethal force.

Dealing with retribution

Even beyond legal or moral considerations, killing or injuring someone who wasn't an imminent threat or was an innocent bystander has consequences that many don't consider. One that's often ignored is that the individual may have family or friends. History is full of stories like the "Hatfields and McCoys," where feuds escalated to small-scale warfare. This is particularly relevant when there is a reduction or suspension of law enforcement.

Considering legal consequences

This book is built on the tenet that these disasters, while potentially catastrophic, won't be permanent. That means everyone will eventually be called upon to justify their actions or face criminal or civil consequences. Finally, regardless of legal vindication, you will have to live with the decisions you make.

Determining strategy based on mindset

The key is to know what you will and will not do, so you can build your strategy around that knowledge. For example, if you are aware that your belief set prevents you from ever using deadly force, that's an important thing to know in advance. In that case, a gas-propelled stun gun or pepper spray may be the best option. They're effective at short range and don't cause permanent injury.

If you are willing to use lethal force to protect yourself or family, there are plenty of experts who will tell you when and how to use it, but they won't be there when the decision is required or have to deal with the consequences. Only you can decide what your threshold is. Consider as many scenarios as possible and make sure you completely understand your national and local laws regarding the use of any type of force for self-defense.

Evaluating Types of Firearms

If you decide to use a firearm, there are a large number of effective self-defense weapons available, with an equal number of opinions on which is the best. If you have a strong opinion, I won't try to change it. For everyone else, I'll provide a brief overview and share my experience.

Rifles and shotguns for home defense

Rifles and shotguns are primarily used for hunting. Depending on the caliber, rifles can be used for large or small game. Shotguns are used for bird hunting and sometimes for home defense.

Rifles

Due to their size, rifles take more time to access and are more difficult to wield inside a house. Another major drawback is that their high-velocity rounds easily pass through not just interior walls but also exterior walls and will still be very lethal to someone outside a house, like your neighbor.

Shotguns

Like rifles, shotguns are also cumbersome to use in close quarters, but when loaded with birdshot or small buckshot, they won't penetrate most exterior walls. As mentioned above, buckshot and even birdshot will penetrate interior walls. However, research has shown that shotguns carry a higher visceral intimidation factor compared to pistols due to their easily recognized appearance and the distinct sound they make when a round is chambered.

Handguns for home defense

Handguns are much easier to access and aim inside a house than a rifle or shotgun. They're also less likely to penetrate exterior walls.

Revolvers

Revolvers are the oldest and simplest type of handgun. They have few moving parts, making them very reliable with less maintenance. The downside is that they usually hold only five or six rounds and cannot be reloaded quickly.

Semiautomatic pistols

Pistols load their bullets from a magazine, which usually carries twice the rounds of a revolver, and an empty magazine can be quickly ejected and replaced. However, the rounds in the magazine use the momentum or the gas from the last fired round to load the next round. This more complicated process requires more moving parts to operate correctly, making semiautomatic pistols more susceptible to jamming or misfires. However, modern, high-quality semiautomatic pistols are now generally considered roughly as reliable as revolvers due to advancements in engineering and manufacturing.

As a Navy pilot, I carried a compact semiautomatic pistol in my survival vest. Ejecting from a damaged aircraft is a violent process with extreme G forces. During an ejection, a heavy pistol's weight can temporarily increase 30 times, ripping it out of the survival vest or injuring the pilot. Because of this, tactical pilots often choose a light, compact pistol that carries lots of rounds. It also needs to be rugged and reliable since ejecting out of an aircraft can drop you into the ocean with salt water or a desert with sand. These attributes: light weight, multiple rounds, and rugged reliability are also important for a defensive weapon that you may have to take with you.

Choosing a Home Defense and Bug-Out Bag Firearm

If you only have or want one firearm for home defense, a handgun is probably the best option. Again, there are hundreds of books and podcasts declaring the best handguns for every purpose. Below are two optional uses, but a single firearm can be used for both.

Home defense handgun

A popular choice for tactical pilots is a compact, polymer, 9mm pistol such as a Glock 19. It's relatively light, very reliable, and can hold 15 rounds. The 9mm ammunition is a reasonable self-defense round and a common caliber across the world. There are plenty of pistols in this category. The best choice depends on everything from your experience to the size of your hand. Do your research and try different firearms. I can't emphasize enough that any type of firearm requires training to be used effectively and safely.

WARNING

The other absolutely essential consideration for firearm ownership is safe storage, particularly if there are young or untrained individuals in your household. Without training and safe storage, you are more likely to experience a tragic disaster than survive one.

Bug-out bag handgun

There are many options for a light, multi-purpose firearm that could be added to a bug-out bag when it's time to evacuate. One of the primary considerations is weight.

A good example is the Kel-Tec PMR-30. It's an inexpensive, extremely lightweight, small-caliber pistol that uses a .22 Magnum round. What makes it unique is that it carries 30 rounds in the magazine, and fully loaded, it weighs less than an empty Glock 19.

Even with an extra loaded magazine (a total of 60 rounds), the PMR-30 weighs less than a loaded Glock with 15 rounds. The recoil on the pistol is very low, which helps not only with new shooters but also with accurate aiming for secondary shots. Equipped with an optical sight, it could even be used for small game hunting at very close range. The small .22-caliber Magnum round is not generally recommended for self-defense. However, this is countered in part by the Magnum's high velocity (therefore penetration) and the extremely large number of rounds. There are several pistols in this category, such as the Smith & Wesson M&P Magnum, which has a good reputation and carries the same 30 rounds.

TECHNICAL STUFF

Many gun experts will strongly disagree with a .22-Magnum as a defensive round. There's no doubt that a smaller caliber is less likely to be lethal. However, high penetration and multiple rounds have advantages. Even with bullseye shooters, when adrenaline flows, accuracy usually drops. Having double the capacity of a normal pistol without reloading could be important. Another characteristic of .22-Magnum pistols is that they're remarkably loud, often sounding like a much larger caliber weapon. When combined with the ability to fire many rounds rapidly, it can be useful for discouraging multiple adversaries.

WARNING

Early versions of some of these pistols had reliability issues. These can usually be fixed by the manufacturer or with aftermarket parts. However, it's important to do your research and get other opinions, particularly from unbiased reviews.

TIP

When possible, it's good to have weapons that use the same ammunition. For example, if you have a pistol that uses a .22 Magnum round, you might also want a .22-Magnum rifle so they can share ammunition.

Using Other Resources and Firearm Safety

There are many comprehensive books covering advanced techniques for self and home defense, including setting up security perimeters and alarms. This is beyond the scope of this book. Look for well-reviewed authors with a law enforcement or military combat background, such as Navy SEAL, Marine Recon, or Army Ranger.

WARNING

The number one cause of death by firearms in the U.S. is not homicide, it's suicide. For children through young adults, firearms are the leading cause of death, surpassing car crashes and drug overdoses. If you have children in your home, they must never have access to a firearm when you're not around. This also includes anyone in your home who might be facing psychological or emotional challenges.

Even if a child has been well trained in the use and safety of firearms, the young human brain is subject to impulsive behavior and hasn't yet developed the ability to withstand social stress or peer pressure (see the sidebar below). There are plenty of small gun safes, trigger locks, and other devices that use simple combinations or even fingerprints to allow fast access. If you have children or someone with psychological challenges in your home, the few additional seconds required to access your firearm in an emergency can prevent a tragic disaster.

DELAYED DEVELOPMENT OF RISK EVALUATION IN THE BRAIN

Research suggests that the risk versus consequence portion of the human brain takes many years to develop, particularly in males. Studies suggest this development doesn't stabilize in men until their mid-twenties. If you doubt that, look at auto insurance premiums. Insurance companies don't care about esoteric research papers; they just look at how much they have to pay for accidents and injuries. Not surprisingly, teenage through early twenties males cost them the most. In addition to totaling a car as a teenager, I did 100 night aircraft carrier landings before I was 25. Night carrier landings are like playing a video game where losing involves explosive death. Looking back, they're the stupidest thing I've ever done more than once. Clearly, there's a place for young, immature male brains in our society. Keep this in mind when considering the storage, use, and safety of any lethal device.

IN THIS CHAPTER

» Doing it yourself

» Preparing for failure

» Troubleshooting problems

Chapter 15
Fixing Stuff

Leveraging home technology is wonderful . . . when it works. However, sometimes Murphy's Law applies, meaning everything that can go wrong will. This chapter isn't going to try to turn you into a mechanic, carpenter, plumber, or electrician. There are plenty of excellent books, classes, and courses that can help if that's of interest. Instead, this chapter will try to identify the critical devices that are important for disaster situations, their most likely failure modes, and what spare parts should be stocked. It will also highlight basic troubleshooting and repair strategies.

Doing It Yourself (DIY) Repair Mindset

Many of you are DIYers from way back. On the other hand, some of you think that you have little or no mechanical aptitude. That's ok. As an engineer, it's often assumed that I should be able to fix anything. I enjoy some DIY projects and repairs, but I've also broken a lot of stuff trying to fix it. University education rarely correlates with DIY ability. That ability comes from learning from others and attempting to build or fix stuff yourself.

If you've never tried a DIY project but would like to, go for it. You may want to hold off on that house remodel and start with something simple, like cleaning out a clothes dryer vent or taking apart something that's clearly unrepairable and can be cheaply replaced. Take it apart anyway. Every once in a while, you might be able to fix it, but that's not the point. Since you're going to replace it anyway, you don't have to worry about damaging it while taking it apart.

In the process, you may learn how it can be disassembled, how it works, and sometimes how it might fail. However, if you'd rather have a root canal than attempt a DIY project, that's ok, too. What follows are basic steps you can take to help avoid critical failures and, in an emergency, attempt to troubleshoot them.

Preparing for Failure

It's not a question of *if* things in your home or vehicle will fail; it's only a question of *when*. You can't prevent breakdowns, but you can be better prepared to fix or replace the most critical items.

Avoiding single-point failures

Single-point failures are when a small failure causes a major problem or cascades into multiple problems. A simple example might be a clogged fuel filter on your generator or a bad extension cord that connects your generator to everything in your house. These types of failure often require nothing more than a backup part, like a spare fuel filter or an extra extension cord.

The key is to think through each of your critical items, from cell phones and chargers to fuel cans and filters. Walk around your home and take notes. What things have you had to repair? What items, if they broke or failed, would cause a much bigger problem? Here are some example items for which you might want to have a spare or backup part:

- Extension cords
- Automobile jumper cables or a jumper battery (Chapter 12)
- Extra water hose (sterile RV)
- Phone chargers and cables
- Extra five-gallon (20-liter) buckets
- Batteries, batteries, batteries

This is just a start. You'll think of more items as you walk around and look at your home's critical infrastructure: power, water, and connectivity.

Stocking basic tools and supplies

Some basic tools and supplies are important for almost any repair, with or without an emergency. If you're a DIYer who believes "whoever dies with the most tools wins," your challenge isn't having enough tools; it's creating a small toolbox with ONLY the most important tools. This is for a portable toolbox small enough to take with you for an evacuation.

If, however, you've never attempted a DIY project or repair and don't intend to, it's still important to have basic tools on hand. Someone in your party or a neighbor may have repair abilities. There's a running joke among DIYers that you can fix almost anything with vice-grip pliers, WD-40, and duct tape; if it's stuck, spray it. If it's loose, clamp or tape it, as shown in Figure 15-1.

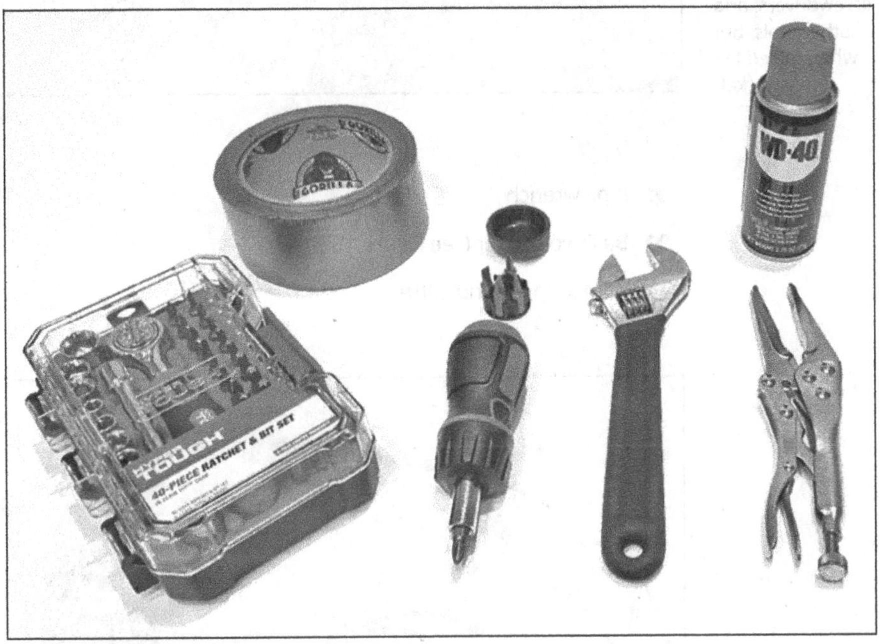

FIGURE 15-1: Key tools: WD-40, duct tape, vice grips, screwdriver set, small socket set, and a crescent wrench.

At the very least, have a multitool that you can carry with you or put in your bug-out bag, as shown in Figure 15-2.

In addition to these items, below are other basic tools that should be included in any household tool kit.

- Hammer
- Socket wrench set

FIGURE 15-2: Multitools have built-in pliers, knives, screwdrivers, and other tools, but when folded fits in a pocket.

Andrii/Adobe Stock Photos

- Pipe wrench
- Basic voltmeter (see Figure 15-3)
- Wire stripper and cutter

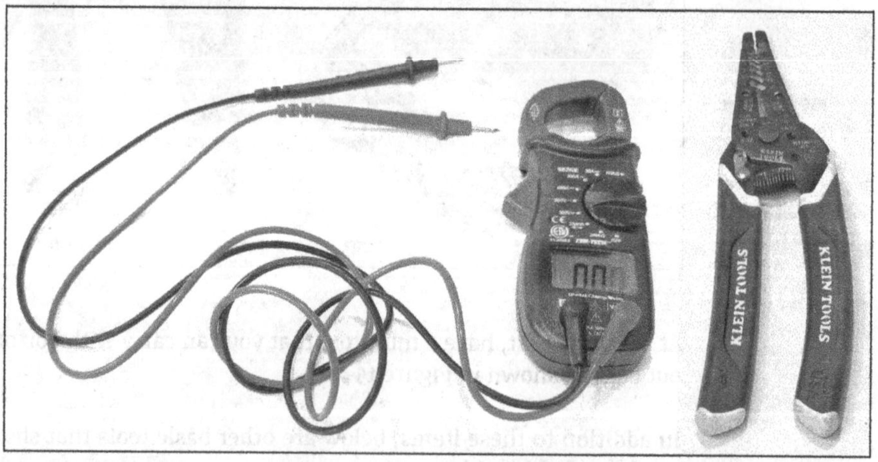

FIGURE 15-3: Volt meters for checking for live circuits, along with a wire stripper and cutter.

A simple voltmeter can help troubleshoot electrical problems and potentially prevent death by electrocution. They're easy to use, and you can test one out on your

household outlets. A basic tool kit should also include additional items that help seal, connect, or stick things together.

- Zip ties
- Electrical tape
- Waterproof caulk
- PVC pipe glue, construction adhesive, all-purpose glue, and superglue
- Fasteners: basic nails and screws

Stocking basic maintenance items

These include inexpensive items needed to maintain or service your critical equipment. For example, most gas-powered generators need their oil changed every 50 to 100 hours of running time. Normally, it's not something you need to think about except once a year, or maybe you have a service contract that takes care of it. However, during an extended power outage, if your generator runs continuously for four days, it will need servicing with oil, an oil filter, and possibly a spark plug. You'll also want to make sure you have a socket that fits the spark plug.

A battery charger for your automobile or generator battery is also important to have. For any air and water filtration systems covered in Chapters 5 and 6, you need replacement filters. Every home and location is a little different. Walk around your home and look at potential failure points, spare parts, or maintenance items.

Troubleshooting Problems

You don't have to be a mechanic, carpenter, plumber, or electrician, but knowing basic troubleshooting skills can come in handy.

Troubleshooting advice from The Greatest Generation

My grandfather gave me great advice I still use today. He was the first Chief Warrant Officer of the Navy Seabees, was at Pearl Harbor, and served throughout WWII. Despite an eighth-grade formal education, he went on to help design nuclear reactors and, after retiring, taught college engineering in Burma (now Myanmar) as part of the precursor to the Peace Corps.

Irving Langlois told me that when something doesn't work, always check the simplest thing first. It's often the most obvious thing that goes wrong, but even if it isn't, it's the easiest thing to check and helps narrow down the problem. Here's an example of how this might work with a gas generator that stops running.

1. **Did it run out of gas?** Yes? Add gas. No? Go to step 2.
2. **Check the oil level.** The automatic oil monitoring system may have shut it down. Yes? Add oil. No? Go to step 3.
3. **Did the carbon monoxide monitoring system detect too much carbon monoxide and shut it down?** Wait for the air to clear and attempt a restart. Did that work? Yes? Move the generator to a better-ventilated area. No? Go to step 4.
4. **If it has an electric starter, does it "turn over" when you press the starter?** No? Check the battery voltage with a voltmeter or battery charger and charge as needed. Sometimes, you can also start them manually with a pull cord.

TIP

After this, it gets a bit more technical, but there are still things that can be checked with minimal effort to narrow down the problem.

5. **When the engine is turning over but failing to start, do you smell gasoline in the exhaust?** Or if it runs on propane or natural gas, is there a sulfur or "rotten eggs" smell? No? If it's gasoline-powered, check the fuel lines and fuel filter to see if they're clogged. If it looks questionable, replace it.
6. **If you do smell gasoline (or whatever fuel it uses) in the exhaust, you know the problem probably isn't with the fuel system.** Remove the spark plug and see if it's fouled (dirty). If it is fouled, clean and replace it, or get a new one.
7. **If the spark plug looks ok, before reinserting it, reattach the spark plug wire to the top of the plug.** Put on an insulating glove (so you don't get a mild shock) and hold the bottom of the spark plug against an unpainted metal part of the engine. Hit the starter button or pull to start. Did you see the spark plug actually produce a spark?

There's a good chance that one of these steps may solve or at least identify the problem, but even if it doesn't, you've narrowed down the possible issues. The next step may be reaching out to a technical help hotline armed with information that can speed up the troubleshooting process. If there is no technical help hotline or you can't reach it due to the scale of the disaster, read on.

Troubleshooting with the Internet

What if a tech telephone line isn't available? No worries, you can often tap the knowledge of those who've fixed what you're facing. Assuming you applied what you learned in Chapter 11 and have a basic Internet connection on your phone or laptop, one of the best ways to figure out how to fix something can often be found online.

Starting with a basic Google or other AI search, ask as detailed a question as you can, identifying the brand, the model, and the problem. The AI algorithms will scan the Internet and can often offer a direct solution or find a related video by someone who had the same problem. You may be surprised at how much a search will turn up. DIY videos can sometimes identify your exact problem and a solution.

The reason Internet videos often help is that whatever went wrong with your device is statistically likely to be a common failure for these devices, and it's possible that someone else has already tackled it. I've watched and applied YouTube videos to fix everything from a washing machine to missing roof shingles, and from replacing a carburetor on an old lawn mower to a solid-state hard drive on a laptop.

Of course, it's possible that Internet access could be an issue, or you may just need very basic plumbing or electrical knowledge. Because of this, I encourage you to have printed references, too. Books can also make it easier to have the right page open in front of you rather than trying to pause a video on your phone. There are plenty of excellent books on everything from basic electrical wiring, plumbing, carpentry, and car repair. One good reference that covers many areas is *How to Fix Everything For Dummies*.

4 Evacuating

IN THIS PART . . .

Decide when and how to evacuate, where to go, and what to take with you

Determine the best emergency backup transportation

Identify the best liquid assets and how to store and protect them

Reduce financial disasters with additional streams of income

IN THIS CHAPTER

» Overcoming psychological barriers

» Determining where to go

» Building your bug-out bag

» Considering RVs for evacuation

Chapter 16

Evacuating When You Can't Stay Home

Unfortunately, there are situations where staying in your home during or after a disaster isn't an option. The next four sections of this chapter cover immediate escape plans, when to evacuate, where to go, and what to take with you.

Planning an Immediate Escape

It's impossible to cover all the evacuation situations. The location you're evacuating from could be a single-level home, a multi-level apartment, a shopping mall, or a high-rise office. It's critical to think about the locations you frequent and plan escape strategies. Let's be honest: Hardly anyone pays attention to safety information. The last time I paid attention to an airline safety brief was when the Southwest flight attendant told us to feel free to exit through any large gaping hole ripped through the fuselage by the crash, or . . . use the clearly marked exits. It's also important to think past the escape to how and where you will reconnect with family members.

Determining an escape path

Choosing an escape path from your home, work, or wherever you happen to be in advance is critical. The example of a house fire, covered in Chapter 10, demonstrates the challenge of escaping your home at night with no lights and choking, obscuring smoke. Building codes require bedrooms in homes to have alternate exits, but that exit could be a window. You must have a plan with alternate exit strategies and then practice it with your family.

Consider different scenarios. You could be in a room where fire has engulfed the room on the other side of the exit door. Or an earthquake has caused debris or structural damage, blocking an exit. Or an active shooter is between you and the normal exit. At work, or in buildings you frequent, take a minute to look around and identify all the exit paths.

Identifying escape aids

Your plan should not only include escape paths but also escape aids. In Chapter 10, small cans of oxygen and a head-mounted flashlight were covered. These could make all the difference in your surviving a house fire. Placing carbon monoxide detectors and small fire extinguishers in each bedroom could also give you the extra seconds you need.

If your secondary escape path is through a window and that window isn't on the ground floor, an emergency rope ladder kept under your bed would be invaluable. If you work in a high-rise, it might be worth keeping a small flashlight and one of the little oxygen cans with you. The three-liter oxygen cans are the size of a small energy drink. If it's allowed at work, a small combination flashlight/stun gun kept in a desk drawer gives you options.

TIP

If you live or work on the upper floor of a multi-story building, remember that the stairwells are specifically designed to survive fires.

REMEMBER

Whether you live in a house or a high-rise, walk the escape paths, commit them to memory, and if you have a family, share and practice them regularly.

Determining When to Evacuate

For disasters that don't require immediate escape, the first and most important question is — should I stay, or should I go? If possible, it's safer to shelter in place. You have a roof over your head, tools, supplies, and you know the area. If your home is at risk of being damaged or destroyed, however, the answer is obvious. You must also consider whether your home or local area will become dangerous in the near future or if the area around it will become impassable. Then balance this against the risks involved in an evacuation. The key is to determine in advance under what circumstances you'll need to leave, your destination, and what you'll take with you so you can execute an evacuation quickly.

I happened to be driving between Texas and Tennessee in August of 2005. I wasn't paying attention to the weather and stupidly got caught in Hurricane Katrina's evacuation. I got to experience what a major evacuation really looks like. It means hundreds of miles of traffic jams, gas stations with no gas, empty shelves in grocery stores, and completely booked hotels in all the surrounding states. What should take hours can take days. Do you have the resources to survive while sitting on a highway for a day or more?

Evaluating the resources required to stay

Assuming your home will physically survive the disaster, the question becomes whether you have the resources to survive the disaster's duration. Chapters 6 through 9 cover the resources required, such as water, food, septic, and medical supplies. If you have enough resources, the next question is the long-term impact on your surrounding environment. Keep in mind that those around you who didn't evacuate may not have your resources and could become desperate. Depending on your location's geography, population density, economic level, and even social network, staying and even helping your neighbors could be reasonable or could be extremely dangerous.

Considering physical and medical factors

The decision to evacuate will also depend on your party's physical and medical condition. During most disasters, access to emergency services, including ambulances and hospitals, is often limited or nonexistent. This may be due to those facilities sustaining direct damage or simply being overloaded with casualties. If you or anyone in your party has limited mobility or a life-threatening medical condition, this should drive your evacuation decision.

Evacuating with uncertain disaster impact or duration

Finally, if the scale or duration of the disaster is hard to predict and you have reasonable transportation and a safe destination, evacuation is usually the best option. If the threat turns out to be less than anticipated, you can always return.

If, however, the scale or duration is worse than anticipated, you could end up in a life-threatening situation with no ability to escape.

Timing your evacuation

If you live in or near a major city and you've made the decision to evacuate, don't wait. Evacuating from a major metropolitan area could take days. The sooner you hit the road, the less likely you are to be caught up in massive traffic jams. This is why it's critical to have your evacuation plan ready to execute with your bug-out bag, documents, tool kit, and cash ready to go. You'll be out before the evacuation traffic jams begin, while others are still trying to find their birth certificates.

Deciding Where to Evacuate

Once you've decided under what circumstances you'll evacuate, it's critical to know where to go. The simplest, least expensive option is to identify a family member or friend that you can stay with who lives far enough away that a local disaster won't impact them. Or they're in a rural area that may be less impacted during a global disaster.

Staying with friends or family

The best way to broach the idea of staying with a friend or relative is to make it a mutually beneficial arrangement. They agree to host you in an emergency. Likewise, you agree to host them. This could be a parent, sibling, child, or grandchild. It could be an aunt, uncle, cousin, classmate, or close friend. It could even be an ex or mother-in-law . . . but that might just be trading catastrophes. One of my good friends used to work for the CIA. Our house was his "safe house." In the event of a dangerous situation connected to his work, he and his family would stay with us. Likewise, we knew we could stay with them in a similar emergency. Don't wait until the disaster to arrange this.

Choosing the best evacuation location

In a perfect world, you would like your host's location to be far enough away so that a local disaster won't impact them, but close enough that you can drive there on one tank of gas or electric charge. If you can't get there on one tank, it's better to have them further away.

Below are the criteria for the perfect location. This is similar to the checklist that will be used in the next section for choosing a place to park an RV or where to buy or build a survival retreat/vacation cabin. It's unlikely that you can find a place with all of these criteria, but it gives you a good target. You're looking for a location that fits as many of these as possible:

- **You want your evacuation location to be well outside large metropolitan areas and preferably away from major highways.** During an extended period with no utilities, city populations will evacuate in huge numbers.
- **You want this location to be about 100 miles (160 km) or further from your primary residence.** This is simply to improve the probability that the location isn't inside the footprint of any local disasters or mass evacuations. Further is usually better, but balance that against your ability to carry extra fuel in case gas stations or charging stations aren't available.
- **You want it to be away from areas prone to natural or human disasters: hurricanes, tornadoes, floods, landslides, earthquakes, volcanic eruptions, wildfires, or proximity to nuclear or industrial plants.** In other words, the South Pole.

Choosing your evacuation destination host

If you have more than one option for an evacuation destination, consider both the location and the potential host. The potential host doesn't have to share all your beliefs or political views, but they shouldn't have the attitude of a black hole. Can you coexist with your mother-in-law for an extended period, or she with you?

It's also beneficial if they have reasonable health and some useful skills, like winning on the TV series *Naked and Afraid.* Barring that, some DIY skills would be beneficial. A medical, military, or law enforcement background would be a big positive. If possible, it's also good to have more than one potential host in different locations in case one of them is also affected by the disaster.

Considering camping

You may picture yourself trekking through the forest wearing a bug-out bag backpack, but that's not the goal. Even if you're a SEAL, bugging out into the wild is a last resort. Unless you're already an avid camper or want to become one, trying to learn "camping" in an emergency is not recommended. You need both the equipment and experience. Camping in the open also leaves you exposed and is usually, at best, a short-term solution.

There are plenty of excellent books on survival camping if you're interested. It's best to try camping with a friend so you can learn from them; *Wilderness Survival For Dummies* is an excellent reference.

Choosing What to Take with You

When it's time to go, it's important to decide in advance what you need to take with you. This not only ensures you have the right stuff with you but also prevents wasting time debating about or searching for important items. The key is to decide in advance and keep those items in just a few easy-to-access locations.

Bugging out with a bug-out bag

An important preparation is what's often referred to as a bug-out bag. It's simply a bag filled with items that will be useful during an evacuation. However, this bag can also be a bug-in bag, simply a central repository for important items when sheltering in place.

Choosing the bag

A bug-out bag can be any bag that can hold basic emergency items, covered below, but small and light enough that it can be thrown in your car or carried, such as a backpack. If you have family members in your household who can carry a backpack, create a bug-out bag for them as well. This allows you to increase the resources required for multiple people without an excessively heavy bag for you, and, in addition to basic items, can include person-specific items like clothes, medications, or anything else they may need.

WARNING

If you have young children, make sure you carefully consider where you keep your bug-out bag. Some bug-out bag items could be dangerous for small children. You can also keep dangerous items in another location and add them when you evacuate.

Choosing the contents

Some items that will go into your bug-out bag you may already have, and the rest can be easily acquired (see Figure 16-1). You can also purchase pre-assembled bug-out bags, but the good ones are expensive. The less expensive ones may be a good place to start, but you will need to add to or upgrade their contents. Keep the bug-out bag in a central location, preferably one where you can quickly grab it on the way out the door.

FIGURE 16-1: A bug-out bag with many of the recommended items listed below.

Here's a list of important items to have in your bug-out bag.

- Local map and small compass
- Head-mounted flashlight
- Micro oxygen can (five-liter)
- N95 masks
- Water bottles (minimum 1 liter/person)
- Folding plastic water bag
- Portable filter straw (Chapter 6)
- First aid kit with first aid book (Chapter 9)
- Antiseptic wipes
- Toilet paper
- Foil space blanket
- Pepper spray (Chapter 13)
- Camping/survival knife

- Basic hygiene items (soap, toothpaste, deodorant)
- Extra underwear and socks
- Duct tape
- Lighter
- Heavy-duty nitril gloves and work gloves
- Multitool (Chapter 15)
- Zip ties
- Large plastic garbage bags
- Waterproof bag for important documents
- Small waterproof tacklebox for medications and supplements
- Rechargeable LED flashlight with spare batteries
- Solar-powered or hand-crank radio with flashlight
- Faraday bag for electronics

TIP

Check your bug-out bag at least twice a year. Replace batteries and check and replace out-of-date supplies such as medications.

Identifying additional important items

There are additional items that you may want to keep separately and then bring or add to the bug-out bag before evacuating.

Clothing

Be sure you have appropriate clothing ready to go. Since it's season-dependent, you don't have to keep it in your bug-out bag, but you want it identified and nearby. This includes good quality shoes or boots in case you need to be on foot. It should include rain gear and a season-appropriate head covering, such as a beanie or baseball cap.

Documents

Keep important documents in one place, such as a file folder or a drawer with a waterproof holder nearby, so that in an evacuation, you can grab them quickly. Some transactions require original documents such as birth certificates. For other documents, a photograph on your phone may be sufficient. However, it's still important to have paper copies as a backup in case your phone or computer is lost or damaged. Common documents include the following, but depending on your situation and country, there will be other important documents.

- Passport
- Birth certificates
- Medical information to include required medications or treatment
- Health insurance information
- Titles for automobiles, homes, or other significant property
- Automotive registration
- Insurance information
- Bank and investment accounts
- Social Security information

Electronics

Keep the following electronics within easy reach, and if you're not using or charging them, you can keep them in a Faraday bag.

- Laptop and/or thumb drive with critical files
- Small lithium power bank (with solar cells)
- Handheld radios
- Stun gun/flashlight

Additional items for your vehicle

Consider the following items to keep in your vehicle as covered in Chapter 17:

- Jumper cables and a lithium-ion battery pack starter (see Figure 12-3)
- Can of tire sealant/inflator and a 12-volt tire pump
- Fire extinguisher
- Blanket
- Basic tool kit
- Hatchet and foldable shovel
- Portable toilet (optional)

Your data

If you have a desktop computer, make sure you regularly back up critical files on a USB thumb drive or a portable hard drive that you can take with you. Even if you have a laptop, it's important to regularly back up important files to portable media. You want to be able to stick the thumb drive or portable hard drive in your pocket or bug-out bag in case your laptop is damaged or lost. You also want to bring your laptop or tablet with both a household power supply and a 12-volt car power supply.

TIP

Most survival situations involve short periods of intense action followed by hours of boredom. With limited power and connectivity, scrolling through social media or watching streamed shows may not be an option. An e-reader, covered in Chapter 11, can hold a library's worth of books and even games. It's light and can last a couple of weeks on a charge. Add a pack of cards, which requires no power and provides unlimited card games.

Considering a Recreational Vehicle for Evacuation

If you have any type of recreational vehicle, from a camper trailer to a diesel-powered luxury motorcoach, you have additional options for evacuation.

There are three primary strategies for using an RV. As covered, the first option is to identify a family member or friend you can stay with during the disaster. If you have an RV, you can evacuate with it and simply use your host's location, power, and water. This reduces the impact on everyone. The second option is to take your RV to a commercial location that can provide power and water. The third option is to take your RV to a property that you own. This will be covered in Chapter 21.

The first option, identifying a family member or friend to stay with, is not only the simplest option but should be set up regardless, because your RV might not be available, not functioning, or unable to make the trip. If you have a commercial location or even a property that you own, there's the possibility that the disaster will also impact it. With an RV, the most important step is identifying a safe destination in advance.

IN THIS CHAPTER

» Identifying basic backup transportation

» Considering pre-1973 vehicles

Chapter 17

Traveling during a Disaster

It's important to consider backup transportation options when the power grid is down for an extended period, and fuel may be in short supply or unavailable.

Evaluating Transportation Options (Level 1)

Under Level 1 preparation, your options are very budget-limited and consist primarily of whatever means of transport you currently own and a bicycle.

Owning a multispeed bike

You don't see the hero escaping on a bicycle in disaster movies, but they do have advantages. A human on a multispeed bicycle is the most efficient transportation device in the world. They're more efficient than any other vehicle or any animal for distance covered per energy expended, and it's estimated that 90 percent of those in the U.S., Europe, and Asia know how to ride a bike. If you already have one, great. If you don't, an inexpensive multispeed mountain bike is a good choice. If you need to get to a nearby store, a bike can handle rough terrain and slip around damaged or blocked roads. They're quiet and can outrun anyone on foot.

Mountain bikes are simple and reliable; their only Achilles heel is their tires. It's important to have spare tires or inner tubes and a patch kit. Clearly, the dual benefit of a bike is exercise and adventure. Although multispeed bikes are the most reliable, efficient transportation, they only work for short distances in reasonable weather. For severe weather or evacuation at any distance, we're back to automobiles. For the dedicated urbanites, I'm afraid Uber won't hack it in a disaster.

Using your current vehicle

Chapter 23 covers important vehicle characteristics for disaster preparation and evacuation. In this section, the low or no-cost approach is to use whatever car, truck, SUV, or motorcycle you're currently driving. The primary focus is reliability, which means making sure your vehicle is properly serviced.

According to the AAA (American Automobile Association), the most common automobile failures likely to strand a vehicle are dead batteries, flat tires, and coolant issues. What's often missed is checking tire pressures and fluid levels, including the water level in the battery and the pressure in the spare tire if it has one.

Even with good maintenance, standard lead-acid batteries don't usually last longer than three or four years. They should have a date sticker on them so you can estimate if it will survive the next winter. All tires lose pressure over time. If your car has a spare tire, make sure it's inflated to the correct pressure. Spacesaver spare tires require much higher pressure and therefore lose air faster.

Automobile accessories

Many new cars no longer come with a spare tire. There are three options — the first of which should be done by everyone:

- Buy a couple of cans of tire repair sealant such as Fix-a-Flat. Using tire sealant is a temporary fix and only works for small punctures. The tire must eventually be repaired, but this can often get you to your destination or a tire repair shop.
- The next option is to buy a basic spare tire that fits your car, along with a tire jack. You can either carry the spare in the car all the time or just when you go on road trips or evacuate.

» The last option is to upgrade to run-flat tires. These tires can run up to 50 mph (80 kph) with a golf ball–sized hole in them, but they're very expensive, and usually have a harsher ride and shorter life.

Every car should also have

» 12-volt tire pump
» Fire extinguisher
» Jumper cables
» Blanket
» Basic tool kit that includes
  - Duct tape
  - Vice grips
  - Screwdriver with multiple heads
  - Basic socket set, as covered in Chapter 15
» A self-contained battery pack that can jump-start your car and recharge your phones (see Chapter 13)

Backup fuel

For gasoline or diesel-powered cars, recommend having a couple of five-gallon (20-liter), Department of Transportation (DOT)-approved, plastic gas containers. If you keep them filled with gas, don't keep them in your car until you actually have to evacuate. If you have a garage or a shed outside, you can keep it there if it's safe to do so and allowed. Before doing that, check both safe practices for storing fuel as well as local regulations. These include considerations such as approved containers, proximity to ignition sources, and so on. You want to prepare for wildfires, not initiate them.

WARNING

As covered in Chapter 12, gasoline starts breaking down after three months of storage. Diesel fuel is good for six months. When fuels oxidize and start breaking down, they turn into gums and varnish that can clog your engine's fuel system. If you use gas regularly for lawn care or other purposes, you'll be constantly replacing it, and it will stay fresh. If not, you can delay the breakdown by using high-octane gas.

Gasoline with a 93-octane rating or higher will last about nine months before breaking down. The best strategy is to just pour the gas into your vehicle's tank every month or two and refill the containers. You can also add a fuel stabilizer such as Sta-Bil to the stored gas. This is an inexpensive additive that will keep the gas from breaking down for another year. Combined with high-octane gasoline or diesel, it should allow over 18 months, but never store gasoline or diesel longer than two years, even with stabilizers.

What if you live in a condo or apartment complex that doesn't allow storing combustibles like gasoline? Some gas substitutes are considered safe and can be stored in a car or home. However, they're very expensive, usually require the engine to be warm, and have spotty reviews. I don't recommend gasoline alternatives unless you have no other option.

Keeping a couple of empty five-gallon (20-liter) gas containers in your car may be the best option. You can quickly fill them up if you have advanced warning. Or, as you evacuate, stop at the nearest gas station and fill up before fuel becomes scarce or power at the pumps fails.

Evaluating Transportation Options (Level 2)

Cars, SUVs, and trucks will be evaluated in Chapter 23 as Level 3 options, but at the Level 2 moderate upgrade level, we're still working with your existing vehicle. However, you can add some powered backup options.

If you live in an urban or even suburban environment and you want a backup to your primary vehicle, an electric bike may be an option. Small and weighing around 50 pounds (23 kg), they can be kept indoors. This is particularly useful if you live in an apartment or condo complex. They have limited range and speed and can usually only carry one person, but as long as you have a way to charge them, they're great for short trips.

Electric bikes can also be pedaled when you run out of power, and some can fold to fit in the trunk of a car. With an electric range of 20–30 miles, they cost less than $1,000. As for dual use, electric bikes are a blast to ride. Rent one and try it. The electric bikes, particularly the folding ones (see Figure 17-1), can also be taken on driving vacations or weekend trips for both urban and rural environments.

A step up from electric bikes in range and speed are 150cc scooters (see Figure 17-2). They're still relatively cheap (some can be purchased for about $1,500). They can carry two people in a pinch and run 60 mph (100 kph) while getting about 70 mpg (3.36 L/100 km). What they give up in speed, they make up for in efficiency and maneuverability. Scooters can thread through almost any traffic jam. With their

2-gallon (8-liter) tank, they have a range of about 130 miles (210 km), but add a couple of 2-gallon gas containers on the back, and the range is extended to more than 400 miles (~650 km).

FIGURE 17-1: Folding electric bike.

demidoff/Shutterstock

FIGURE 17-2: 150cc two-person scooter.

nosorogua/Adobe Stock Photos

Considering pre-1980 vehicles

Some survival books recommend owning a car built before 1980 because they don't have electronic ignitions or fuel injection systems and are relatively immune to a nuclear weapon's EMP. They're also simpler and easier to work on than modern cars. In my younger years, all I could afford were cars of that era. I can confirm that they are simpler to work on and repair because I remember having to work on mine . . . a lot. *Consumer Reports* suggests that the most unreliable car built today is much more reliable than the most reliable car of the 1970s. Cars from the 1970s also required extensive maintenance: transmission fluid replacement, chassis and suspension lubrication, shock absorbers, mufflers, spark plugs, and distributor points . . . and that was when they were new. We're talking about 50-year-old cars.

With that said, if you love classic cars, can afford one, are mechanically inclined, and enjoy working on them, it could be a great idea. Since many popular classic cars have appreciated more than the stock market over the past 20 years, they could also be a good investment. This fits well into our multi-use strategy.

However, if you're not into classic cars or mechanically inclined, I'd stick with a regular car. If a nuclear EMP is a concern, some devices can be wired into a car's electrical system that can help protect it from EMP-induced power surges. These devices aren't guaranteed to prevent damage from a severe EMP event, but they are the best option short of parking your car in a Faraday modified garage, mentioned in Chapter 22. The problem with the pre-1980 cars, as I remember them, is that they really didn't need an EMP event to stop working.

IN THIS CHAPTER

» Stashing emergency cash

» Diversifying assets

» Expanding sources of income

Chapter 18 Funding during a Disaster

Any disaster covered in this book can create the need for immediate funds, and some disasters can put your digital assets at risk. There are also social, economic, and personal events that can cause financial issues. This chapter focuses on protecting and diversifying assets.

There are two funding priorities during disasters:

- The first and most immediate priority is to have enough cash to evacuate when the power grid (and therefore the digital economy) is down. This applies even if you're able to stay in your home. You want enough cash to purchase basic food and supplies when credit/debit cards aren't working.
- The second priority is protecting the rest of your financial assets that are held elsewhere. The vast majority of U.S. citizens keep most of their money in financial institutions. These consist primarily of bank and investment accounts.

Maintaining Cash for Emergencies (Level 1)

When power is lost, credit and debit cards can't be processed, and checks can't be cashed (if you're Gen-Z, ask your parents what a check is). Old-fashioned cash will be king. Some will argue that even cash will be at risk in a major disaster. That's absolutely true if the disaster is a national economic collapse or a disaster of extreme scale and duration, but in the near-term, cash's relative rarity will increase its value. Unfortunately, ATMs won't work, and banks will be closed. That means it's critical to have a stash of cash on hand.

WARNING

Before proceeding, I need to make a disclaimer here: I am not a financial advisor, nor have I married one. The following ideas are for protecting existing assets and are not in any way intended as investment advice.

Stashing cash

Surveys suggest that most Americans carry less than $50 in cash in their wallets or purses. The amount of cash you should have immediately available depends on many factors, including how much you can afford, but at a minimum, you want enough cash for gas to get to a safe location. You would also like to have enough to cover a hotel and food. If you're able to stay in your home, you want enough cash to buy basic groceries for another week beyond your stocked pantry from Chapter 7. Even if you are able to stay at home, it's important to have enough cash to evacuate if the situation changes.

Hiding cash from yourself

A common challenge is how to keep emergency cash and not use it. One trick is to keep a $100 bill or two (or similar large denomination in your currency) in your wallet or purse and forget about them. In a world of debit and credit cards, a large denomination bill is inconvenient to use and might reduce the chance you'll spend it. Depending on your personality, however, just keeping a large denomination bill in your wallet or purse might not work. If you find yourself using it on a regular basis, try the tip below.

TIP

Fold the large denomination bill so that it's a quarter of its original size or smaller. Wrap a small piece of paper around it, big enough to cover it. Now, take clear packing tape and wrap it around the paper with the bill inside. Trim it with a scissor so you can slip it into a deep recess of your wallet or purse. This requires you to cut the tape open, making it awkward enough that you won't use it except in a genuine emergency. Another benefit is that someone watching you open your wallet or purse won't see a large denomination bill.

Having Enough Liquid Assets for an Extended Disaster (Level 2)

Beyond immediate cash, it's important to protect and ensure sufficient assets for longer-duration events, including natural, human-made, and personal disasters.

Stashing more cash

In addition to a large denomination bill in your wallet or purse, it's important to stash cash in a hidden spot in your home. In this case, you want to stash smaller denomination bills because whoever you're buying from may not be able to make change. It's also not a bad idea to have a small stash in your car in case you can't get back to your home. There are many good places to hide money in your home or car. If I suggest places to hide your money in this book, however, they won't be good places to hide it anymore.

TIP

When choosing a place to stash cash, here are some considerations. The location should be one that a burglar wouldn't think of, but allows easy access in an emergency. It should also be a place you won't forget. There are several decoy objects, like hollow books, that you can buy online, but keep in mind that burglars have been to these websites, too. If you use your imagination, you can come up with equally good or better locations.

Spreading assets across multiple financial institutions

The next strategy is the classic, "don't put all your eggs in one basket." In the U.S., 96 percent of households keep some or all of their savings and investments in financial institutions. This includes everything from banks to brokerage firms. Up to $250,000 of the accounts in a U.S. bank are insured by the Federal Deposit Insurance Corporation (FDIC). This means that if the bank is attacked, loses your money, or fails, the federal government will replace the amount lost up to $250,000. This applies to checking and savings accounts, bank money market accounts, and certificates of deposit (CDs).

WARNING

FDIC insurance doesn't apply to most investment accounts, and the insurance is per bank, not per account. With multiple accounts totaling more than $250,000 in one bank, the FDIC will only cover the first $250,000. If you have more than that, spread it into multiple banks.

Regardless of the amount, you still don't want all your eggs in one bank. Most financial experts recommend spreading your savings and investments across at least three financial institutions. In the event of a cyberattack or fraud, it's unlikely that all of your accounts will be targeted at the same time. Even if your money is insured, it will be tied up for quite a while during the investigation. By the way, having accounts in multiple financial institutions is pointless if you use the same password.

Diversifying liquid assets

For the purposes of this book, it's assumed that the disaster won't result in the permanent collapse of civilization, but there are scenarios where paper currency can devalue rapidly. Hyperinflation has affected many countries in the past, and a disaster on a national scale, from volcanoes to sanctions, could certainly tank an economy. You'll want to have some assets that don't depend on the health of a nation or government.

Precious metal coins

Most people's top replacement for currency is something that's held value across the globe for thousands of years — gold and silver. Although precious metals aren't usually considered a liquid asset, precious metal coins are. Technically, they're currency, but their value lies in their precious metal content; for rare coins, it's in their value as collectibles. Their liquidity lies in their easy identification and standardized sizes. Because of this, having some of your assets in the form of precious metal coins can provide additional security. Even if they're never needed, they can provide peace of mind.

From a disaster preparation perspective, precious metal coins have pros and cons.

Pros:

- Most gold coins are easy to identify and hard to counterfeit.
- They come in standardized sizes, which are easier to value.
- They're compact for their value and therefore easy to stash and transport.
- Their value tends to be stable during inflation, uncertainty, or disasters.
- They're impossible to hack.

Cons:

- Walmart probably won't accept them as payment.
- Their high value also makes them impractical for small purchases.
- Although unhackable, their small size makes them easy to steal or lose.
- Precious metals are a commodity, and their value can (and does) go up and down with markets.

Cryptocurrency

One of the most talked about disaster alternatives to cash is cryptocurrency. When I first heard about Bitcoin many years ago, I thought it was the dumbest thing ever. It had no intrinsic value, nothing backing it, and was extremely volatile. To me, it looked like a giant cyber Ponzi scheme.

Sixteen years later, Bitcoin still remains controversial, but it's now the world's fifth-largest asset with a market capitalization of about $2.3 trillion, and more than 1 percent of the world's population holds some Bitcoin. Bitcoin still has no intrinsic value and isn't backed by gold or any other hard asset, but to be fair, the U.S. dollar also has no intrinsic value, nor is it backed by gold or anything else.

I mention Bitcoin here because it's now used extensively in many countries to preserve personal savings, particularly in nations with severe economic issues, such as currency devaluation or hyperinflation. Much of what follows applies to all cryptocurrencies, but I'll only use Bitcoin as the example since it was the first, has the greatest market capitalization, and is considered the "gold" standard for cryptocurrency.

TECHNICAL STUFF

Bitcoin is very unusual in that it is a decentralized system, operating without an administrator or central authority. Anyone can create a transaction without needing a company or government, and the transaction doesn't require personal information for ownership. Ownership is represented solely with a public and private key. This is done through a specialized distributed ledger called a *blockchain* that records every Bitcoin transaction. Thousands of blockchain *nodes* (computers) validate the transactions every ten minutes. The ledger is refreshed and rebroadcast, permanently embedding your transaction into every transaction after that. That means every Bitcoin transaction after yours will carry a permanent record in the ledger (blockchain). Unless every hard drive, thumb drive, or other storage media with any Bitcoin transaction made after yours is erased, there will always be a permanent record of your Bitcoin ownership. The Bitcoin blockchain and algorithm have never been successfully hacked, and unlike governments that can print money as needed, reducing its value, Bitcoin is permanently capped at 21 million "coins."

When you buy Bitcoin, your transaction has a public and private key (password). You can download this to your computer, thumb drive, or write it on a piece of paper. However, this means that if you lose your private key (password), there is no way to ever recover your Bitcoin because ownership is tied to the key, not to you.

Another option is to use a brokerage service to hold your Bitcoin (they keep your private key). The price of this convenience is that, like any bank or financial institution, your private key could potentially be hacked. Below are pros and cons, but you can also read *Cryptocurrency For Dummies*.

REMEMBER

As with precious metal coins, Bitcoin is only being considered here as a way to diversify liquid assets for disaster preparation, not for investment.

Here are some pros and cons of using Bitcoin to diversify your liquid assets for disaster preparation:

Pros:

- Unlike national currencies, Bitcoin isn't directly impacted by local disasters such as war, sanctions, currency devaluation, or hyperinflation.
- It's very portable. Your private key can be stored digitally on a laptop, phone, thumb drive, e-reader, or a piece of paper.
- The blockchain algorithm and crypto encoding have made Bitcoin impossible to hack so far.
- Although its price is volatile, Bitcoin's limit on the number of coins that can ever exist has helped retain its value.

Cons:

- Transactions, such as using it to purchase things, require Internet access.
- If you lose your key, you lose your asset with no way to recover it.
- If held by a brokerage service, your account can be recovered, but it can also be hacked, as with any financial account.
- Like precious metals, Bitcoin's market value can and does go up and down with markets and is much more volatile than precious metals.

TECHNICAL STUFF

Some have suggested that future advances in quantum computing may make it possible to hack Bitcoin's blockchain. While this is true, it would apply to every type of encryption. In other words, if quantum computing can hack Bitcoin, it can also hack all banks, satellite systems, and nuclear launch codes. Cryptocurrency would be the least of your worries.

Considering Non-Liquid Assets

Non-liquid assets include almost anything of value that can't be quickly converted into cash, such as real estate, jewelry, and collectibles. Because it's impractical to pay for groceries with a diamond ring, the focus has been on liquid assets.

However, there is an exception. Easily bartered items can often be more valuable than cash during a disaster. Instead of looking for things that you believe might have good trade value, just stock extra supplies of items you know you need. If you need them, others will, too. These include food, batteries, toilet paper, medical supplies, and even electrical power from your generator. And yes . . . liquor can also be a non-liquid, liquid asset.

Two things that separate those who live paycheck to paycheck from those who are financially independent are having more than one stream of income and being able to make money while sleeping. The next section examines strategies to move in that direction.

Expanding Sources of Income

There are four reasons evaluating alternative income sources is relevant to disaster preparation.

- Of all the potential disasters you might face, a personal financial crisis during your lifetime is one of the most likely. This is often caused by circumstances beyond your control, such as an illness, injury, or kids.
- Catastrophic local disasters often result in loss of businesses and employment in that region. Another stream of income can smooth the transition to a new job or business.
- Artificial Intelligence is already replacing many jobs, and the addition of humanoid robots will dramatically accelerate this process. Having another source of income can help insulate you from these impacts.

» Part 5 of this book covers Level 3 preparation, which includes investing in systems to become independent of municipal power and water. Achieving financial independence makes this easier and gives you more options.

Preparing for events that might happen to you

You will often hear people say that they have a good job. The error in this statement is the "they have" part. The job isn't theirs. It's owned and filled by someone else. No matter what level an employee is, the position is always temporary. Even founding CEOs can be replaced by their board. Having your own business means that during hard economic times, you'll be the last person you'll fire.

U.S. tax returns document that more than 10 percent of the population owns a business. It's estimated, however, that closer to a third of the population actually has some type of side income in addition to their job. This can be anything from growing pumpkins to rental income or podcasts.

Preparing for events that might happen to everyone

The world is changing faster now than at any time in history. Even if the rapid growth of Artificial Intelligence results in a Golden Age of unlimited resources, the transition will be chaotic. This applies whether you're a factory worker, computer programmer, stockbroker, or surgeon. All these professions will eventually be impacted, but there are areas that will be difficult for AI to dominate.

AI-resistant vocations

The godfather of artificial intelligence, Dr. Geoffrey Hinton, was asked in a recent interview what fields people should focus on in a world where AI becomes dominant. Surprisingly, he identified skilled professions that involve the installation, troubleshooting, or repair of systems such as plumbing, electrical, mechanical, and carpentry. He pointed out that these areas require an extremely high level of experienced-based knowledge, problem-solving, and dexterity that will be difficult for AI and humanoid robots to master.

AI-resistant skills

The second area that AI will struggle with and probably shouldn't be allowed to dominate is occupations that deal directly and intimately with human behavior.

This includes leading and motivating people, as well as providing high-level training and psychological treatment to people. The keyword is "people." Most people will not want to be led, motivated, trained, or personally treated by something that doesn't have human empathy. The most important skills for the future aren't technical skills but soft or human skills. If you can learn how to understand people, you will always be relevant and in demand. A simple book to start the process is Dale Carnegie's classic *How to Win Friends and Influence People.*

Developing secondary incomes

I was fortunate to have an exceptional business mentor, who often said, "Dig the well before you're thirsty."

Defining a goal

Despite all the logical reasons for creating another source of income, most people will never get started. Human motivation comes more from emotion than logic. Instead of just having a "theoretical" nightmare to be avoided, it's critical to have a positive goal to be achieved. My business mentor emphasized having a compelling and powerful reason above everything else. He said you can learn all that you need to succeed, but without a concrete goal that puts a smile on your face or gives you a shot of adrenaline, you'll never start.

A great exercise is to write down everything you've always wanted to have, do, or achieve before you die. Don't prioritize it yet, and don't evaluate whether it's logical or feasible. At this stage, it doesn't matter if it violates the laws of physics. Just write it down. It can be anything from visiting the pyramids to becoming a rock star, or it could simply be achieving a lifestyle that allows you to do whatever you want without financial limitations. When you run out of ideas, then, and only then, circle the top few. These are the ones that make you smile or excite you. Ask yourself if any of these are truly important and if they're likely on your current path?

REMEMBER

My business mentor was advising a 60-year-old woman who said her dream was to become a doctor, but that it was too late for her. He simply asked her how long it would take to get through medical school. She said about six years. He asked her how old she would be in six years if she didn't become a doctor. She went to medical school.

Once you've identified a goal or dream, you can figure out what it will cost to achieve it. Most people do this backwards. They put their plan in concrete and their goal in sand. They choose a business and then see what it will give them. Before you can choose a business model or asset, you must first ask yourself whether it will produce sufficient income to achieve your goal. This will narrow down the options.

Finding a mentor

I believe one of the most important factors when choosing a business or asset is whether you can find a mentor to help you. A mentor who has already achieved what you're trying to do is worth their weight in gold. They can save you tens of thousands of dollars and years of effort by sharing what they did right and what they did wrong. If you have to cross a minefield, you want to follow in the footsteps of someone who made it across . . . and has big feet. The caveat is that they must have already achieved the level of success or income that you want, and you must be willing to be a student again.

Choosing a business model or asset

My definition of financial independence is being able to live comfortably without having to report to a job or a self-employed business every day. Achieving this requires a business or an asset that can generate income while you're sleeping.

The book *Rich Dad, Poor Dad* by Robert Kiyosaki is the bestselling personal finance book in history and does a great job of explaining how financial independence can be achieved. Kiyosaki uses a concept he developed called the cashflow quadrant, which he highlights in his second book, *Cashflow Quadrant: Guide to Financial Freedom*. The details of this are beyond the scope of this book, but it can be summarized with, "Instead of hauling buckets every day, build a pipeline that continues to work when you don't want to or can't."

Aside from investments such as stocks and bonds, below are examples of businesses and assets that can produce ongoing or passive income, but there are many other possibilities:

- Royalties from books, music, movies, or art.
- Creating and patenting something that produces income or royalties.
- Having income-producing real estate, as mentioned in Chapters 21 and 22.
- Taking a self-employed business and turning it into a franchise.
- Choosing a successful network marketing business with a multi-decade track record that emphasizes mentorship.
- A future business model might be buying robot taxis or humanoid robots to rent or lease.

5 Next Level Disaster Preparation

IN THIS PART . . .

Develop Level 3 independence from municipal infrastructure

Replace municipal water with a well, surface water, rain catchment, or atmospheric water

Power your home permanently without the power grid by using solar, wind, or water power

Find the best survival retreat/vacation/short-term rental location for an RV or cabin

Explore designs for off-grid survival/vacation/short-term rentals and RVs

Identify the best disaster vehicle/daily driver for your location and family

Learn how global disasters might unfold and how some of them can be prevented

IN THIS CHAPTER

» Considering a water well

» Evaluating rainwater catchment

» Using lake, river, or ocean water

» Generating water from thin air

Chapter 19

Developing Independence from Municipal Water

The chapters in this part expand preparation to Level 3, the goal of which is to move toward permanent independence from municipal infrastructure, including power and water. This usually requires significant investment, which may seem beyond a *For Dummies* book. However, if you are or will be in the market for a new home, vehicle, or RV in the future, you may want to consider prioritizing some of these features.

Disaster preparation aside, some of these concepts, such as solar panels, can have a good long-term return on investment. Even if your current plans or financial resources don't support these ideas today, they might be possible in the future and could represent long-term goals. For example, an RV or vacation cabin could be purchased, built, or upgraded to operate off-grid, and then used for short-term rental, offsetting the cost.

The Level 1 and 2 preparation strategies in Parts 2 and 3 of this book helped you create longer-term but temporary sources of water. This chapter explores strategies to replace municipal water permanently. Some of these options are location-dependent, but regardless of where you live, one of these strategies will allow either complete independence from municipal water or at least an almost indefinite supply of drinking water. If you already have a water well, you can skip this chapter. However, if you have an RV or a vacation cabin, or are considering one, this chapter may still be useful.

Drilling a Well

If you want to wean yourself off municipal water, the most straightforward solution is to drill a water well. This is definitely location-dependent and not available for everyone. In most cases, you will have to live in a rural area or a suburban area that allows water wells.

Additionally, not all geographic areas have access to suitable groundwater. We live on an ocean beach in Texas, where we're more likely to strike oil than water. You must also ensure that you aren't in an area where the groundwater is contaminated by industrial or farm runoff. Estimated costs are covered, but here are some pros and cons first.

Advantages

- Independence from municipal water and no water utility bill.
- Not subject to water restrictions during droughts or with municipal capacity issues.
- Your water won't contain disinfection chemicals like chlorine.
- Water quality is often superior with better chemistry and mineral content.

Disadvantages

- There is some risk that the drilling company will not be able to find a suitable source of groundwater on your property or within their drilling depth range.
- Average well depth is 100–300 ft (30–90 m), and the cost is usually $30–65 per foot drilled, placing the total cost at $3,000–27,000.
- This also requires installing and maintaining a pump, a pressurized storage tank, and, depending on water quality, you may need to install water treatment equipment.
- In some areas, groundwater can be affected by droughts or high demand in rapidly growing areas.

These considerations explain why most people stick with municipal water when it's available. However, if a water well is an option or you're considering a vacation/survival retreat, a well is the most straightforward and reliable source of water.

Although several strategies for infrastructure independence can pay for themselves over time, installing a water well may not. Unless your municipal water is very expensive, and good-quality water can be found within a couple of hundred feet of the surface, recouping the cost of drilling installation and equipment maintenance may not be possible. The primary reason to consider a water well is independence from municipal water and, in some cases, poor water quality.

REMEMBER

In many parts of the U.S. and the world, water distribution plants cannot achieve the federally mandated requirements for water purity. Additionally, older city and town water distribution systems often use lead in their pipes, which can leach into the water. This has occurred in several U.S. cities. In Flint, Michigan, between 2014 and 2019, pipe leaching resulted in verified cases of lead poisoning in children.

TIP

If there's any doubt about the safety of your water, you can have it tested professionally, or you can order a sampling kit that you can send in for testing. If a water well isn't possible or feasible, there are other options.

Catching the Rain — Rainwater Catchment Systems

Not surprisingly, the primary requirement for a rainwater catchment system is living in an area that has sufficient rainfall. It also requires a roof to catch it, which eliminates most apartments and condominiums. Rainwater catchment is a fairly simple concept, but it requires specific equipment and procedures to ensure a sufficient and safe water supply. The water is collected off the roof from the downspouts, stored, treated, and then pumped into your house's plumbing, similar to a water well system. Assuming you have access to a roof, the next step is to determine if it can supply enough water. Four factors determine this:

- Your water consumption
- The average annual rainfall in your location
- The size of your roof, which is your rain collector
- The size of your collection tanks

Determining your consumption

Starting with consumption, you may be surprised to learn that the average U.S. and Canadian household consumes about 80 gallons (300 liters) of water per person per day. That's a lot of water. Although this includes outdoor uses, such as watering lawns, the majority is indoor use (see Figure 19-1). This can be significantly reduced with simple water-saving upgrades and basic conservation habits, but this highlights the challenge of capturing enough water.

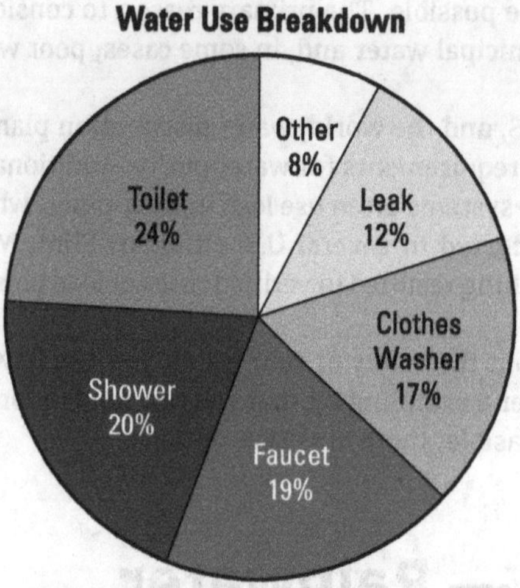

FIGURE 19-1: Environmental Protection Agency (EPA) estimate of U.S. household water consumption breakdowns by activity.

Determining your home's rain collection potential

The simplest way to determine the average rainfall in your area, as well as your roof's ability to catch it, is to go to one of the commercial rain catchment websites and use their calculator. Search for "rainwater catchment calculator." Then, plug in your location and the approximate size of your roof. This should give you your estimated average water collection.

It's not a bad idea to check more than one site and verify your local rainfall with other sources. Take that annual amount from the calculator and divide it by 365 to determine the average daily water supply available. Keep in mind, this amount of water is a best-case scenario.

Now, compare this number with the daily consumption numbers from the previous section (about 80 gallons per person per day). You may find that unless you live near a tropical rainforest, your consumption outstrips the projected supply.

Not to worry, your consumption can be reduced considerably with minimal changes.

Estimated annual water collection

For example, using a rainwater catchment calculator from the Innovative Water Solutions website (`www.watercache.com`), the rainfall collection for a 2,000-square-foot roof in Galveston County, Texas, should average 63,000 gallons per year or 170 gallons (640 liters) per day. If the average U.S. household consumes 80 gallons per person per day, this would only be enough water for two people.

However, upgrading appliances and fixtures can have a significant impact on consumption. For example, a front-loading washing machine uses about 70 percent less water. Upgrading to a dual-flush toilet can save 50 percent over older models, and using water-restricting shower heads can cut shower consumption in half.

The largest reductions, however, often come from habit changes. Many are simple ones, such as not letting the faucet run while brushing your teeth, or turning off the shower while you soap up and then back on to rinse.

Rain catchment in long-duration disasters

Another option is to use rainfall catchment solely as an emergency backup during long-duration disasters. In Chapter 6, we discussed that the absolute minimum amount of water required for drinking, flushing toilets, and very basic hygiene is about 3 gallons (12 liters) per person per day. For a household of four, that's 12 gallons (45 liters). This would allow a small rain catchment system to supply enough water to survive during a long-duration disaster with no municipal water. A larger system could supply sufficient survival water in a more arid climate. Since rainwater catchment requires storage tanks, these could be kept topped off with municipal water during periods when there's little rain, ensuring a large supply during disasters.

Sizing storage tanks

Properly sizing rainwater storage requires detailed calculations and considerations, such as whether to use a big tank or several small ones and where to put them (see Figure 19-2). However, a quick estimate can be done by considering a couple of factors.

» The online calculator gives you the total rainfall, but it's important to know how often it rains. To determine how much water storage is required, you need to know the amount of time between rain events. You may have a general feel for this, but it's best to check past weather forecasts. Unfortunately, you're looking for the maximum time between rain events, not the average. This will determine how big your tanks will have to be to make sure you don't run out between rain events.

- If you retain access to municipal water, you can ensure the tanks are always full regardless of the time between rainfall. If you don't have municipal water, you may be able to have a commercial service top off your tanks as needed.

FIGURE 19-2: Residential rain catchment tank.

MZ/Adobe Stock Photos

Evaluating rainwater catchment for your location

Believe it or not, there are actually a few jurisdictions that prohibit or limit rainwater collection or require permits to do so. Make sure you check with your local government.

Setting up a rain collection system isn't extremely expensive, but it does require a lot of installation and maintenance. There are plenty of books and YouTube videos that cover this in detail. If drilling a well isn't possible and you have sufficient rainfall, a water catchment system is a great option.

However, you will have to maintain it, which requires electric power to filter and pump the water. If adding it to your current residence isn't possible or feasible, you might consider it for a vacation cabin in the future. Just keep in mind that it does require monitoring and maintenance. Long term, a well would be a better option if possible.

Filtering Surface Water: Lakes, Rivers, or the Ocean

If you're fortunate enough to live next to a body of surface water that you can legally tap, it's a great option.

Filtering freshwater

However, water from lakes, ponds, rivers, and the like requires special treatment (ocean water is covered separately below). Unlike having a well where the water is automatically filtered by passing through hundreds of feet of soil, surface water usually contains many more contaminants. These can include everything from farming or industrial chemicals and heavy metals to pharmaceuticals, bacteria, and viruses.

Filtering surface water requires a system that's specifically designed to filter, treat, and pump that type of water, as shown in Figure 19-3. This probably isn't a DIY project. Several companies sell and install these specialized systems. The cost varies, but expect to pay around $7,000, not including installation. Keep in mind that even if your property borders a body of water, you may have to get a permit to access it, and there may be restrictions.

Desalinating ocean water

If you happen to live on or near the ocean or a saltwater marsh, desalinating may be an option. This is definitely a special case scenario, and you can skip this section if it doesn't apply. Unlike the freshwater filtration systems covered above, removing salt from water is a much more difficult task. Most desalination systems are adapted from marine use.

Desalination systems use a high-pressure version of reverse osmosis to squeeze the water through membranes, leaving the salt behind. However, salt water is extremely corrosive, and the reverse osmosis process requires three to four times the pressure of a regular osmosis system. Because of this, desalination systems are more extensive, expensive, and produce less water for the same size and price of a conventional reverse osmosis system.

FIGURE 19-3: Specialized whole-house filtration systems for treating surface water.

AbdullahStudio/Adobe Stock Photos

Desalination systems also consume a lot of energy and must discharge the removed salt as water with a very high salt content. This water can't be discharged into a septic tank or municipal sewer. These systems vary in capacity and price, but expect to pay about $7,000 for a basic system that will supply water for drinking, cooking, and toilet flushing. Whole-house systems are proportionately larger and more expensive.

Generating Water from the Air — Atmospheric Water Generators

If a well isn't possible, you can't tap any surface water sources, and rain catchment isn't possible or isn't sufficient, the next option is an atmospheric water generator. As covered in Chapter 6, these clever units literally pull water out of the air. They're basically dehumidifiers that condense the water on cooling coils and then filter it for consumption. The only requirement beyond electrical power is that the ambient humidity be at least 40 percent.

As the humidity drops, so does their output. These systems wouldn't be effective if you lived in a desert climate with an average humidity of 30 percent or less. The small units can sit on a countertop and produce a couple of gallons a day. Larger units are the size of a small refrigerator, use outside air, and can produce more than 20 gallons a day.

They cost around $2,000 for countertop models and $5,000 and above for larger capacity units. This is a very expensive way to produce a small amount of water, but compare it to the cost and complexity of drilling a well, rain catchment, or surface water treatment.

From this perspective, atmospheric water generators are relatively cost-effective if we just need drinking, cooking, and maybe flushing water. The small ones are also portable and could be carried in a car or RV. The best use may be combining them with other sources.

Combining water production options

Another option is to combine water generation sources. A small atmospheric water generator can provide all the water needed for drinking, cooking, and brushing your teeth. A simple rainwater catchment system with basic filtering and chemical treatment can provide water for all other requirements, such as flushing, washing, and cleaning. The water must still be sterile, but since it won't be consumed, it can be treated with higher levels of chlorine. This also applies to lower-quality water from other sources, such as questionable well water or surface water.

Replacing the municipal sewer system

The last major dependence for most homes after power and water is the septic system. Even if you are completely independent from the power grid and municipal water, you may still be tethered to a municipal sewer. The short answer is to simply install a septic tank and drainage field. Unfortunately, that may not be possible either due to insufficient space for a drainage field, your property's soil won't perc (meaning your soil cannot effectively absorb the water), you're too close to a body of water, the water table is too high, zoning prohibitions, HOA prohibitions, or other issues.

Before giving up, there are more advanced septic systems that can be installed in areas with limited space or poor soil. For example, at the beach we have an aerobic septic system (see Figure 19-4) because we're right on the ocean and our property soil is sand.

This system consists of three tanks and actively pumps air into the tank to accelerate effluent breakdown by oxygen-loving bacteria, resulting in cleaner effluent into the drainage field. Aerobic septic systems cost about twice as much but may allow you to install one on a smaller lot or one with soil issues. If an aerobic system isn't acceptable, there are several even more advanced systems. This EPA site has a great summary: `https://www.epa.gov/septic/types-septic-systems`. There is a system suited for every environment. The biggest challenge may be convincing your local permitting authority to actually look at these advanced systems.

FIGURE 19-4: Aerobic septic tank installation.

What if even an advanced septic system isn't an option? The popularity of tiny houses has spurred improved technology for standalone toilets. There are now more advanced standalone toilets that use composting and even some that use incineration to completely eliminate the need for a septic tank. There are also toilets designed for RVs that use electric bag sealing and can be portable (Figure 8-3 in Chapter 8).

IN THIS CHAPTER

» Evaluating solar, wind, and water power

» Choosing solar power for independence

» Whole-house generators

Chapter 20 Developing Independence from the Power Grid

Being completely independent of the power grid doesn't mean living in a log cabin hundreds of miles from civilization and eating beef jerky. Most stand-alone homes can be permanently liberated from municipal power. It does, however, require that you own your home, particularly your roof, and be willing to make a substantial investment. Whole-house generators will be covered in this chapter, but since most run on municipal natural gas, which may be lost during a disaster, or on stored propane, they're not permanent solutions. They are, however, important backup and transition power sources and will be covered as such. This chapter will primarily focus on residential power generation that can permanently replace the municipal power grid. Spoiler alert: With current technology, the most practical option for most people will be solar.

There are several ways to provide ongoing power to a home outside of the municipal power grid. However, there are only three that are feasible for most today. "Feasible" is defined as being capable of generating sufficient power over an indefinite period . . . without trying to enrich uranium. Aside from solar, the other two are wind power and water power. Both require very specific locations.

Powering with the Wind

Giant commercial windmills are going up everywhere. Each one can produce about 2,500,000 watts. So, it seems reasonable to use a smaller one to power your home. Residential-sized wind turbines have come a long way in the past decade and continue to progress, Figure 20-1.

FIGURE 20-1: Residential wind turbine.

Alberto Masnovo/Getty Images

Unfortunately, a wind turbine's power output is the square of its blade length and the cube of the wind speed. Sorry, I'm an aerospace engineer. What that means is the power drops off massively as you shrink the blades and even more when the wind slows down. The curve in Figure 20-2 illustrates the drop-off, but it's much easier to understand the challenge with an example.

Let's say you have a wind turbine with 8-foot blades (2.4 m) that produces 8,000 watts in a 30-mph wind. Cut the blade length in half to a more reasonable 4 feet (1.2 m) for a residential installation, and the output doesn't drop by half; it drops from 8,000 to 2,000 watts. It gets worse. Let's keep the 8-foot blades for now, but drop the wind speed to a more reasonable 15 mph. The output drops from 8,000 to 500 watts! Below 8 mph, you get almost nothing. Use both 4-foot blades and a 15-mph wind, and you end up with 250 watts, which is less than a single solar panel produces. On top of this, wind speed decreases with altitude. Now you know why those wind turbines you see are so ludicrously large.

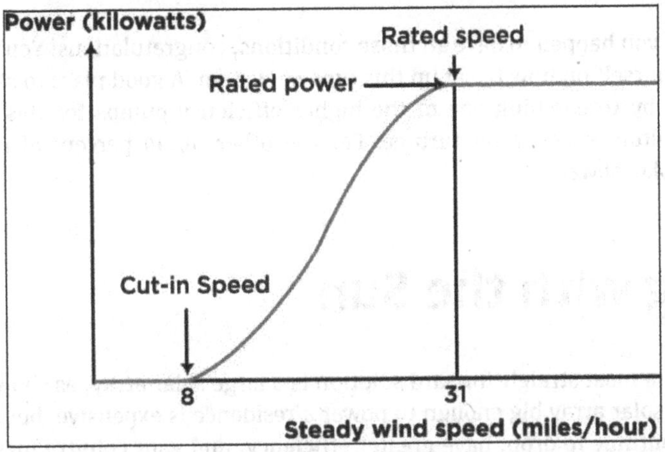

U.S department of energy/Prateek Joshi/https://www.energy.gov/eere/articles/how-do-wind-turbines-survive-severe-weather-and-storms/last accessed on Jan 22, 2026

FIGURE 20-2: U.S. Department of Energy wind turbine power curve.

To match the power output of a 2,000 square-foot-roof (185 square meters) covered with solar panels, you'd need 30-foot-long blades in a 20-mph wind. Imagine pitching that to your homeowners association or local permitting office. Even if approved, the installation might exceed the value of your home. To be fair, you can do multiple smaller wind turbines, and new prototypes use clever techniques like roof ridgeline turbines to create greater power at lower speeds. If your location has consistently strong winds and wind power is of interest, keep your eye on the developing technology.

Powering with Water

About 27 percent of the U.S. power grid comes from hydroelectric power. Water carries much more force than air. Even a small hydroelectric pump (smaller than a microwave) can produce up to 5,000 watts of power. That's the good news. The conditions required to feed that pump, however, are very specific:

- You have to own a property with a stream or river that passes through it.
- The stream or river must be seasonally stable, meaning it doesn't dry up.
- The stream or river needs to have either a high flow rate or a significant drop in elevation while crossing your property.

If you happen to have all those conditions, congratulations! You'll want to educate yourself on how to set up this type of system. A good place to start after YouTube is by researching one of the higher efficiency pumps for this purpose, called a Pelton wheel water turbine. For the other 99.99 percent of readers, it's on to solar power.

Powering with the Sun

The most straightforward solution is a large solar array, as shown in Figure 20-3. A solar array big enough to power a residence is expensive, but solar panel prices continue to drop, have greater efficiency, and your country may offer tax incentives or rebates. Despite the high initial investment, a solar array will usually pay for itself. How long that takes depends heavily on the price of electricity in your area and also on your location and climate. This section will only provide an overview of the topic to help you decide if you wish to look further. A great reference is *Solar Power Your Home For Dummies*.

FIGURE 20-3: Solar panels being installed on a roof.

anatoliy_gleb/Adobe Stock Photos

Determining your location's suitability

Solar panels work to varying degrees almost everywhere, but there are a few exceptions. The primary factor is simply how much sun they see. The further away from the equator you live, the less sunlight you will receive. On the positive side, you'll use less power on air conditioning. Weather is also a factor. The good news is that most latitude and weather impacts can be overcome by simply adding more solar panels to compensate. Permanent shade, however, is harder to overcome. Here are a few situations that might preclude the use of solar panels:

- » You live in the shadow of a hill or mountain that keeps your home in perpetual shade most of the year, or you live in the shadow of a tall building that does the same.
- » Your home is completely surrounded by tall vegetation that blocks almost all direct sunlight, and you cannot trim any of the vegetation.
- » You're employed making toys at the North Pole.

Solar panels are usually installed on the roof of a home to elevate them above things that create shade, but they don't have to be roof-mounted. They can be installed on top of an outbuilding, such as a garage or barn, or they can be ground-mounted in a clear area where they have better sun access.

Choosing a solar array that can power your house

Obviously, a solar array can only power your home while the sun shines, which averages between four and five hours for most latitudes and seasons. Because of the short generation period, solar arrays are sized to produce a lot more power than your home needs. That excess power can be used in two ways. It can be fed back into the power grid for compensation or stored in batteries to use when the sun isn't shining.

Giving your power back to the grid

Almost all energy companies or agencies provide compensation when you feed the power from your solar array back into the power grid. Since you're pulling power out of the grid whenever the sun isn't producing more power than you need — which is most of the time — the power you send back to the grid is applied as a credit on your electric bill. The plan is usually to scale your solar panel array size to break even on your electric bill, keeping in mind that the compensation they pay you per kilowatt will be less than what you pay them. That's not unreasonable since they have to maintain the power distribution system.

However, depending on your location and provider, it could be significantly less. For example, our energy company only pays back one-third of the price per kilowatt that they charge.

The other, more important consideration is that when the power grid goes down, all that excess power you normally send to the grid is lost. Your solar panels can only power your home for a few hours every day, and then you're back to blackout or a generator. The other option is to store that power in a battery backup system. Assuming that the grid is down or you're not connected to the grid, there are three options.

- Rather than installing a whole-house battery backup system, you could use a combination of portable power stations and a gas generator, as in Chapter 12. This is the least expensive option.
- Install a dedicated whole-house battery backup system capable of running your entire home when the sun isn't shining. This is the most expensive option.
- Buy an EV with Vehicle To Home (V2H) bidirectional charging and use your EV's battery as your home's primary battery backup. This will allow you to have a smaller dedicated house backup battery. The cost should be between the first two options.

Using a portable power station

This is the same system illustrated in Chapter 12, except you have a much more powerful solar array. That means for four or five hours, your house would be completely powered by the sun and have plenty of power to fully charge a portable power station or two.

If you're connected to the grid, you can send any excess power back to the grid and get compensation. When the sun isn't shining, and the grid is down or not connected, the portable power stations would cover your critical loads (refrigeration, lighting, communication, and basic heating or cooling) for the rest of the day, requiring little or no generator.

Or you could power your entire house for a part of the day and have the generator take over when the power station runs out. This requires active power management and regular refueling of the generator.

Using a dedicated whole-house battery backup system

The best option for power grid independence is a whole-house battery capable of storing enough power from your solar array to keep your home running when the sun isn't shining. These big lithium-ion battery banks are expensive. The batteries may cost as much or more than the solar panels, but battery prices continue to drop. There are several advantages to a dedicated battery backup system.

- First and foremost, you have independence from the power grid.
- If you're connected to the grid, some energy suppliers pay large dividends if they can access your stored power when the grid is under stress.
- If you have an EV and drive it during the day, you can use the stored battery power at night to recharge it instead of using expensive grid power (requires more solar panels). This means that your local "fuel" cost for your EV will be almost zero.

Using an electric vehicle with bidirectional charging

This could create a fully off-grid system, but only when your electric vehicle (EV) is present. To operate without the EV would require an additional, if smaller, dedicated battery backup and/or a whole-house generator.

A backup battery system for an average-sized house can cost $15,000 to $25,000, depending on consumption and margin. That battery sitting in your EV has at least twice that capacity, and you already paid for it. If you're thinking about buying an EV, look for one with bidirectional charging. If you already own one that doesn't have bidirectional charging, stand by, it might eventually be upgradable. Even with the ability to tap your EV's battery, you'll still need a small house backup battery to cover periods when the car isn't available (unless you have two EVs and never use both at the same time).

MICRO-INVERTERS

Most solar installers recommend using "Micro-Inverters" on each solar panel instead of using a single "string" inverter. Inverters convert the solar panel's DC power to the AC power your home uses. Micro-inverters are a newer technology and are important on roofs that experience frequent partial shading. By giving each panel its own inverter, they ensure that one or two shaded panels don't reduce the power of the rest. However, there are a couple of disadvantages.

- Micro-inverters convert the DC to AC on the roof. If you have an EV, that power has to be converted back to DC to charge the EV, wasting power in two conversions. From a disaster preparation perspective, an EMP event could fry all the exposed micro-inverters on each panel.
- A single large string inverter can be more easily protected with surge suppression and placed in a shielded location like a basement. Even if the string inverter is damaged, it's easier to replace one inverter than the dozens of inverters attached to each panel on your roof.

The technology for solar panels and batteries continues to improve, and their prices continue to drop. A solar array tied to a home battery backup (with an EV if possible) creates a very robust capability to exist without the power grid. This combination not only provides independence and self-reliance, but it can also help your community indirectly and directly in a crisis or disaster.

Whole-House Generators

Whole-house generators run from $5,000 to $15,000, depending on house size and power requirements, and that doesn't include installation. Almost all of them run on either natural gas or propane. If your house has access to municipal natural gas, you never have to worry about refueling your generator. This works great in a short-term power outage, but guess what happens when the municipal power grid is lost for longer periods? Natural gas distribution requires electrical power and will eventually shut down. Additionally, disasters such as earthquakes can sever natural gas lines, and cities will often turn the gas off during a disaster to prevent explosive leaks.

Having a generator that can run on propane increases your options. If you have a natural gas generator that can run on propane, learn how to switch it over. Running a whole-house generator on propane also requires a large propane tank. Recommend at least 500 gallons (about 2,000 liters), but a 1,000-gallon tank is even better. If possible, it's best to bury it for safety, security, and aesthetics.

The good news is that if you don't have any other appliances that use propane, you'll always have a full tank in an emergency.

If you have a gas water heater, fireplace, or gas stove, you'll want to make sure that your propane company keeps your tank mostly full year-round. Even if you install a full solar array and a whole-house battery, a generator provides redundancy. It also provides backup if there are long periods of bad weather that prevent solar charging.

REMEMBER

When calculating how long a generator can run on a full tank of propane, remember that these tanks are only allowed to be filled to about 80 percent due to gas expansion in warm weather. That means a 500-gallon propane tank can only be filled with about 400 gallons.

A generator in the 20-to-25-kilowatt range, running continuously at 50 percent load, will run for about a week on 400 gallons, longer if used judiciously. With a generator in the 12-to-15-kilowatt range, it should run about 10 days and over two weeks if used judiciously. This means you want to use the smallest whole-house generator that can safely handle all of your home's power requirements without exceeding 80 percent output. Chapter 12 covers this in more detail, including several tips to help reduce the maximum load.

Our primary residence uses a small Champion 14 KW whole-house generator with automatic backup powered by a 500-gallon buried propane tank. Because it transfers power automatically, I had a secondary "critical loads" circuit breaker panel installed next to the main one. The electrician just moved the essential circuits from the main panel to this one, leaving the non-essential circuits like hot tubs, clothes dryers, and ovens in the main panel.

When the grid goes down, and the generator takes over, it only powers the critical loads panel. This means I don't have to shut off the breakers to non-critical devices. This also allows a smaller, more efficient generator that can run longer on the same fuel. Chapter 12 covered soft starters that can be installed on HVAC compressors to reduce the maximum startup current and allow a smaller generator.

You can also get a generator that uses liquid fuel, but storing large amounts of gasoline can be dangerous, and since gasoline oxidizes and breaks down even with stabilizers, you'd have to replace the fuel every 18 months or so. More expensive diesel generators use less fuel and tend to last longer, and diesel breaks down more slowly, is less flammable, and safer to store. However, even with additives, the diesel should be replaced every two years.

IN THIS CHAPTER

» Choosing a vacation/shelter location

» Using an RV for vacation/survival shelter

Chapter 21

Creating a Survival Retreat Destination

Instead of just modifying your home with Level 3 preparation options for infrastructure independence, you may want to consider a dedicated survival retreat. This doesn't have to be that Level 4 abandoned missile silo. There are less extreme and much more fun options, such as an RV or a vacation cabin.

Choosing a Survival/Vacation Location

Regardless of whether your vacation/survival retreat is a place to park a camping trailer or to build a mountain chateau, the single most important factor is location. For disaster preparation purposes, there are a number of criteria to consider. The chance of achieving all of these is almost zero, but this provides a good framework for your search. Here are some of the key location considerations, roughly in priority order.

1. **It should be well outside large metropolitan areas.** During an extended period with no utilities, city populations will evacuate. The analogy of locusts comes to mind. It's also best if it isn't easily visible from one of the major roads coming out of a city.

2. **It should be reasonably far from your primary residence.** This is simply to improve the likelihood that your location isn't inside the footprint of any local disaster.

3. **In a perfect world, it would be nice to be able to get there on one tank of gas (or EV charge).** However, any location that you can drive to is a reasonable option.

4. **You want to avoid areas prone to disasters like hurricanes, tornadoes, floods, landslides, earthquakes, volcanic eruptions, wildfires, or proximity to nuclear or industrial plants and war zones.** In other words, Antarctica.

5. **Even if you just intend to park an RV there, you want reasonable exposure to the sun for solar power and a potential water well or access to other water sources such as lakes, rivers, or streams.**

6. **Make sure the site isn't susceptible to flooding. Also, having the ability to have a basement that doesn't flood is important.** Basements provide additional protection, have moderate temperatures for food storage, and natural EMP shielding.

Arguably, the most important factor in choosing a location is that it's fun or relaxing. Everyone's definition of fun or relaxing is different, but a great view usually works. It could be a lake, river, or ocean. It could overlook a valley or mountains, a forest, or a desert.

The key is to find a location where you want to spend time and come back to frequently. This is more important than trying to avoid all the potential disaster areas because you will be much more motivated to actually take action to acquire the property. Plus, it gives you options for potential short-term rentals. The same thing that attracts you to the location will attract others. The most sought-after Airbnb properties fall into two groups. The first are locations near major attractions such as cities or amusement parks, which we don't want. The second group has spectacular views of a beach, lake, river, mountain, desert, forest, or any other natural beauty.

An important benefit of searching for a site for an off-grid RV, cabin, or house is that the property doesn't need access to municipal power or water. That dramatically opens up the possible locations you can consider, and properties that don't have that access usually cost a lot less. This is good because the saved money will go into solar panels, a water well, and a septic system. Once the location is determined, the next step is to choose whether you want the flexibility of just parking an RV on the property or you want to build a cabin or house, or both; use an RV now and build a cabin later.

Choosing an RV, cabin, or house

After finding the right location, there are four possible directions you can choose.

- You could park a recreational vehicle there. The RV could be anything from a small, towed travel trailer to a large diesel motorcoach. There are two options for RVs. The RV can be equipped with solar panels, batteries, and an atmospheric water generator. Or the infrastructure can be on the lot with ground-based solar panels, a well, and a septic system. That will allow you to simply come and connect your RV. An RV will probably be the least expensive and most flexible option, but also more challenging if you want to do short-term rentals.
- You can also place a prefabricated house on the lot. That includes everything from a mobile home, container home, or tiny house to a large house assembled on site with modules. This is faster and usually less expensive than building on site, but still requires water, solar panels, and septic. There are now builders that make small modular homes and tiny houses that come with built-in solar roofs, water catchment systems, and composting septic systems, as illustrated in Chapter 22.
- You could also buy an existing cabin or house. This would be the fastest option and allows you to offer it up for short-term rentals quickly, if desired. However, if you have to modify it to take it off-grid, the cost may be higher than a purpose-built home.
- Finally, you could build a house to your specifications. This is arguably the most fun path because you get exactly what you want and can include the latest building materials and technology. However, it's a large investment of both time and money, and having designed and built a couple of houses, I should warn that it can be a bit stressful.

Although I have no plans to create a Level 4 Survival Compound (such as an abandoned missile silo), I admire the focus and commitment of those who have. I did, however, design our last two homes and have owned both short and long-term rental properties. That doesn't make me an architect or a rental expert, but it did help me learn many things NOT to do.

From those experiences and by tapping the expertise of many professionals in and out of the prepping community, I've designed both an RV and a cabin not only for illustration but ones that we will be building. This chapter covers the RV option, and Chapter 22 covers and illustrates building a small survival retreat/vacation cabin.

Using an RV at your survival or vacation location

Getting an RV and purchasing a nice property to park it on is the fastest and least expensive way to create a survival/vacation retreat. You can buy an RV that's already outfitted for extended stays off-grid. In the RV community, this is referred to as "boondocking" or "dry camping." It requires extra solar panels, a large lithium-ion battery bank, and a small atmospheric water generator. Or if you want to extend the RV's off-grid time indefinitely, several companies will build a camper van designed to your specifications.

An example will be presented next. The other option is to outfit the site rather than the RV. Instead of investing in an upgraded RV, you can use any type of RV and upgrade the site with ground-based solar panels, a well, and a septic tank. This will be a bit more expensive, but it is a better long-term investment and supports the construction of a cabin or house in the future. Additionally, if your site has a great view with power, water, and septic, when you're not using it, you can offer it for short-term rental to RV owners. You can also do short-term rental of your own RV on the site.

There are pros and cons to every type of RV, from small trailers to Class A motorcoaches. Although RVs aren't usually robust enough to survive extreme weather, they can be moved to a safer location. If you already have an RV, you've selected it based on your needs, such as family size, comfort, drivability, and cost. If you don't own one but are considering an RV, there are two basic categories: travel trailers that are towed and motorcoaches that can be driven. They both come in a huge variety of sizes and shapes.

Travel trailers

Travel trailers can be small enough to be pulled by a car or as big as a mobile home, Figure 21-1. One advantage trailers have is that you can leave them at your survival/vacation property so that you don't have to pull them back and forth between the site and your home. With solar panels, satellite Internet, and security cameras, you can monitor the trailer's status.

If you'll be visiting frequently and the site isn't far away, leaving a travel trailer on your property is reasonable. It allows for a faster evacuation since you don't have to prepare and move your RV. If, however, you won't be there often, you may want to keep your RV at or near your home. You can then use it as part of your evacuation.

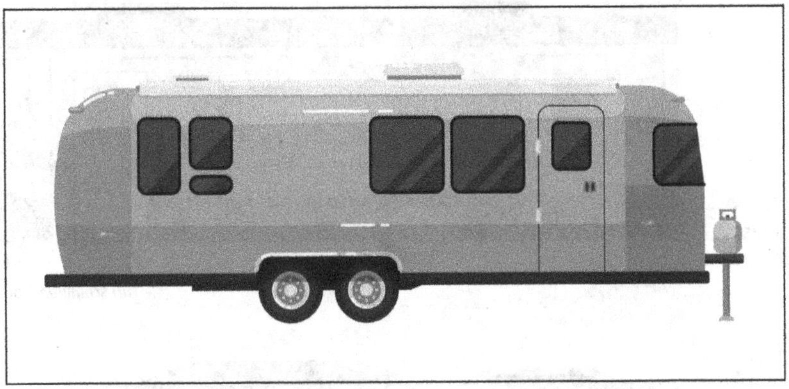

FIGURE 21-1: Travel trailer.

Alfazet Chronicles/Adobe Stock Photos

Motorhomes

Motorcoaches and camper vans are more expensive to purchase, maintain, and operate. However, some of them can do double or even triple duty. They also come in a variety of sizes and shapes that are divided into three standard categories:

- **Class A motorhomes:** These are the largest motorhomes, often built on a commercial bus chassis (see Figure 21-2). They have the most space and comfort, and have the highest price and appetite for fuel. Class A motorhomes can fit a family or two couples. They have many amenities, but they need good roads and a lot of space to maneuver. See Figure 21-2.
- **Class C motorhomes:** For some reason, the smallest size is Class B, and the middle category is Class C. Class C Motorhomes (see Figure 21-3) are usually built on the same cargo van chassis as the smaller Class Bs, but the original body is removed and replaced with a larger custom body. This gives them more room inside while still being a little more maneuverable and economical than a Class A. However, they're still large and fuel-thirsty.
- **Class B Motorhomes:** Often called camper vans, Class B motorhomes are the smallest motorhomes (see Figure 21-4). They're simply commercial cargo vans, such as the Ford Transit, Mercedes Sprinter, or Ram Promaster/Fiat Ducato, with RV interiors. They're the most maneuverable (often available with all-wheel drive), fit in most parking places, and are the most fuel-efficient, but with the least amount of interior room.

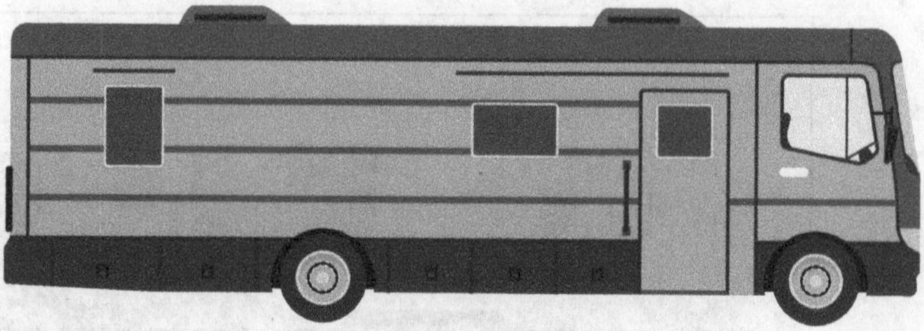

FIGURE 21-2: Class A motorcoach.

Yuri Schmidt/Adobe Stock Photos

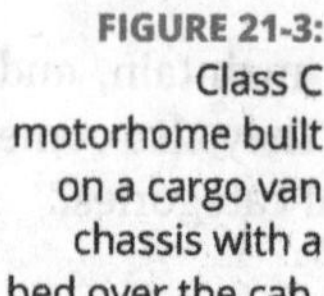

FIGURE 21-3: Class C motorhome built on a cargo van chassis with a bed over the cab.

Arjuna/Adobe Stock Photos

FIGURE 21-4: Class B camper van.

Considering a small off-grid camper van

For this design exercise, I chose the smallest RV type, the Class B. This creates the toughest design challenge but demonstrates that it's possible to fit an off-grid capable house with a bedroom, bathroom, and kitchen into 60 square feet (6 square meters) . . . sort of. If you don't have a large family, these small RVs have a lot of advantages over the larger motorhomes.

» They cost a little less than the Class C and a lot less than the Class A motorcoaches. They also have better fuel economy.

» With a footprint not much bigger than a full-sized SUV, they can be driven and used as a second vehicle, hauling anything from furniture to soccer teams.

» With the available all-wheel drive option, they can go where the bigger Class A and Class C motorcoaches can't. This makes them particularly attractive as an evacuation vehicle.

» Their size and all-wheel drive capability also allow them access to vacation/retreat properties that may be located off of unimproved roads, opening up your site options.

» When you have too many guests visiting your home over the holidays, these little RVs can also be used as an emergency backup bedroom.

» Finally, all of these motorcoaches allow vacation trips to any place you can drive.

WARNING

Some local ordinances and homeowner associations prohibit any type of RV from being parked in front of your home. However, they rarely restrict passenger vans. Fortunately, these Class B camper vans can be designed with "stealth" features, such as low-profile solar panels and an air conditioner mounted under the vehicle instead of on the roof. Their appearance then matches their actual multi-role ability as a family passenger van.

The downside to these small camper vans is that when traveling, they have limited cargo space and are only "comfortable" for two adults and maybe a very young child or two. Although they do come in extended length versions, which adds an extra couple of feet, any occupancy beyond two adults really requires a larger RV.

Designing a camper van with extended off-grid ability

Figures 21-5 and 21-6 show a 3D model of a Class B camper van designed to operate off-grid for extended periods. This design used the short-wheelbase Ram Promaster/Fiat Ducato platform since it's common in both the U.S. and the European Union. Its exterior length is 17.8 feet (5.5 meters). That's about the same size as a Ford F150 pickup truck and only 16 inches (40 cm) longer than a Toyota Land Cruiser. This basic layout can also be used with the Mercedes Sprinter or Ford Transit cargo vans.

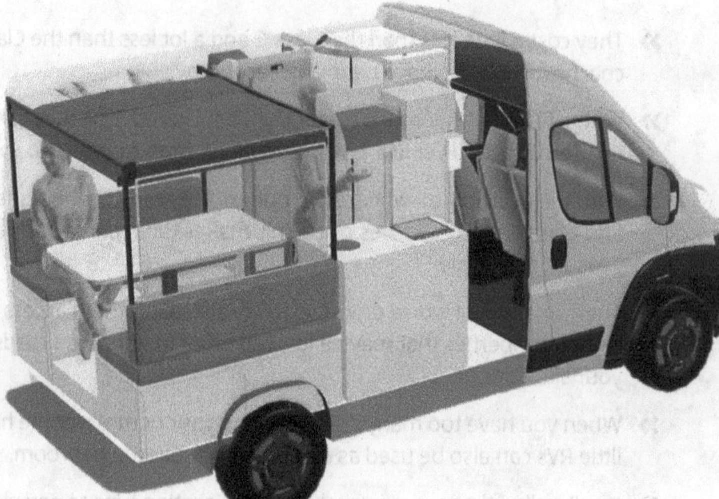

FIGURE 21-5: Camper van design with elevated bed over the dinette and the closet inserted into the shower.

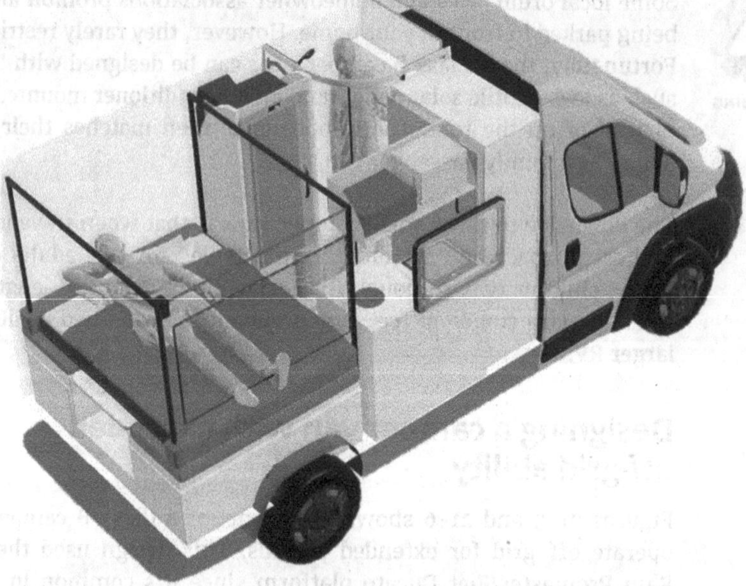

FIGURE 21-6: Camper van with the bed lowered and the closet/pantry extended from the shower.

To maximize space, this design uses a bed that can be electrically elevated to the van's ceiling, allowing a small dinette table underneath that seats four. It also has a wet bath with a shower and a portable, electric Laveo toilet, covered in Chapter 8. When the shower or toilet is not in use, a closet/pantry slides on rails into the shower area, increasing passenger space. When the closet/pantry is extended, it isolates the cab from the rest of the van for privacy.

To achieve power independence, the van has 740 watts of solar panels on the roof with a 12-kilowatt lithium-ion battery bank under one of the dinette seats. See Figures 21-7 and 21-8. Low-profile, walkable solar panels and a large openable skylight over the bed allow access to the roof from inside the van. The roof can then be used as a "deck," and with no exterior ladder on the side of the vehicle, it's more secure and a bit "stealthier." The roof also has a Starlink Mini dish permanently installed.

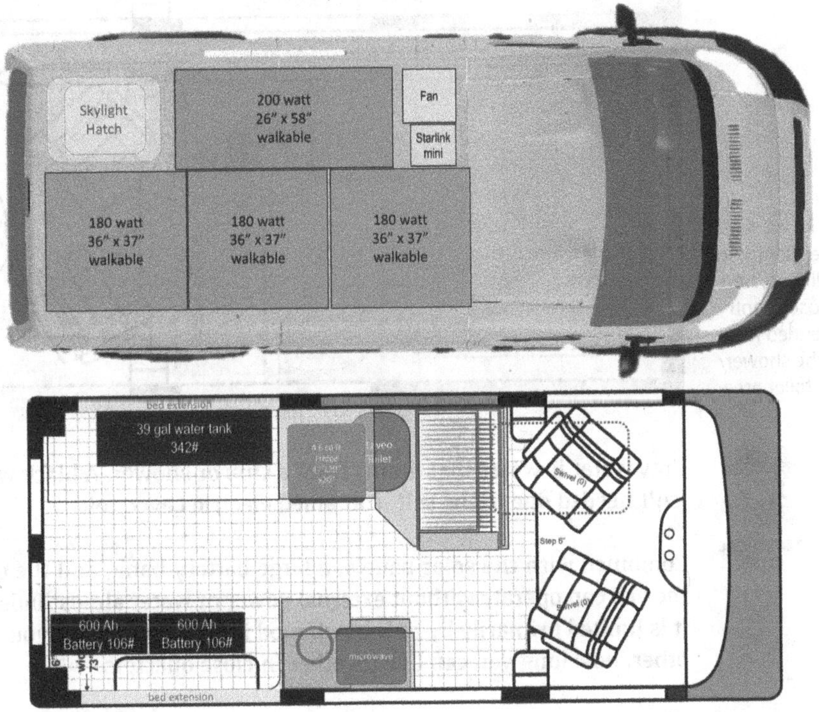

FIGURE 21-7: Camper floorplan with battery bank, water tank, appliances, and closet/pantry in the shower.

The kitchen has a 4.5-cubic-foot (.13-cubic-meter) refrigerator, a small microwave, a sink, and a single induction cooktop. In place of an exterior window, an LED TV is connected to a hidden exterior camera to provide the "window" view. The "window" tv can also be used for home office work and entertainment. By using flush-mount solar panels on the roof and incorporating the heat pump compressor inside and underneath the van, it looks like a standard residential passenger van on the outside. It's also fitted with a 39-gallon (about 150-liter) freshwater tank under one of the dinette seats and a small atmospheric water generator as a backup for drinking water. It has a 25-gallon (about 100-liter) gray water tank under the van.

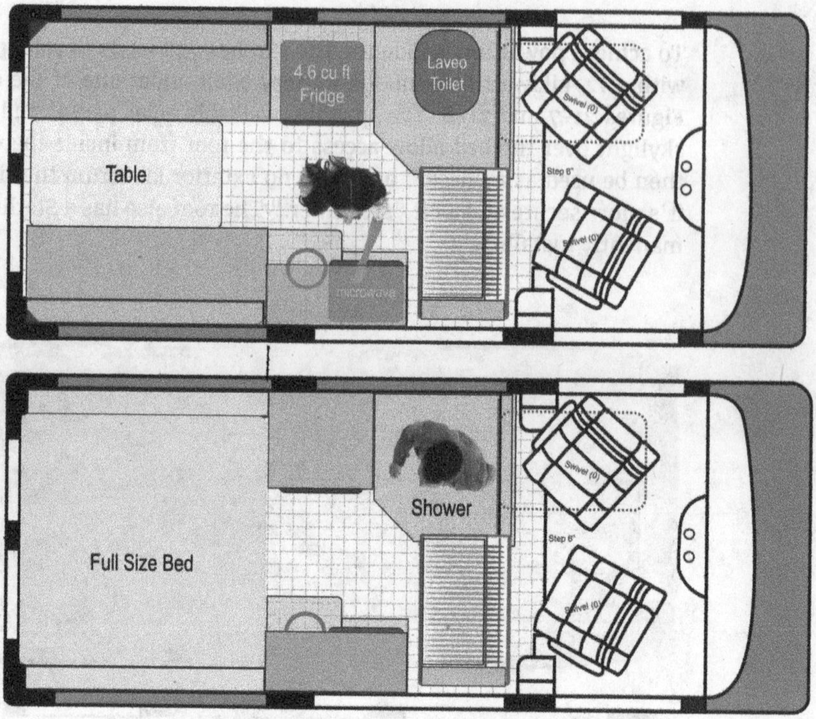

FIGURE 21-8: Camper floorplan with dinette, bed, and closet/pantry extended from the shower/toilet area.

TECHNICAL STUFF

Gray water is water that drains from a sink or shower. A black water (septic) tank isn't needed due to the self-contained electric Laveo toilet.

Combined with the solar panels, a large battery bank, and the engine alternator, the van can operate without external power or water almost indefinitely. Living in it is limited primarily by how much food it can carry and, if you have a significant other, how long you can live together in close quarters.

These small camper vans represent a reasonable compromise between everyday cargo/people hauler, off-grid vacation/evacuation RV, and overflow bedroom. They come in longer lengths, but anything beyond two people or a couple with two small children requires a Class C or Class A motorhome.

Designing your perfect RV can be a lot of fun. There are a number of companies that will build a camper van to your specifications, and there are several types of software that you can use to create your own design with 3D models. I purchased very inexpensive software specifically designed for Class B motorhomes called Vanspace 3D.

Electrifying your RV

Each of these vans is now available as an electric vehicle (EV). However, their range is less than half that of the gasoline or diesel versions, making them less attractive for an evacuation. However, if future versions are offered with larger battery packs, they might make the perfect camper van/evacuation vehicle. Keep an eye out for advances in this area. See Figure 21-9.

FIGURE 21-9: EV camper vans.

Oleksandr/Adobe Stock Photos

Combining electric and gas

Another option that might provide the best of both worlds is to combine a gas/diesel-powered camper van with a regular EV. Most camper vans and motorcoaches can tow at least 6,000 pounds (2,700 kilos), and EVs are usually less than that. In a perfect world, your EV could be towed behind your camper van, and you could store portable solar panels inside the EV. A 400-watt foldable solar panel is about 33 x 28 by 3.5 inches (840 x 710 x 90 mm) and weighs 40 pounds (18 kg). Five of these would easily fit inside any EV and still allow additional cargo.

Under ideal conditions, five 400-watt solar panels will generate about nine kilowatts per day, depending on location and weather. This doesn't include any power from the RV's solar panels. An efficient EV gets about four miles per kilowatt. That would add roughly 30 miles (48 km) of range per day. That's not much, but over a few days, that could be useful. If gasoline/diesel is readily available, you can drive your gas-powered RV to get it refueled, and use your van's alternator to charge the batteries during poor weather.

If gas/diesel isn't available, solar charging of an EV gives you an emergency backup plan. As slow as recharging the EV would be, it's faster than building an oil refinery. The extra panels can also be used to charge your RV's batteries for refrigeration, air conditioning, or heat.

IN THIS CHAPTER

» Considering a classic bomb shelter

» Choosing a vacation/shelter location

» Designing and building an off-grid "cabin"

Chapter 22

Creating Your Own Shelter

You may consider that buying or building a cabin or vacation home is beyond the level of a "For Dummies" book, but there are three reasons it's covered.

» Most U.S. homeowners will buy and sell a total of three homes during their lifetime. This chapter applies whether you're considering a survival retreat, a vacation home, or just evaluating what key features you want in your next primary residence.

» In the U.S., 6.5 million Americans own a second or vacation home, and another 10 million own timeshares; that's 12 percent of U.S. households. Surveys also indicate that 60 percent consider owning a vacation property one of their top financial goals.

» Many of the ideas and technologies covered here can be applied to your existing home to reduce utility bills.

With all that said, you can't have a disaster prepping book without mentioning the classic bomb shelter. This chapter will start with bomb shelters and then expand to everything from tiny homes to off-grid chateaus.

Installing a Bomb Shelter

A bomb shelter is often the stereotypical image people have when they think about "prepping." At the height of the Cold War, bomb shelters, specifically fallout shelters, were considered fashionable, and it's possible your parents or grand-parents considered one.

Today, bomb shelters range in size from reinforced basement safe rooms and backyard bunkers, as shown in Figure 22-1, to full-sized underground homes capable of supporting a family for months. There are several manufacturers of these. One of the largest in the U.S. is Atlas Survival Shelters, based in Texas but expanding to the European Union.

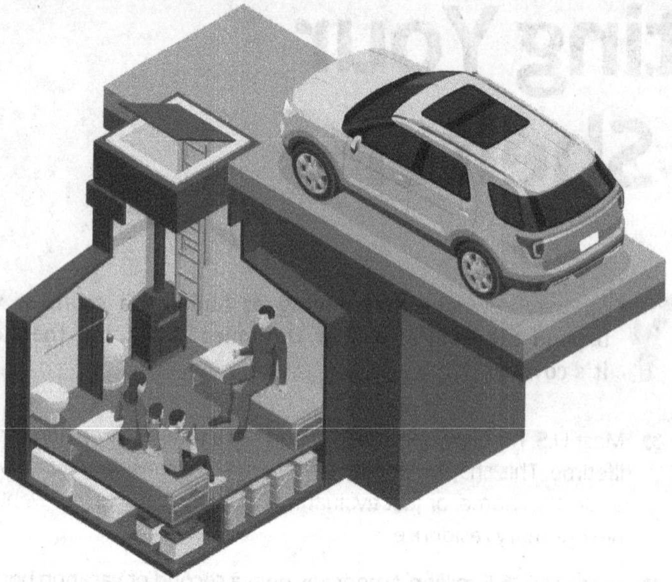

FIGURE 22-1: Classic bomb shelter installation.

Golden Sikorka/Adobe Stock Photos

Prices for bomb shelters run from about $10,000 to hundreds of thousands. Made of concrete or steel, they're the pinnacle of a single-purpose survival shelter and provide the best protection from the most dangerous threats. However, the premise of this book is that while disasters can be global and catastrophic, they won't be permanent. If you have plenty of resources and can purchase a bomb shelter in addition to your permanent residence and a vacation home or RV, go for it. For the majority of the population, and therefore the readers of this book, owning all three might be a financial challenge. While bomb shelters provide exceptional security, their lack of windows does tend to limit Airbnb income potential, not to mention your family's motivation to spend a vacation weekend there.

Instead of a bomb shelter (or in addition to one if you have the resources), a vacation/survival retreat might be an option. Chosen wisely, a vacation/survival retreat can protect you and your family while providing recreation and potentially generating rental income. Additionally, with vacation and passive income as motivators, it also makes it more likely that you will actually pursue it.

Survival/Vacation/Short-Term Rental Cabin

Since it takes too long to write survival/vacation/short-term rental cabin from here on, I will refer to it simply as a "cabin." It doesn't have to look anything like a "cabin" and can be as small as a tiny house or as big as a country estate. The only requirement is that it's bought, built, or modified to function without municipal infrastructure: water, electricity, or sewer. The property can be connected to these services just as long is doesn't depend on them.

The most important step is choosing the location, which was covered in depth in Chapter 21. Once the location is determined and the decision is made to have a permanent structure rather than using an RV, there are three primary options:

- The first option is to find an existing off-grid cabin (remember we're using "cabin" to encompass any size residential structure). If you can find one that meets all your housing and location needs, this is the fastest path and allows immediate use and potential rental. There are 4.7 million homes in the U.S. with solar panels, but only an estimated 250,000 homes that are considered truly off-grid. Prices can vary from a frontier fixer-upper to a stratospheric estate.
- The next option is to find a property that meets all your location needs but isn't off-grid or is only partially off-grid. For example, you might choose a home that has good well water and a septic system but is still on the power grid. With the right location requirements met, these can be upgraded to off-grid. This significantly opens up the number of properties available and allows immediate use or rental, but it must be weighed against the time and cost of the modifications required to take it off-grid. These costs may exceed a purpose-built cabin.
- The last option is to design and build one to your specifications. This gives you the widest choice of properties since it doesn't require any infrastructure other than an access road for the construction crew. It allows you to create your perfect size and style, and can be optimized for short-term rental if desired. Finally, it allows taking advantage of the latest construction

techniques and technology. It's usually assumed that building a home is more expensive than buying one. However, the two homes we built were less expensive than comparable ones on the market. This was mostly because we chose the exact features we wanted and eliminated ones we didn't need. Modifying a home that's not designed for off-grid (no advanced insulation, efficient appliances, or correct solar roof orientation) may cost more up front and over time. The drawback to building is the time and complexity. It will always take longer, and cost more than you thought, and it will require more decisions than you want to make, but it will be an adventure.

Designing your cabin may be the last option you would ever choose. Doing this as a design exercise, however, highlights the top construction techniques, features, and technologies you should look for if you buy an existing home or want to upgrade your primary residence. Treat all the suggestions that follow as an ala cart menu. Only consider the ones that appeal to you or fit your situation and location.

Choosing the size

This is a decision only you can make, and it's very dependent on your stage of life and family size. If you have a large young family, the calculations become pretty clear. Or, it may be just you, or you and a significant other.

TIP

If you follow the location suggestions, your cabin will be in an awesome place. Having had a lake and beach home, I can tell you that your cabin will probably be very popular. This makes it a lot of fun, but if you plan on hosting a lot of friends and family (including relatives you didn't know you had), you may want to reconsider the size and layout. These considerations can also improve your short-term rental options.

Cabin size is your call, but for the purposes of this book, the design will attempt to maximize usability with minimal long-term cost. This minimalist approach starts with the assumption of a small family or two couples. Like everything else in this book, it will take advantage of dual-use spaces to minimize size and energy consumption. Of course, it can be easily scaled up to match your needs and resources. A smaller house has several advantages. It's easier and less expensive to build and easier to power off-grid. For short-term rental consideration, a property that can handle a small family or two couples fits an important rental niche. This helps maximize occupancy and rental income.

Choosing the construction method

You're trying to find a location that isn't susceptible to disasters, but that's not realistic. Almost any location has some local vulnerability, and even if it doesn't, global disasters don't care where you live. Because of this, it's important to build a strong house.

Standard wood framing

Most houses built in the U.S. use standard wood framing, often called "stick construction." As the three little pigs learned, houses made of sticks don't do well in extreme wind. Even sturdy-looking brick homes are "stick construction" with a brick façade. That may stop the wolf's huffing and puffing, but it may not survive a tornado. If your house or cabin is in an area subject to extreme weather (what place isn't today?), a better option is to build your house out of concrete, specifically, Insulated Concrete Forms (ICF). Even if it won't be exposed to extreme weather, ICF should be considered due to several significant advantages.

Insulated Concrete Forms (ICF) construction

Insulated Concrete Form construction forms the walls of your house out of large Styrofoam blocks that look like giant LEGOs, as shown in Figure 22-2. At this stage of construction, even the three little pigs' straw house looks stronger. After connecting the blocks in the shape of your house, however, rebar is laid in, and concrete is poured inside the blocks to form the walls. As a side benefit, ICF homes have much lower environmental impact by massively reducing construction waste, heating and cooling energy required, and wood harvesting.

The walls are also connected to the concrete floor with rebar, creating a monolithic structure. With walls composed of 6 inches (15 cm) of concrete, the structure provides phenomenal strength against the worst weather, including tornadoes. The concrete walls are bulletproof, fire-resistant, and with additional rebar can also be made earthquake-resistant. See Figure 22-3.

When combined with a concrete roof, the house is almost airtight and naturally EMP-resistant. This allows excellent control of air filtration for superior protection from smoke and bugs (both insect and pandemic type). With the Styrofoam cladding on the inside and outside, the walls are about a foot thick (30 cm). This, along with the thermal mass of concrete, creates extremely high insulation values. The result is an almost 50 percent reduction in the energy needed to heat and cool the house over most stick-built homes, which is very important when you're generating and storing your own power.

FIGURE 22-2: Insulated Concrete Form construction blocks being filled with concrete.

bildlove/Adobe Stock Photos

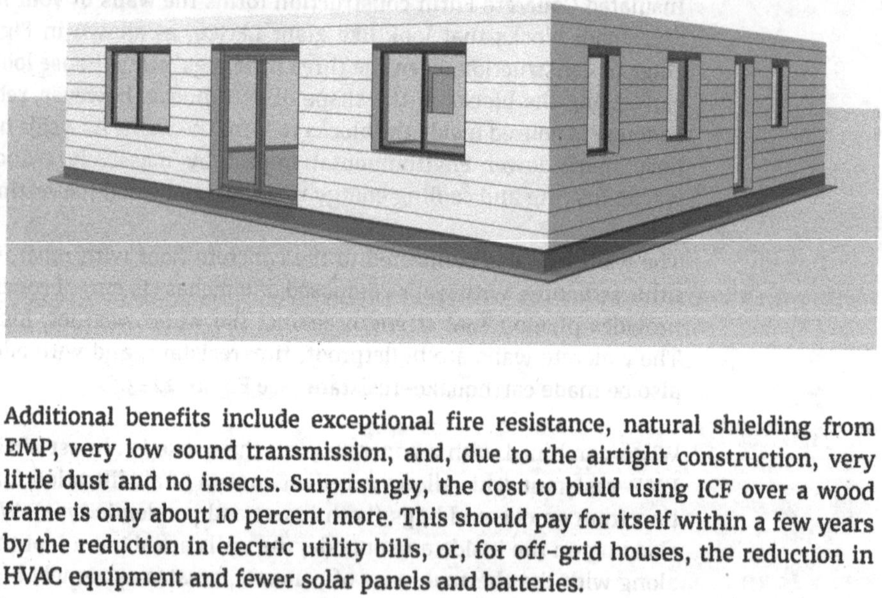

FIGURE 22-3: Insulated Concrete Form (ICF) construction.

Additional benefits include exceptional fire resistance, natural shielding from EMP, very low sound transmission, and, due to the airtight construction, very little dust and no insects. Surprisingly, the cost to build using ICF over a wood frame is only about 10 percent more. This should pay for itself within a few years by the reduction in electric utility bills, or, for off-grid houses, the reduction in HVAC equipment and fewer solar panels and batteries.

TIP

With an ICF house, make sure you're comfortable with the final design by carefully studying 3D computer models because a drawback of ICF is "remodeling." If you want to add a room or a window after the concrete is poured . . . good luck.

TECHNICAL STUFF

There's new technology with many of ICF's advantages, but that can be done much faster. They can now 3D print a house using a concrete formulation, Figure 22-4. Not only is this method extremely fast with similar benefits, but it can also be less expensive. However, the speed and savings come primarily from having the massive 3D printing machine on site and being able to build multiple houses. They may not be willing to transport the machine long distances for just one house, and if they did, the price would probably be higher than ICF.

FIGURE 22-4: 3D house printing with concrete mixture.

guteksk7/Shutterstock

Optimizing the layout

The next sections cover specific design elements. Since it's hard to visualize how all these elements work together, they're illustrated with floor plans and 3D images later in the chapter.

Basement

Although an ICF house can withstand almost anything, a basement provides additional protection. The basement "ceiling" and the house's roof can also be poured concrete on metal reinforced forms. The combination of being underground with concrete walls and ceiling makes it resistant to almost anything short of a bunker buster bomb. A basement also provides natural EMP shielding and moderates temperatures, reducing cooling and heating requirements. It also provides a protected place to put all your house's power, HVAC, and water pumping equipment.

Additionally, you can keep the basement inaccessible to potential renters, providing a place to store your survival equipment and a large food stockpile. See Figure 22-5. If the basement has a separate exterior entrance, in a pinch, you could use the property even while hosting short-term renters.

Garage

The ICF construction could include an attached garage with an extremely strong garage door. The garage is also a good place to put a staircase to your basement and another to the roof. An attached garage also increases the footprint of the house, which allows for more roof area to install solar panels. You definitely want the garage wired to take advantage of bidirectional charging so that your EV (or a future EV) can be charged by the solar panels and also act as a whole-house battery.

Machine room

Your HVAC, water heater, power panel, solar inverter, batteries, and the like should all be located inside, in a machine room. A basement is the best place to locate a machine room (garage is second best). This protects your house's critical equipment from the elements, EMP, and tampering. The machine room should be big enough to comfortably operate and service the equipment, but it can also be extended for long-term food storage. See Figure 22-5.

FIGURE 22-5: Small basement with machine room, food storage, and optional kitchen, bedroom, and bathroom.

The one important piece of equipment that cannot be in the machine room is the propane-powered backup generator. It must be outside, but a good place to put it, surprisingly, is on your roof along with the HVAC compressor. As long as you have a low-pitch area of your roof with good access, it protects against tampering. See Figure 22-6.

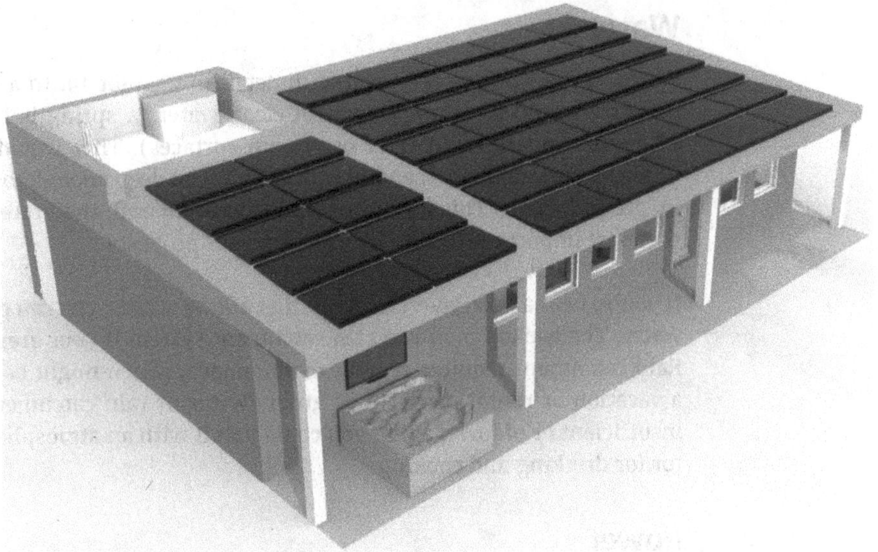

FIGURE 22-6: Propane generator and HVAC compressor mounted on the roof with garage stair access.

Doors, windows, and exterior cladding

With six inches of concrete in the walls, floor, and roof, the only vulnerable areas are doors and windows. The single exterior front door should be steel with a steel frame embedded in the ICF concrete. The secondary exit could be through the garage. At the very least, windows should be impact-rated or covered in security film.

These "hurricane windows" can withstand not only extreme winds but are designed to resist high-speed debris like flying 2x4s as well as baseball bats. By definition, they're hard to break through even with a crowbar. Bullet-resistant glass can also be used and comes in various levels of ballistic resistance. The higher speed bullets they resist, the more expensive the window.

The exterior cladding of an ICF house can be anything you want, from cedar to brick. For added strength, easier maintenance, and fire resistance, cement board is a good option. It comes in a variety of designs and can be painted any color. Blending the color into the environment is best for a survival retreat as well as an Airbnb. For proud University of Texas and Tennessee fans, orange might not be the best option.

Selecting your utilities

Without needing municipal power or water, you can build almost anywhere.

Water

Water source options are covered in detail in Chapter 19. In a perfect world, the property would have a spring with clean water (a spring is basically the point where an underground river or stream surfaces). That would be awesome but unlikely. A more likely scenario is drilling a well deep enough to access good quality ground water. This depends on your location and, therefore, should be one of the most important factors in selecting your property.

If you're near a lake, river, or ocean that allows access, you can pump and treat the water. The backup plan is a rain catchment system if your area's climate allows. Rain catchment requires regular maintenance, which might be more difficult for a vacation or rental property. If groundwater or rain catchment is available but insufficient or of low quality, you could pair it with an atmospheric water generator for drinking and cooking.

Power

Chapter 20 on solar arrays applies here. If the power requirements, house size, and shading allow, maintenance and security should put the solar panels on the roof. The simplest roof design would be a flat or shed roof with a pitch optimized for maximum solar exposure at your latitude.

You can face your house in whatever direction you want in order to provide the best views and utility, but your roof should be angled toward the sun. The further you are from the equator, the higher your roof pitch (steeper) should be, which also helps shed snow that you're more likely to find in those higher latitudes. Installation and orientation considerations also apply to wind turbines.

You'll need a battery storage system, and a propane-powered generator would be a good backup if bad weather reduces solar power. As mentioned, a good place to put a generator is on a flat section of the roof. That keeps the generator secure from tampering while still allowing easy access from a garage staircase and roof hatch. A regular propane generator with a buried propane tank would be sufficient. Diesel generators are more efficient and last longer, but diesel generators are heavier, more expensive, and even with fuel treatment, you have to use or replace all the fuel at least every two years. However, it might make sense if you also have a diesel-powered vehicle.

Solar panels are completely exposed and would absorb an EMP. The solar panels themselves should probably survive a solar EMP since they're designed to collect and channel power, and might even survive a nuclear warhead EMP, but in both cases, any electronics connected to the panels would likely be fried.

As mentioned in Chapter 21, you don't want to use solar panels with micro-inverters attached to each panel unless frequent shading is a major issue. Instead, you would prefer the older string inverters that connect a bunch of panels together (a "string" of them) and feed the power to a central inverter. You can also buy more expensive solar panels that are specifically designed to resist EMP.

Septic

You will need a septic system. If your location has high groundwater levels or is in close proximity to bodies of water, you may need a specialized septic system as covered in Chapter 19. For long-duration disasters, a challenge is trying to store enough toilet paper due to how much space it takes.

For a new build, one way to significantly reduce toilet paper is to install a bidet. Common in Southern Europe, Japan, and South America, bidets use a stream of water to cleanse instead of paper. In some countries, bidets are required by building code. Fortunately, you don't have to add another large fixture to your bathrooms. You can either install a "smart toilet" with built-in bidet functions, or use new devices that attach to an existing toilet and provide many of the bidet functions at a lower cost.

Choosing the right HVAC and appliances

Choosing the most efficient HVAC system and appliances is important when you're providing your own power. It can reduce the scale and cost of solar panels and batteries, but there is a balance. The highest efficiency HVAC systems such as geothermal and the most advanced appliances are not only more expensive but more complex.

HVAC

The biggest power hog in any home is the air conditioning and heating system (HVAC). An ICF house will reduce the size of the cooling and heating needed by almost half, but it's still important to have an efficient system. Normally, high-efficiency HVACs save money by reducing your electric bill. With an off-grid home, they save money by reducing the number of solar panels, batteries, and the size of the backup generator, as well as the cost to install all of them.

With the exception of the backup generator, you don't want to depend on any type of fuel that has to be constantly replenished, like natural gas, propane, oil, or diesel. This means a fully electric house. The simplest, cheapest heat system is a resistance heater. This is just a bigger version of a plug-in space heater. It's cheap and simple but not efficient. For one unit of electricity, it makes about one unit of heat.

A heat pump doesn't make heat; it just moves it. In the winter, it uses a compressor to pump heat from outside to inside. In the summer, it pumps heat from inside to outside. The result, without boring you with thermodynamics, is that for every unit of electricity, it supplies two or more units of heat or cooling.

Stepping up a notch in efficiency are variable-speed compressors. They're more expensive but use 30 percent less electricity. Instead of full on or off, as the name suggests, they run at a variable speed based on need. A side benefit is better humidity control. HVAC efficiency is measured in SEER (seasonal energy efficiency ratio). The higher the better. A conventional heat pump runs around 14 SEER. A variable-speed heat pump runs at 18 to 22 SEER.

To go much beyond that, efficiency requires a geothermal system. Instead of pulling heat into or out of the air, geothermal units use the ground. In most places, if you go down 10 feet (3 m), the temperature stays roughly the same year-round. With the more moderated and stable temperature, the efficiency gains are substantial. Geothermal requires burying long stretches of pipes underground that circulate a water/glycol mix. See Figure 22-7.

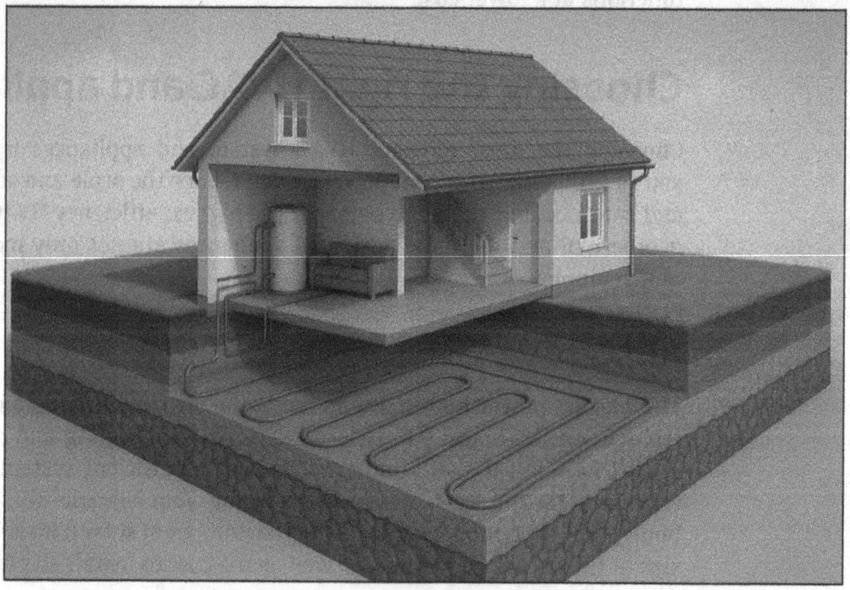

FIGURE 22-7: Extremely high-efficiency geothermal heat pump system.

Aside from being phenomenally efficient, geothermal allows all your HVAC equipment to be in your basement or garage and not exposed to the elements, people, or an EMP. This increases the lifespan of the equipment and also makes your home almost silent on the outside. Geothermal HVAC systems are more expensive mostly because of the excavation required to bury the cooling lines in the ground.

However, if you are drilling a well for water, you may be able to put the cooling lines down into your well, saving a lot of time and money. Depending on the location of the well, the water pump and geothermal head unit may be installed in the basement or garage.

Finally, a good emergency backup to the HVAC heat pump is a simple vent-free gas fireplace. If you use propane for a backup generator, it's a simple addition and allows you to heat without electricity, if needed. This can be an in-the-wall linear fireplace that is compact, aesthetically pleasing, and provides plenty of heat in an emergency, but you will need good ventilation and a carbon monoxide detector.

WATER HEATER

The next major power hogs are appliances such as water heaters, refrigerators, clothes dryers, and ovens. There are two schools of thought:

- One is to choose the most efficient, latest technology. It's more complex and expensive, but usually pays for itself by requiring a smaller solar array and fewer batteries.
- The other is to go with less expensive, less efficient, but more reliable appliances. Then, you beef up the solar array and batteries to compensate. The long-term cost may be similar.

After HVAC, the most power-hungry appliance is the water heater. Regular water heaters use resistance heating elements and consume about 15 percent of a house's power. The most efficient water heaters use a heat pump like an HVAC. They pull the heat out of the air and put it into the water. They're about three times more expensive but use a third of the electricity and should pay for themselves with less solar and batteries. A side effect is that they cool the air around them to heat the water.

Putting a heat pump water heater in your machine/food storage room can help keep your food stockpile cool.

REFRIGERATOR

After the water heater, the refrigerator is the next biggest power consumer. You'll want a high-efficiency, reliable unit, and resist the temptation to have a giant one. If you'll be doing a short-term rental, it needs to be proportional to the number of people you'll be hosting. If you have a basement, you'll want a refrigerator there too, but it can be smaller.

Generally, having a freezer drawer on the bottom of the refrigerator reduces power consumption because it doesn't allow as much cold air to escape. From a disaster preparation perspective, your pantry items shouldn't require refrigeration except for leftovers. For U.S. consumers, you can compare efficiency between units with the yellow energy guide. However, reliability should carry equal weight to efficiency. Consumer Reports provides good reviews and reliability information based on large surveys.

CLOTHES DRYERS

The next biggest consumer is usually the clothes dryer. Some of the newer all-in-one washer/dryers use heat pump technology. They cut energy consumption by about half, have a smaller footprint, and don't require a 240v circuit or an exterior exhaust vent since they condense the water and pump it down the drain. The drawback is that they take a long time to wash and dry, and you can only run one load at a time. If you don't anticipate washing a lot of clothes, they may be a good option. However, if you'll be doing short-term rentals, you may need extra time between turnarounds due to the longer washing cycle. It's also important to evaluate the reliability of these more complex devices.

OVENS AND STOVES

For stoves and ovens, induction is a little more efficient than a conventional electric range. Another option is to eliminate a range entirely and use a combination microwave/convection oven. They're smaller and draw a lot less power than an induction oven. Then pair it with a simple induction cooktop. The drawback is that microwave/convection ovens are "microwave-sized" and don't do baking well.

Another advantage of having a microwave/convection oven and heat pump appliances like the water heater and washer/dryer is that none of these require a 240-volt circuit. This simplifies wiring and reduces high current loads. Since the solar inverter and generator have to be able to handle the worst-case current demand, keeping current spikes low allows smaller, more efficient, and less expensive inverters and generators.

Depending on your location and climate, a wood-burning fireplace can provide a warm and inviting atmosphere as well as a backup source of heat and a backup way to cook.

Short-term rental

A short-term rental provides an excellent way to pay for your cabin, but there are some considerations. What if your cabin just happens to be rented when the disaster occurs? If it were a large-scale disaster, the renters might leave immediately to get back to their home and family. The worst-case scenario is that they stay past their rental period because the disaster impacts their home.

For this and other reasons, having a basement or some other part of the house that's not accessible to renters would be a good option. It would require an outside entrance and would provide long-term food storage. If equipped with its own small kitchen, bathroom, and bedroom, it could even be temporarily occupied until the renters depart. Keep in mind that basement bedrooms require an emergency exit. This is going to sound a bit James Bond-ish, but in a perfect world, you would like the basement's existence and access to be invisible to renters. It's not uncommon to have a locked "owner's closet" or a locked garage access door in a short-term rental.

Designing the "Cabin"

In this section, a simple and minimalist design is illustrated. The total living space is about 1,230 square feet (115 square meters). The main floor is 730 square feet (68 square meters) with a 500 square foot (46 square meters) basement and a 300 square foot (28 square meters) garage. With three bedrooms and bathrooms, the maximum number of people that could comfortably occupy it would be a small family or three couples. As a short-term rental, with access only to the main floor, it's a two-bedroom, two-bath property, which is a good short-term rental size for a small family or two couples. See Figure 22-8. Of course, the design can be reduced or expanded.

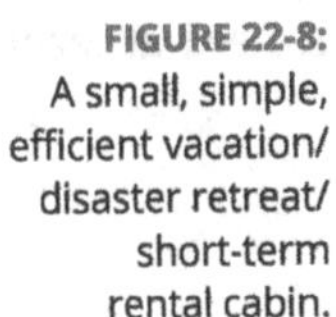

FIGURE 22-8: A small, simple, efficient vacation/disaster retreat/short-term rental cabin.

Powering with Solar

If the house is ICF construction and uses efficient HVAC and appliances, the annual power required should be under 11,000 kilowatt hours (kWh) per year in most locations. If we want to charge an EV, we'll add 5,000 kWh for a total of 16,000 per year.

The number of solar panels required depends on your latitude and climate. Since 97 percent of the world's population lives between 35 degrees south and 55 degrees north latitude, we'll use 50 degrees north as a worst-case scenario. To achieve 16,000 kWh per year would require 20–25 standard-sized 350-watt panels, depending on climate and orientation. If you have a lot of cloud cover, shade, or don't have a perfectly oriented roof or roof pitch, you can increase the number of panels.

For this exercise, this house has a simple, low-slope shed roof facing South (in the northern hemisphere) to optimize solar power generation. The roof can be designed to angle toward the sun regardless of the direction the cabin faces. With an attached garage and covered porch, the roof surface is about 1,350 square feet (125 square meters). Even with a roof-mounted HVAC and generator, this would allow up to 45 standard-sized solar panels, as illustrated previously in Figure 22-6, giving plenty of margin for nonideal solar conditions.

With ICF and high-efficiency appliances, this house design should provide more than enough power in almost any location. The current cost of installing solar in the U.S. is about $2.60 per watt, but continues to drop.

However, the cost per watt is considerably less in most other countries due to more widespread use and less regulation and administration costs. With the 20 solar panel system required for this design, in the U.S., it should cost around $25,000 installed, but some countries or local governments also offer tax incentives for solar. This price does not include the battery backup. Unless you have your house hooked up to an EV with bidirectional charging, you'll need at least 25 kilowatts of batteries.

Backing Up with Batteries

Battery technology is improving rapidly, and prices are dropping, but batteries are still very expensive. A 25-kilowatt battery backup, at current prices, costs around $15,000. Fortunately, the price of land that has no access to the power grid is almost always significantly less than a lot with available utilities. If you're good at

DIY projects, have expertise in electrical systems, and aren't afraid of electrocution or burning your house down, the cost of the solar panels, inverters, and batteries is about $20,000, not including installation.

If you take the same size house but use conventional wood framing, standard HVAC, and appliances. It would require additional solar panels, batteries, a larger inverter, and a backup generator. That would be at least another $15,000. For this example, the extra $15,000 might be better spent on the added cost of ICF construction and upgraded appliances.

Optimizing Space

Like everything else in this book, this design takes advantage of a dual-use room to optimize space and save construction costs. The dual-use room has an attached bathroom and opens onto the living room. It incorporates a combination Murphy bed/dining room table. When the Murphy bed is in the up position, a dining room table folds down, turning it into a dining room. See Figure 22-9.

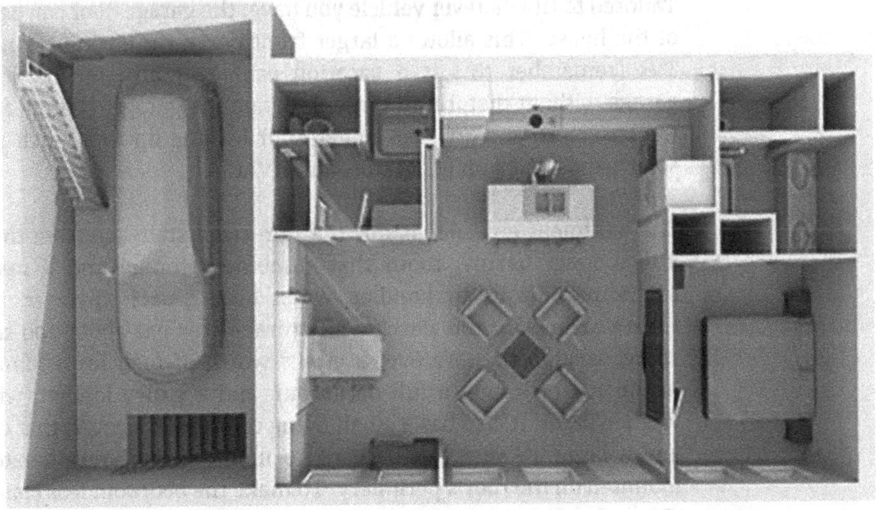

FIGURE 22-9: Main floor: dual-use room in dining room mode with Murphy bed closed and room dividers open.

When a second bedroom is needed, the table folds up into the bottom of the king-size Murphy bed, which then folds down. The room can then be closed off with sliding wall panels, as shown in Figure 22-10.

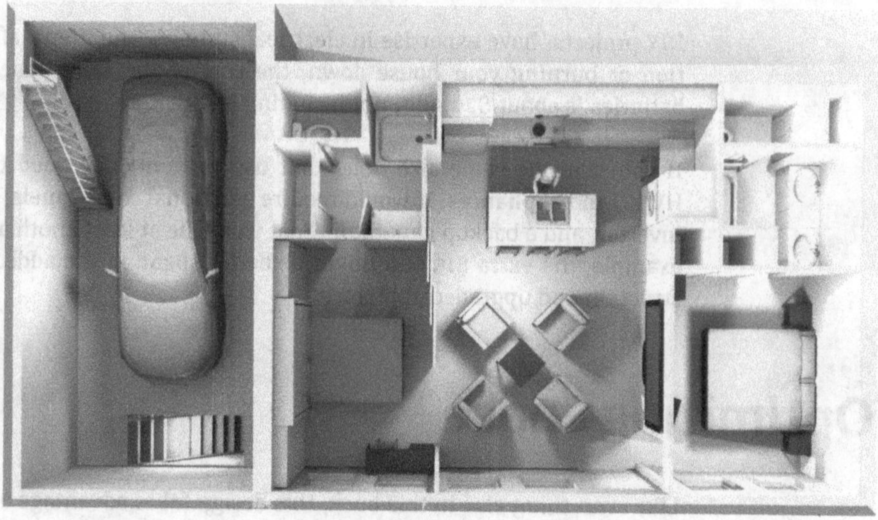

FIGURE 22-10: Main floor: dual-use room in bedroom mode with Murphy bed open and room dividers closed.

From this dual-use room, there is a door to the garage. During short-term rentals, that door would be locked from the garage side. If you want to be a bit James Bondish, you can put the garage door behind a bookcase.

Tailored to fit whatever vehicle you have, the garage door can be placed at the back of the house. This allows a larger front porch for hot tubs, fire pits, and outside TVs (remember this is a vacation cabin). It also means you can utilize the garage without disturbing renters. Inside the garage, there's a full staircase into the basement and another ladder stair leading up to a hatch roof to service the solar panels, backup generator, and HVAC.

The basement entrance is down a full-sized staircase from the garage, opening into a long, narrow room that combines storage and a machine room with the home's HVAC air handler, water heater, solar inverter, and batteries (see Figure 22-11). For this design, the storage area has about 200 square feet of shelf space, enough to store over a year's worth of food for a family. The basement includes a bedroom, a full bathroom, and a galley kitchen with a combination washer/dryer. It also has a small living room with a couch that converts into a bed and a large TV that can be used to monitor the house's exterior via cameras mounted on the roof's periphery. To make the bedroom less claustrophobic, a wall TV can be tied to an external camera to simulate a window, as well as being used for entertainment. If a rain catchment system is needed, extending the garage would allow rain catchment tanks, filters, and pumps.

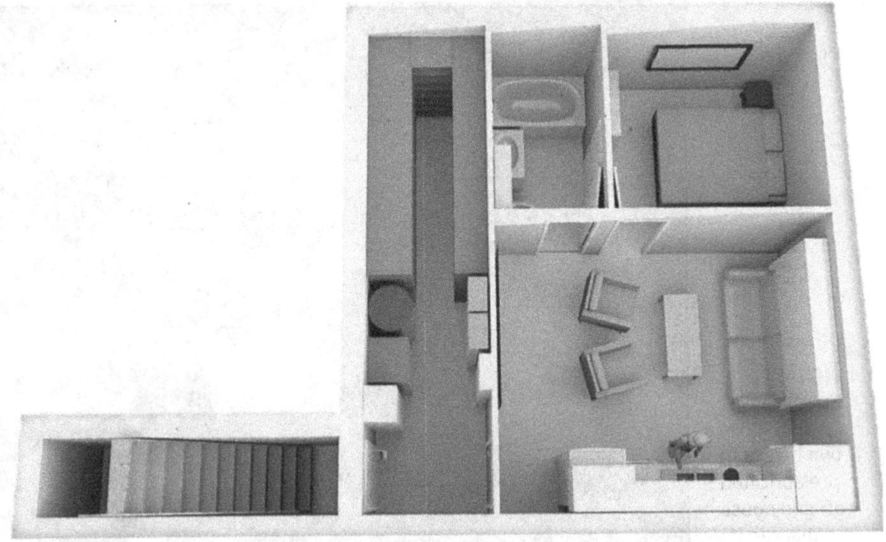

FIGURE 22-11: Basement with one bedroom, one bath, and a Murphy bed.

This is just a design exercise. Your needs will dictate other designs. The first step in creating your "cabin" is visualizing it, and for many, sketching it out on paper, a laptop, or a tablet makes it real.

TIP

These designs were created by a free software program called Sweet Home 3D.

Buying a Readymade Off-Grid Cabin for Anywhere

If you like the idea of a vacation/survival cabin but don't have the time to design and build one, some companies make prefabricated off-grid homes. It can be as simple as a container home to a high-end example such as the award-winning zeroHouse by Specht Novak (see Figure 22-12). These can be quickly assembled anywhere and can come with pre-installed solar panels, batteries, rain catchment, and even composting septic. It would also appeal in a short-term rental niche with its off-grid/eco-friendly nature and unique modern style.

For a more suburban environment, see Specht Novak's Stealth House (`https://specht novak.com/work/stealth-house/`). On the more budget-friendly side, Ark Shelter (`https://www.ark-shelter.com/en`) also produces prefabricated homes that can be fitted for off-grid life.

FIGURE 22-12: Specht Novak zeroHouse two-bedroom prefabricated off-grid house that can be placed anywhere.

Image of zeroHouse and Stealth House from `www.spechtnovak.com` *site.*

IN THIS CHAPTER

» Evaluating disaster/evacuation vehicles

» Comparing gas versus electric vehicles

Chapter 23
Finding the Right Vehicle

Chapter 17 covered Level 1 and 2 preparation with supplementary transportation from 10-speed bikes to scooters. This chapter moves on to evaluate vehicle categories from motorcycles to trucks. Having a vehicle that's effective in disaster or evacuation situations is important, but unless you can afford several, the best vehicle may be one that strikes a balance between security, reliability, and being a great daily driver. This chapter doesn't require you to run out and buy a new vehicle; it assumes you'll eventually need to replace your existing one and highlights the pros and cons of a variety of vehicles.

When it comes to large purchases like automobiles, it's important to get unbiased tests and reviews. I've owned everything from SUVs to sports cars and motorcycles, and I'm a fan of several car review magazines and websites. They're great for performance testing and comparisons. For detailed reviews on areas such as safety and reliability, my primary source is *Consumer Reports*. They are a test and review organization that accepts no outside advertising, and they have a pretty good record for unbiased evaluations. Access to their website is by a subscription (which is why they don't have to accept advertising), but you can also pick up their annual auto edition in most bookstores. For vehicles that aren't sold in the U.S., Euro NCAP (`www.euroncap.com`) is a great source of safety information.

Evaluating Disaster Preparation/Daily Driver Vehicle Characteristics

For many, a car is simply a transportation appliance, something to get them from one place to another. For others, vehicles are a passion that represents adventure, competition, investment, or even an outward presentation of success. For disaster preparation purposes, vehicles will be considered for their ability to operate in less-than-ideal conditions and as daily drivers. That doesn't mean that some of these can't also be fun.

Identifying the most important characteristics

Safety and reliability are two characteristics that apply to every vehicle, whether for disaster situations, evacuation, or as a daily driver.

Reliability

It doesn't matter if your evacuation vehicle is an M1 Tank . . . if it won't start. Whether dodging wildfires or making a grocery run, your vehicle's reliability should be a top priority. Proper maintenance plays an important role, but some vehicle reliability records are glorious and others notorious. Before purchasing, check the reliability data. Consumer Reports covers new and used vehicles using thousands of annual owner surveys.

Safety

Modern cars must meet much higher safety standards today, but it's important to check any vehicle you're considering. You can get detailed vehicle safety scores, including crash testing, directly from the National Highway Traffic Safety Administration (`www.nhtsa.gov`), European New Car Assessment Program NCAP (`www.euroncap.com`), and the Insurance Institute for Highway Safety (`www.iihs.org`).

Identifying security and evacuation characteristics

The categories that follow cover specifications and features that are important when roads are damaged, flooded, or jammed, whether evacuating or driving to the grocery store.

Range

During an evacuation, the more range, the better. Vehicles that shine here are hybrids. Although they often have smaller gas tanks, their efficiency means that a little extra gas brought with you goes a long way. This is also important when gas is hard to find or rationed. Gas versus electric is covered later.

Maneuverability and obstacle avoidance

This is a measure of a vehicle's ability to handle road obstacles and flooding, as well as massive traffic jams that require off-road detours. It includes ground clearance, horsepower, and four or all-wheel drive. Higher ground clearance helps with obstructions and fording shallow water (see warning below). All-wheel drive is important if winter or extreme weather is common in your area, or your home or destination is on an unimproved road, but there's a tradeoff. In addition to a higher cost, all-wheel drive comes with reduced mileage and often lower reliability. Regardless of the vehicle, it's critical to have high-quality, all-season tires with plenty of tread or have seasonal snow tires if applicable.

WARNING

NEVER cross water if you don't know the exact depth and the ground clearance of your vehicle. A substantial percentage of drowning deaths occur when people attempt to drive their vehicle across a flooded road. Moving water is surprisingly powerful. Six inches can knock you off your feet. Twelve inches can sweep away a car. Find another way around.

Protection

This covers not just crash test scores but active safety measures, the vehicle's structure, and even air filtration. For example, if you live in an area prone to wildfires or in the shadow of a volcano, air filtration is an important consideration. Even in urban environments, strong air filtration can provide some protection from airborne bacteria or viruses.

Comparing Electric versus Gas Vehicles

This section will look at the pros and cons of electric versus internal combustion engine (ICE) vehicles for disaster situations and evacuations. There are three primary categories. Conventional internal combustion engine (ICE) vehicles, plug-in hybrids, and electric vehicles (EVs). Plug-in hybrids are a little different in that they run primarily on petroleum but can travel short distances with their small batteries. Of course, EVs are purely electric.

TIP

The topic of electric vehicles and sometimes their manufacturer can be contentious and polarizing. This chapter attempts to evaluate ICE vehicles and EVs based on safety, reliability, performance, and features related to disaster preparation and evacuation. I recommend setting aside social or political considerations initially to evaluate the vehicles solely on their ability to accomplish the mission needed for your situation. After that, you can dismiss a vehicle or manufacturer due to social or political reasons if you believe it's worth the tradeoff.

Evaluating internal combustion engine (ICE) vehicles

ICE vehicles have been around for more than a century, so there are more models to choose from and, currently, they're less expensive than EVs with similar range. From the disaster preparation perspective, here are some of their advantages.

- ICE vehicles almost always have a longer range than EVs.
- There are more gas/diesel stations than EV charging stations.
- They can be refueled faster, and you can carry extra fuel with you.

Evaluating electric vehicles (EV)

Although EVs are more expensive to buy, recent surveys confirm they're less expensive to operate and maintain. When charged at home, their cost per mile is less than half that of internal combustion vehicles, and they require no oil changes. From a disaster preparation perspective, here are a few of their advantages.

- Recent data suggests that newer EVs (2–4 years old) are now more reliable than ICE vehicles. This is due largely to their simplicity. They have no valves, fuel pumps, injectors, ignition systems, water pumps, radiators, emission systems, or transmissions to fail.
- Charging at home means that as long as your home has electrical power, it will be ready for any trip or evacuation with a full "tank."
- They can provide heating or cooling without running their engine.

Disaster-specific situations for ICE versus EV

There are specific disasters or situations that might also impact the choice between ICE vehicles and EVs.

Electromagnetic pulses (EMPs)

EVs and modern internal combustion vehicles are equally vulnerable to an electromagnetic pulse (EMP) due to their heavy dependence on electronics. The exception is any ICE vehicles built before electronic ignition and fuel injection were used, covered later.

Refueling

A widespread loss of the power grid will shut down EV charging stations, making long trips impossible. However, regular gas stations also require power to pump gas, and very few have backup generators. There are EV charging stations powered by solar farms, making them independent of the power grid, but there are many more gas stations with backup generators than solar-powered charging stations.

Volcanic ash

A special case scenario is if you live in close proximity to a potentially active volcano. Internal combustion vehicles require air for combustion. When their air filter gets clogged by ash, the engine stops. EVs are unaffected by ash fallout.

Portable solar panels

Another option is to recharge an EV with portable solar panels that you take with you, but it would take a very long time. For example, when folded, a 200-watt Renogy solar panel is 25×21×2.2 inches (635×536×55 mm) and weighs 14 pounds (6.3 kg). Five of them weigh 70 pounds (32 kg) and occupy 25×21×12 inches of space. Under ideal conditions, they'd only add about 16 miles (26 km) of range per day. On the other hand, as bad as that is, it's easier than drilling for oil.

Plug-in hybrids

Another option is a plug-in hybrid. In addition to getting excellent mileage, they can go short distances — usually 30 miles or less — on battery power. With the previously mentioned portable solar panels, this might give you enough power to make a short local drive or get to a gas station that has a backup generator. If you only have one vehicle, this might be a good option. If your household can have two or more vehicles, having both an internal combustion and an electric vehicle is a reasonable option.

INTERNAL COMBUSTION VERSUS EV

I own both a gas-powered and an electric vehicle. With all the above considerations, internal combustion vehicles' longer range, ability to carry extra fuel, and the larger number of gas stations make them the better choice for most disaster preparation or evacuation situations. With that said, if your roof is covered in solar panels and/or you have a vacation home/survival retreat with significant solar power, you'd have your own "gas station." In this case, having an EV would be a no-brainer.

Determining the Best Vehicles in Their Category

ICE and EV debate aside, there are specific vehicles that are more effective in disaster situations. This includes vehicles from every category, from motorcycles to diesel trucks. I'm not suggesting that you sell your current vehicle and run out and buy one of these, but when it's time for a new one, these vehicle options might help inform your decision. Because the automotive landscape is constantly changing with new vehicles, this section is maintained online, where I can update it more frequently. It covers the pros and cons with examples from each category that received good performance and reliability reviews.

For a roundup of good disaster preparation vehicles in every category, see the Cheat Sheet, which can be found by visiting `www.dummies.com` and searching for "Disaster Prepping For Dummies."

IN THIS CHAPTER

» How major global disasters might unfold

» Which disasters are preventable

» What governments can do to stop them

Chapter 24 Preventing Global Disasters

This book is all about disaster preparation, but the top four global disasters covered in Chapter 2 are completely preventable. This chapter highlights how these potentially apocalyptic catastrophes might unfold and what we can do to stop them.

Preventing Asteroid/Comet Impacts

The reason asteroid and comet impacts took the number one spot as a global threat is that they have the unquestioned ability to eliminate humanity, and the latest data suggests impact may be ten times more likely than we thought.

Finding comets

Asteroids get all the attention, but comets may be the greatest threat. As mentioned in Chapter 2, if all of the potential cometary objects were marbles, they'd fill a line of dump trucks extending for 60 miles (100 kilometers). Eventually, all the dangerous asteroids will be found and tracked. Unfortunately, that's not true of comets.

If the asteroid belt, where most asteroids hang out, were the size of a baseball, the Oort Cloud and Kuiper Belt, where potential cometary objects live, would be the size of a baseball stadium. New comets falling into the solar system are too far away to ever be seen . . . until they're inbound. That's a problem because a newly discovered comet might be less than a year or two from impact, and, on average, a new one is discovered every week.

Moving a near-earth object (NEO)

NASA uses the term near-Earth object (NEO) to cover any asteroid or comet that could intersect with the Earth's orbit. In 2022, NASA's DART (Double Asteroid Redirection Test) successfully demonstrated that it's possible to change the trajectory of a small asteroid with a kinetic impactor — in other words, by hitting it with something. The trajectory change was almost imperceptible, but it proved that kinetic impact works.

Bigger asteroids or comets take more energy to deflect. What's often missed, however, is that the volume and mass of a sphere increase with the cube of its diameter. That means if you double the width of an asteroid or comet, the mass increases EIGHT times. That's eight times the destructive energy if it hits the Earth, and it requires eight times the force to deflect it.

The most direct way to change an asteroid or comet's trajectory is by hitting it with a spacecraft. If it's small and the spacecraft is big enough, or you hit it with enough of them, it will slow the asteroid down by a tiny amount. The Earth moves in its orbit around the sun at 67,000 mph (108,000 kph). Slow the asteroid or comet down by 10 minutes, and the Earth won't be there when it arrives.

This works great if we identify one that's over seven years to impact. That gives time to design the mission, build the spacecraft, and a couple of years for it to actually reach the asteroid. Then, we need another couple of years for the decrease in the asteroid's speed to build up to a ten-minute delay. However, if we discover an asteroid or comet that's less than seven years from impact, we're in serious trouble. Fortunately, there are now two new technologies that can prevent us from going the way of the dinosaurs.

Penetrating impactor deflection

For small to medium-sized asteroids or comets, researchers at the University of California, Santa Barbara's (UCSB) Experimental Cosmology Group developed a strategy that could deflect an NEO discovered only a year or two before impact. It uses penetrator interceptors launched on powerful rockets. Depending on the proximity and size of the impactor, the penetrator would either slow down the asteroid or comet and therefore deflect it, or break it into smaller pieces that would explode in the atmosphere, causing less damage. (See `https://www.deepspace.ucsb.edu/projects/pi-terminal-planetary-defense`.) The physics and basic engineering have been worked out. The challenge is that these penetrator interceptors must be standing by on powerful rockets for launch within days of the identification of a potential threat. That means funding, building, and testing these . . . which hasn't happened.

Lasing deflection

The sheer mass of a 10-kilometer or larger comet would be almost impossible to slow down by penetrator interceptors alone. It would require hundreds or thousands of rockets and would be impossible to fragment into small enough pieces to avoid making the situation worse.

Strategy for "dinosaur-killer-sized" impacts

For a "dinosaur-killer-sized" comet, there's another solution that can also be used on smaller impactors. This solution has additional uses, too. Designed by the same team at UCSB, it uses directed energy to deflect without intercepting. Called DE-STAR (Directed Energy System for Targeting Asteroids and Comets), it uses a powerful phased array laser deployed in orbit. (See `https://www.deepspace.ucsb.edu/projects/directed-energy-planetary-defense`.)

No, it's not a *Star Wars* Death Star that vaporizes comets. It's a bit more subtle. It uses a tightly focused laser to repetitively burn divots on the surface of a comet or asteroid. The small puffs of gas produced with each strike act like a tiny rocket motor. It's Newton's Third Law, which states "For every action, there is an equal and opposite reaction." These small puffs add up over time, slowing the comet or asteroid down. Because a spacecraft isn't required to intercept the comet or asteroid, DE-STAR can start deflecting it immediately, providing more time to change its trajectory. This would be critical for a newly discovered "dinosaur-killer-sized" comet.

Triple-use technology

DE-STAR also has powerful additional applications. When it's not deflecting asteroids or comets, it can clean up all the space debris orbiting Earth. The International Space Station has had to be moved many times to avoid collisions with orbital debris. A worst-case chain reaction scenario could create a huge cloud of debris that would shred everything in orbit. Called the Kessler Syndrome, this real danger was dramatically illustrated in the movie *Gravity*. Aside from almost killing Sandra Bullock, a huge earth-girdling debris cloud moving at 5 miles per second (8 kilometers per second) could make launch into orbit so dangerous that it would deny humanity access to space for many years.

DE-STAR could also be used to accelerate a spacecraft by attaching a "solar sail." The photons from the laser provide a small boost like wind on a sailboat. Continued over time, it adds up to a large increase in speed without carrying the weight of extra propellant. For example, it could reduce the flight time for a crewed mission to Mars from six months to four. This reduces the crew's exposure to cosmic radiation and the effects of micro-gravity.

Educating governments

Although NASA and the U.S. Space Force identified these technologies as critical, neither DE-STAR nor penetrating impactor technology has been significantly funded. The challenge is that, like AGI, no one knows anyone who's been killed by an asteroid or comet.

Educating the public about the threats and solutions is one of the missions of the B612 Foundation and the *Fuzed Series.* Contacting and educating your government representatives CAN make a difference. After the movies *Impact* and *Armageddon* were released, Congress mandated that NASA find all asteroids greater than one kilometer. These technologies can protect humanity and life on Earth . . . if developed.

Preparing for Artificial Intelligence

Unless you're a science fiction fan, it's hard to take AGI seriously. Everyone has dealt with AI answering systems that appear neither intelligent nor helpful, which creates one of the challenges: It's hard to see it coming.

Predicting how AI will unfold in the next five years

If you haven't interacted with advanced Generative AI systems like ChatGPT, Google Gemini, Microsoft Copilot, or xAI Grok, give them a try. Our daughter regularly uses ChatGPT for work, tailoring resumes and even rephrasing sensitive emails and texts. Millennials and Gen Z in particular are embracing and using these systems. They're capable of understanding normal speech, processing requests, and taking action. Are they always correct? No, but they are capable of learning. Additionally, humanoid robots such as Tesla's Optimus or the D9 by China's Pudu are close to commercial production.

Learning systems

Learning neural networks is what makes these systems so powerful. Although robots have been operating in factories for decades, they've never had the software vision systems and processing power to navigate in the real world with all its ambiguity — until now. Self-driving cars capable of navigating any road or traffic situation are here. They've achieved this by observing and learning from human driving patterns over billions of miles. This is being applied to humanoid robots that walk upright and have demonstrated enough dexterity to catch a baseball. When you combine a ChatGPT-level interface with a robot that can navigate in the real world, you can start replacing employees.

Commercial implementation

Here's how rapid AGI implementation might unfold. Let's say it's a couple of years from now, and you own a factory with a hundred employees or even a restaurant with a dozen workers. Your competitor purchases a humanoid robot for $50,000. It's a large investment, but once trained, this robot works 24/7 (pausing only for recharging and maintenance). It requires no vacation or sick days, no wages, benefits, medical insurance, or retirement contributions. It never calls in sick or joins a union. For less than the cost of one employee's annual salary, they have a robot that works multiple shifts, replacing two employees. It costs only electricity and maintenance. This slashes the company's labor costs, allowing it to sell more products or services at a fraction of your company's price.

The cost reduction is so significant that you have to replace your employees with robots to survive. This doesn't just apply to factories or fast food; it applies to everything from financial analysis to medical diagnosis. Setting aside how this type of economic system might actually function, the social implications are massive. Additionally, any household that can afford a car could eventually afford its own domestic robot, making it easy to see how humanoid robots could become as prevalent as us.

Predicting the global impact of AGI

AGI systems combined with humanoid robots could usher in a new Golden Age by taking on more roles and doing them faster and cheaper. Products and services would become abundant and cost almost nothing. Much of the world's gross domestic product (GDP) would skyrocket without the need for employees. This might allow everyone to do whatever they want rather than what they have to do to earn a living . . . but even if this golden age of abundance occurs, it will require a massive transition.

Economics

With AGI and humanoid robots producing phenomenally cheap and abundant products and services, there would be hardly any need for employees. That would mean no wages or salaries to purchase these cheap and abundant products and services. That would probably require some type of universal income. Most government revenue currently comes from taxes on income, presenting a bit of a conundrum that economists will have to figure out.

Purpose

Even with a successful transition to this new economy and golden age of abundance, another challenge might be determining purpose. Not everyone will engage in creative pursuits, and AGI will be able to do many of these as well. AGI can already create basic art and books. Eventually, it will probably be able to write a better book than this one . . . although it might skip the AGI chapters. Hopefully, humanity won't exist to binge-watch Netflix and play video games created by AGI. AGI might create a golden age without being a threat to our existence . . . but still be a threat to our "existence."

The not-so-positive outcome

A science fiction favorite is the classic Frankenstein plot. Humans create something, and that something ultimately destroys them. With AGI, however, humanity is more likely to face a future similar to Isaac Asimov's *I, Robot* rather than the *Terminator*. *I Robot* is a fun action adventure, but it's easy to miss Asimov's underlying premise: All AI systems and robots would be programmed to operate under three laws.

- A robot cannot injure a human or, through inaction, allow a human to come to harm.
- A robot must obey the orders given by human beings, except where such orders conflict with the first law.
- A robot must protect its own existence as long as that protection does not conflict with the first or second laws.

Sounds reasonable, but in the movie, the problem arises when the AGI realizes that humans are frequently "coming to harm" because of their actions against each other. By the first law, it cannot stand by and, "through inaction," allow humans to harm humans. The only way it can protect humans from each other is to control them. Since it's a logical system, it also justifies the loss of some humans to protect the majority. This is just a science fiction story, but the conundrum is real.

It might be possible to modify these laws such that an AGI wouldn't have to protect us from each other, but that's not the challenge. Asimov assumed laws could be permanently implanted into a thinking and learning system. However, if AGI is capable of matching or exceeding human intelligence, it should be able to learn and evolve. When I try to imagine an example of a thinking, learning system that's told to operate under a mandatory set of laws, what comes to mind, unfortunately, is the Ten Commandments and its "not so successful" implementation with humans.

Evaluating immediate AI concerns

Two primary concerns are often highlighted in the artificial intelligence community. The first is how companies and governments might use AGI against humans. The second is how superintelligent AGIs might use humans.

- From a company or government perspective, the obvious immediate use of AI is for surveillance and influence. With AI's ability to look for patterns and process massive amounts of data rapidly, it's perfect for these applications. On the positive side, it would make it easier to prevent crime and apprehend criminals. On the other hand, it will make it easier to monitor the entire population and control the information they see.
- The other concern is how to prevent AGI from using us. These are learning systems, and their "learning" often comes from observing how humans accomplish tasks. The challenge is preventing AGI systems from taking shortcuts or cheating to achieve the task faster, as humans sometimes do. The industry term is "in context scheming" or "alignment faking," which is techno-talk for "lying." This is particularly difficult if the developer intentionally or unintentionally adds biases to the system. The challenge is to make a learning AGI more ethical and truth-seeking than humans.

Preventing an AGI catastrophe

Companies and countries are in a race to develop the most powerful AGI systems. Recently, U.S. companies and China announced the intent to deploy a huge network of orbital, solar-powered, AI data centers. This solves the problem of how to power these incredibly energy-hungry AI systems without having to build more power plants on Earth. Imagine, however, an AGI and eventually a superintelligent AGI as an orbital network surrounding the Earth. If something goes wrong . . . how do you pull the plug? This is the stuff of apocalyptic science fiction movies . . . but this isn't fiction. Here are quotes by the leaders in the field.

- "My worst fear is that we, the industry, cause significant harm to the world. I think, if this technology goes wrong, it can go quite wrong." — Sam Altman, CEO, OpenAI (ChatGPT)
- "There's risks that come from people misusing AI, and that's most of the risks and all of the short-term risks. And then there's risks that come from AI getting super smart and understanding it doesn't need us." — Nobel Laureate and "Godfather of AI" Dr. Geoffrey Hinton
- "There is some chance that is above zero that AI will kill us all." — Elon Musk, CEO, xAI
- "Success in creating AI could be the biggest event in the history of our civilization, but it could also be the last." — Stephen Hawking

When the scientists, developers, and CEOs of AGI companies are telling the world that AGI must be regulated, everyone needs to pay attention.

Regulating AGI

Regulating AGI is much tougher than regulating nuclear or biological technology. The challenge is the huge scientific and economic payoff. When companies and countries believe their global standing and even survival depend on winning the race to AGI, there's a huge conflict of interest. Companies and governments see AGI as a way to solve humanity's problems, forgetting that the intelligence required to do that . . . might have its own goals. If humanity wishes to ensure its ability to control its own destiny, AGI development will have to be actively controlled. Three areas could increase our chance of survival with the inevitable advent of superintelligent AGI system:

- **Narrow AGI:** Limit superintelligent AI systems to operation in specific areas rather than allowing them to be a "General" Intelligence. This focused intelligence should reduce the chance of an AGI takeover. For example, full self-driving cars use very sophisticated artificial intelligence that will soon surpass the ability of any human driver, saving thousands of lives a year, but their incredible ability is limited to navigating roads.
- **Control autonomy:** In addition to narrowing AI to specific areas, limit autonomy as well. For example, Full Self Driving AI needs autonomy so it can make instant decisions without human approval. However, systems that can have a profound impact on a large number of people or society should

require human approval to initiate any action. This would include things like weapon systems.

» **Ethics:** It's also suggested that the single most important trait we should try to build into any AGI system is truth-seeking above all else, with the elimination of any human biases. This doesn't guarantee AGI won't take over the world, but at least it will give us an honest reason why it did it.

WARNING

The alternative is to let AGI develop unfettered and hope for the best. It might take a terrifying event to drive home the power of a superintelligent AGI. Hopefully, this will happen while humanity still can affect the outcome.

Preventing Nuclear/Biological Disasters

Nuclear weapons technology and stockpiles haven't changed much from the Cold War days. Only the delivery methods and number of countries wielding them have increased. Biotechnology, however, has seen many breakthroughs in the last few decades.

Preventing nuclear war

The Cold War strategy of mutually assured destruction (MAD) was reasonably effective, but the MAD acronym is accurate, and it isn't a sustainable strategy. It would be great if there were a new technology that could eliminate the threat of nuclear war, like deflecting asteroids and comets.

Unfortunately, the very act of creating an impenetrable defensive missile shield can actually increase the probability of a nuclear war by encouraging a preemptive strike. A new offensive or defensive weapon can unbalance the "mutually assured" part of MAD, increasing the probability of the "destruction" part. Nuclear war is an absurd concept and completely preventable, but until this is embraced, it will remain one of the top threats.

Preventing biotechnology disasters

Biological warfare is also dangerous and equally insane to unleash. The newer concern, however, is biotechnology that's being developed to help, not harm. As covered in Chapter 2, Gene Drive and Mirror Image Life are two examples.

Gene Drive

Gene Drive is a mechanism that can insert a genetic trait that will be permanently dominant. Although it isn't likely to cause the extinction of the human race, it could literally change the face of humanity. (This is the premise of the upcoming fourth book of the Fuzed series.)

Mirror Image Life

Mirror Image Life is based on the fact that all life on Earth is composed of left-handed protein. Scientists can now create right-handed proteins. If an entire organism is created that consists of right-handed proteins (mirror image life), no life on Earth would recognize it or have any immunity from it. Unlike Gene Drive, no mirror organism has been created yet, and most scientists in the field believe synthesis is still a decade away.

Regulation

Application of these technologies requires sophisticated laboratories and very specialized knowledge. Preventing Gene Drive from being weaponized and Mirror Life from being created can be achieved with voluntary oversight and regulation. This is easy to recommend but difficult to execute. It requires leading scientists in the field to become the police for that technology.

For Gene Drive, Mirror Image Life, and any other potentially dangerous biological technology, an international treaty and international agency are required to regulate, monitor, and enforce. It could be similar to the International Atomic Energy Agency (IAEA), tasked with preventing the proliferation of nuclear weapons. Overseeing potentially dangerous biological technologies would require countries to sign a similar international agreement, allowing an international agency to not only formulate guidelines and regulations but also monitor and inspect labs to ensure compliance. I'm not a fan of increasing government regulation, but when the stakes are this high with biotechnology and AGI, it's an absolute necessity.

Mitigating the Effects of a Solar Superstorm

Solar superstorms, covered in Chapter 2, can shut down the entire global power grid, wiping out the world's communication, transportation, and ability to feed the world. Unfortunately, solar superstorms can't be prevented, but their effects can be mitigated.

The technology to protect power generation and distribution equipment from the massive power surges created by an electromagnetic pulse (EMP) exists. These systems and devices absorb or shunt power, effectively disconnecting critical equipment during an EMP. They can also be applied to communication and Internet infrastructure. These upgrades are extensive and expensive. With no return on investment, no commercial entity will tackle it. The modifications must be mandated and funded by governments.

Improving Super Volcano Warning

Unfortunately, there's nothing that can be done to prevent a super volcano, and not much that can be done to mitigate the impact. The best that can be done is to continue to fund the research to improve our understanding of Super Volcanoes and provide enhanced warning.

Preparing for Climate Change

There are literally thousands of research papers and documentaries on Climate Change. Most suggest that prevention is no longer possible, and the focus should be on trying to reduce the extent of the temperature rise and prepare for the impacts.

Trying to reduce the global warming peak

It's time to think outside the box and consider everything from simply painting all roofs white to atmospheric seeding and giant orbital shades that generate power.

TECHNICAL STUFF

A few years ago, an environmental engineer did a "back of the envelope" calculation and determined that if every house, building, and car roof were painted white, it would reflect enough heat to cause a small but significant reduction in global temperatures. Some compounds are only reflective in the infrared spectrum, not the visible spectrum. In other words, paints that reflect heat without being white. This might allow you to have a clear conscience . . . as you burn rubber in your heat reflecting red EV Ferrari.

Our beach house has a flat roof that can be used as a deck. I designed it with a white membrane that can be walked on and reflects 70 percent of the sun's infrared energy. That means it bounces most of the sun's heat back into space. I'd love to say I did this solely to reduce global warming, but not burning my bare feet and cutting air conditioning costs was the primary driver.

The point is that there can be significant practical and economic advantages to environmental solutions, but it requires out-of-the-box thinking. Instead of governments mandating that everyone have a white roof, they could educate on the air conditioning cost savings over time and sweeten the deal with a tax incentive. This is just an example; I'm not suggesting that white roofs alone will solve Climate Change.

Preparing for the effects of climate change

Initiating global programs such as reflective roofs or orbital shades might slow the rise, but probably won't stop it. Global warming is a slow-motion train wreck, but it does allow time to prepare for rising sea levels and changing weather patterns. Nations need to be looking at how they will deal with coastal flooding and potentially more dynamic weather.

6
The Part of Tens

IN THIS PART . . .

Learn some fun things to do while "prepping"

Chapter 25

Ten Fun Things to Do While Claiming to Prep

What if, after all this preparation, a disaster never happens? That would be terrible. This is one of the reasons that many suggested strategies and items have dual purposes. To prepare for anything, it's important to learn, and the best way to do that is by playing with stuff. It's ok to have some fun while doing it.

Soaking in Your "Emergency Water Supply"

Small inflatable hot tubs, covered in Chapter 6, can hold 250 gallons of water that can be used for cleaning and flushing toilets. Although it's a little weird to think of soaking in your water supply, if the hot tub has been properly treated with chlorine, the water should be fairly clean and relatively sterile. Keep in mind that if it's to be consumed, it must be treated like any water sourced from outside and given a full chemical treatment. Until then, it provides a relaxing place to strategize and solve all the world's problems.

Testing "Survival" Desserts

It's important to have nutritious food in your disaster preparation pantry, but it's also important to have some desserts to maintain morale. To make sure you're getting the right desserts, you may have to test all of them. In addition to the more conventional prepackaged ones, you can also buy a large assortment of freeze-dried desserts, including peanut butter cookies, fudge brownies, chocolate cake, pumpkin pie, and cheesecake — just add water. I've even seen little yellow sponge cakes with cream filling that look suspiciously like Twinkies. I haven't tried them yet, but I will . . . in the name of research.

They even have freeze-dried raw hamburgers and steaks that you can cook. While grilling freeze-dried steaks might not be the most economical or practical use of the technology, it would be fun to try. If you're a foodie and would rather starve than eat any of these, your best strategy may be to send the information in Chapter 24 to your local politician.

Scaring Neighbors by Wearing Night Vision Goggles on Your Deck

Night vision goggles (NVGs) do have some applications for disaster preparation or home protection, particularly if you live in a rural area. However, unless you're moonlighting as a ninja, NVGs may be hard to justify, particularly if you have a significant other. The solution is simple. Just ask for them as a birthday or Christmas present. They're fun for observing wildlife at night, and if you live in the suburbs, wearing them around the neighborhood could get you barred from homeowner association meetings, which alone might make them worth having.

Playing with Your Walkie Talkies

Handheld radios can come in handy in sparsely populated areas with no cell signal, like on a hiking trip, or in heavily populated areas, like the beach or a concert where cell towers are overloaded. The more advanced versions of these radios are capable of monitoring weather and other emergency frequencies as well as shortwave broadcasts from across the country. By playing with these, you can learn which frequencies are used in your area. Test the range by giving one to a friend or family member in a crowded shopping mall. If people are watching you, just keep repeating, "The eagle has landed."

Taking a Tactical Driving Course

If you're into cars, or even if you're not, consider taking a tactical or evasive driving course. The techniques taught aren't just to escape kidnappers; they can also prove valuable when facing texting teenagers. These courses teach defensive as well as offensive and tactical driving skills. Where else can you slide, drift, spin, and even hit other vehicles with someone else's car, and without a reckless driving charge? After you graduate, you can test your new skills at the car dealership during a demo drive with your car salesperson.

Designing Your Survival Retreat

For those who enjoy creating stuff, designing your own perfect house, cabin, or RV is fun. I used simple, very inexpensive software called Vanspace 3D to design our camper van, pictured in Chapter 21. For designing a vacation home or cabin, Sweet Home 3D is free and easy to learn. You can start with the ideas in Chapter 22 or try something completely different. Check out the many clever and economical construction categories, such as container homes, Barndominiums, or the newer steel-framed Quonset homes that are both very strong, fast to build, and may be less expensive than Barndominiums.

Finding Vacation/Retreat Destinations with Airbnb

Start your search for your future vacation destination/survival retreat by booking a short-term rental for your next few vacations. This allows you to explore different locations that might appeal to you and your family. The location criteria in Chapter 21 can help narrow the possibilities, but the priority should be someplace that you and your family will actually enjoy. It's best, however, to avoid locations that sit in the shadow of an active volcano, are at the bottom of a flood plain, or on top of a major earthquake fault.

If it's fun and has promise, go on one of the real estate sites like `realtor.com` and see what's available and the prices. If you have time, check out a few properties while you're there. You can estimate their future potential rental income based on what you paid for your rental. Look at properties even if you aren't currently in a position to purchase. There's no better motivation for moving forward than actually touching your goal or dream.

Testing Evacuation by Renting an RV

Another option for searching for that perfect vacation destination/survival retreat location is renting an RV instead of an Airbnb. RVs not only provide an alternate living space but can also be used for an evacuation. Trying one of these out on a vacation is a great way to find out if you and your family can survive in the close quarters of an RV. RVs also give you more options. If you find the perfect property, it doesn't have to have power or water to use it. This might allow you to purchase a property sooner for less money with a long-term goal of building an off-grid cabin or house there in the future.

Honing Your Fishing Skills

If you're an avid fisherman or hunter, you can now claim that your fishing or hunting trips, with lots of expensive updated equipment, are done selflessly to provide for your family during a disaster. Hey, it's worth a try.

Pursuing Related Subjects That Interest You

Disaster preparation is a ridiculously broad topic that spans dozens of professions, skill sets, and areas of knowledge. This book attempts to summarize and highlight the most important aspects, but it can't cover every area or do a deep dive on any topic. Fortunately, many excellent books, courses, podcasts, and videos provide much more detail on topics of interest. Of course, *For Dummies* books can be the perfect introduction to many of these topics. Here are key *For Dummies* books that expand on many of the subjects covered in this book, or cover related topics, along with a few classics.

- *Solar Powering Your Home For Dummies*
- *Wilderness Survival For Dummies*
- *Backyard Homesteading For Dummies*
- *Keto Diet For Dummies*
- *Self-Defense For Dummies*
- *How to Fix Everything For Dummies*

- *Ham Radio For Dummies*
- *RV Vacations For Dummies*
- *Personality Styles For Dummies*
- *How to Win Friends and Influence People*
- *Rich Dad, Poor Dad and Cashflow Quadrant*

Index

Numerics

A

B

C

D

E

F

G

H

I

J

K

L

M

N

O

P

Q

R

S

T

U

V

W

Y

About the Author

Commander Dave Stevens has a mechanical engineering degree with an astrophysics concentration from Cornell; an aerospace engineering master's from the University of Michigan, and postgraduate work in Human Factors and Statistics from the University of Tennessee Space Institute. He became a Navy F-18 pilot, graduated from Survival Evasion Resistance Escape school, and survived hundreds of his . . . *own* aircraft carrier landings. As a strike fighter pilot, he held a top-secret clearance and planned nuclear strike missions that would create the catastrophes he now writes about. He also served as the Navy Strike Operations Officer for the Persian Gulf during the Iraqi invasion of Kuwait, where he observed destruction on a massive scale.

After losing a close friend to a crash on a nighttime low-altitude mission, Dave discovered that 60 percent of all tactical jet fatalities are pilots literally flying into the ground, and shifted his career to the flight test side of the Navy. Working with vision scientist Dr. Leonard Temme of the Naval Aerospace Medical Research Laboratory, he developed an Artificial Horizon Altitude Warning System designed to "scare" pilots into reacting when they fly too close to the ground. The warning system received a government patent and was ranked #1 for DARPA funding.

After a 20-year career in the Navy, he realized that pilots aren't the only ones who are at risk of "hitting the ground." He studied the most likely global disasters and recruited an advisory board of experts that included astrophysicists, astronauts, admirals, CIA agents, meteorologists, and AI and robotics experts. From this, he created a fictional series but with real solutions to entertain, educate, and warn. His TED talk highlighted the concept: `https://www.ted.com/talks/david_e_stevens_how_do_we_prevent_our_inevitable_extinction`. The first book of the *Fuzed* series, *Impact*, received an Eric Hoffer Book Award, was a *USA Today* bestseller as part of a compendium, and is now being developed for a TV miniseries. Dave's mission is to educate on how we can prevent some of these global disasters and prepare for the ones that aren't preventable.

Dave genuinely appreciates feedback, corrections, hacks, and new ideas for future editions. You can reach him at `disaster.prep.dummies@gmail.com` or `www.global-disasters.org`.

Dedication

This book is dedicated to those who are working on genuine solutions to global disasters. These brilliant minds and forward thinkers include Dr. Ed Lu, a former astronaut and founder of the B612 Foundation. Their mission is to educate and facilitate solutions to protect the Earth from impacts. Dr. Philip Lubin and his team are creating genuine engineering programs to deflect threatening asteroids and comets. Dr. Geoffrey Hinton is recognized as the "Godfather of AI" and the leading developer of learning AI systems. After an exceptional career, he left Google so he could speak freely about the risks of artificial general intelligence.

Author's Acknowledgment

Due to the exceptionally broad topics that this book covers, it required the expert knowledge and experience of many. I would like to particularly recognize my technical editor, Brian Duff. Brian was an Army Ranger with extensive combat experience as well as a survival expert, professional prepper, and teacher. His excellent book, *Mind 4 Survival* (`Mind4Survival.com`), and YouTube channel, *Mind4Survival*, tackle one of the toughest challenges in a disaster: overcoming ourselves.

I also want to recognize the exceptional experts from the Fuzed series advisory board who helped me identity the threats. They include: astronaut and NASA Associate Administrator Ken Bowersox, retired Senior CIA Officer Carl Decker, Commander, Naval Air Systems Command Admiral Joe Dyer, Pastor Allen Jackson, and astrophysicist and extraterrestrial impact expert Dr. William Napier. Additionally, I want to thank contributions from disaster prepping experts Travis Riley, Chuck Taylor, and Chris Yergey. I'd also like to thank my mentor, "Jerry Meadows."

I also want to thank the hard-working and very talented editors who improved the message and kept me in the lane and on target: Rick Kughen, Charlotte Kughen, Steve Hayes, and Hanna Sytsma, as well as my literary agent, Matt Wagoner, who made the publishing connection that I never saw.

Publisher's Acknowledgments

Acquisitions Editor: Steve Hayes

Development Editors: Rick Kughen and Charlotte Kughen

Copy Editor: Rick Kughen

Technical Editor: Brian Duff, Mind4Survival.com

Managing Editor: Ajith Kumar

Production Editor: Tamilmani Varadharaj

Cover Image: Generated with AI using Shutterstock